The PROGRESSIVE APPROACH to LANGUAGE

Kinder 1

HAZEL DOMINGO BABIANO

DONOVAN DOMINGO BABIANO

Authors

Complete with: teacher's guide, songs, games, and suggested activities for the different language skills and for the different learning areas (THEMATIC)

The Progressive Approach to Language Kinder 1

ISBN: 978-971-625-377-1

📍 First RVC Building, 92 Anonas Cor. K-6th Streets,
   East Kamias, Quezon City
📱 Tel. Nos: (02) 8426-5611 | (02) 8573-2380
📠 Telefax No.: (02) 8426-1274
✉ Email: inquiry@stmatthews.ph
🌐 Website: www.stmatthews.ph

Note: This book was prepared with the utmost care and scrutiny.

Errors which may be discovered while reading the book will be corrected

in the next printing. The publisher guarantees the replacement

of books received and found to have physical defects like binding

and printing, provided that the defects are found before use.

Just call telephone nos. (02) 8426-1274 or (02) 8426-5611.

The books will be replaced immediately.

Published by **St. Matthew's Publishing Corporation**

PREFACE

The mastery of language is possibly the most essential skill that a child needs to acquire in his early years. After all, during this primordial stage the child   is nearly one hundred percent dependent upon an adult for his learning. The child needs to be able to comprehend simple verbal cues and decipher hand gestures and facial expressions, and from here he should soon progress to the discovery of the significance of written symbols. Without first learning this rudimentary language of his early instructors, the child cannot move on to other concepts such as writing, math, and science. Thus, communication is the basis of early learning and development.

Not every child, however, can be communicated to in the same way. While some children would have no trouble understanding visual signals and symbols, other children would learn better when something is spoken or sung to them; others would need to touch something physical and tangible in order to have a mental grasp of a concept; still others would learn best when their whole bodies are engaged in the learning activity—through clapping, miming, acting, or dancing. Every child, being a unique individual, has a unique way of learning.

It is with this in mind that we crafted the activities in this book. We've included more action games and songs here than we've ever done in a previous incarnation of The Progressive Approach to Language series. We've also included suggested activities for the different areas of language development—the receptive (reading and listening) and expressive (writing and speaking) language skills. Thus, every type of learner—be he visual, auditory, or kinesthetic—can fully participate in the learning process. Furthermore, children will not only learn the correct usage of words but will also be trained to comprehend both written and spoken language and to express themselves clearly and confidently. We hope that this out-of-the-box approach to book-writing would serve to demonstrate what educators need to always remember: that teaching, when made enjoyable, is a thousand times more effective, a thousand times more efficient, and a thousand times more lasting for the child.

Each child may have a different way of learning, but they ALL learn BEST when they are having FUN!

Teacher Hazel Domingo Babiano
Teacher Donovan Domingo Babiano

TABLE OF CONTENTS

FIRST QUARTER
EVERYTHING ABOUT ME

Lesson	At the end of the activities, the child should be able to:	NI	S	E
1	1. tell something and answer questions regarding oneself			
	2. tell the names of classmates and make proper introductions			
	3. gain self-confidence through socialization			
	4. tell one's gender			
	5. differentiate boys from girls			
	6. identify the clothes that boys and girls wear			
	7. identify the parts of the body and tell the use of each part			
	8. master the things that he or she can do with his or her body parts			
2	9. use greetings in communicating with others			
	10. tell when to properly use these greetings			
	11. pronounce words and greetings correctly			
	12. acquire self-confidence through role-playing			
3	13. use polite expressions in day-to-day activities			
	14. know when to use these polite expressions			
	15. practice the act of courtesy and politeness at all times			
	16. develop self-confidence in interacting with others			
4	17. tell how a person feels through facial expressions			
	18. know the different emotions a person has			
	19. tell what a person is trying to tell through gestures			
	20. use facial expressions and gestures in communicating with others			
5	21. use he and she correctly			
	22. pronounce words clearly			

Legend:

NI — Needs Improvement   S — Satisfactory   E — Excellent

LESSON 1

ALL ABOUT ME

Telling About Oneself

Guide: Introduce your name to the class by singing "H *is for Hazel*" while putting some actions to it. Let everybody sing, using each pupil's name and changing the action for each beginning letter.

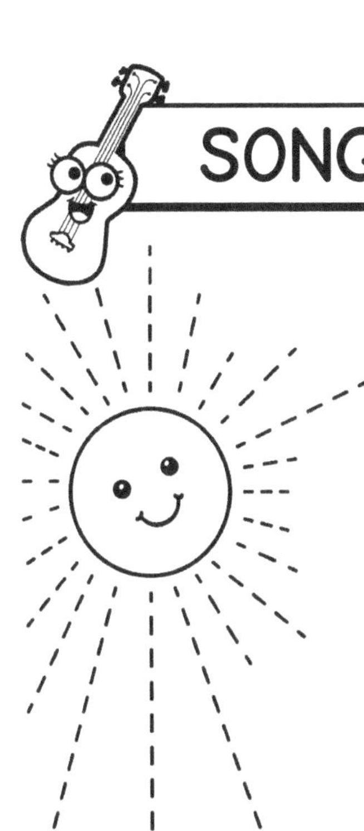

(Tune: "*C* **is for Cookie**")

H **is for Hazel**

H is for Hazel,
And Hazel is my name.

H is for Hazel,
And Hazel is my name.

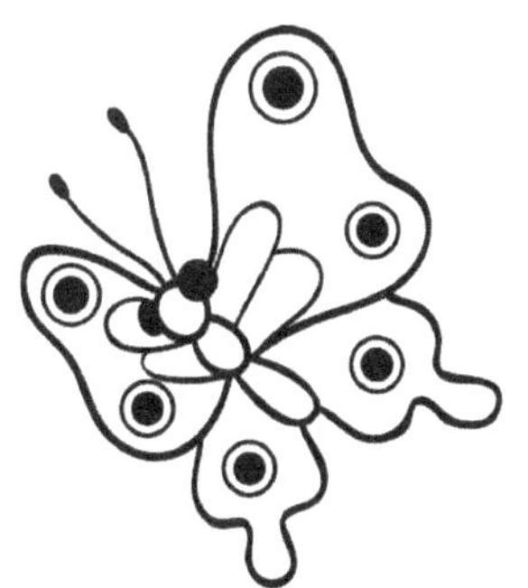

H is for Hazel,
And Hazel is my name.

Oh, Hazel, Hazel, Hazel
*Is my name.

Variation for * is "Starts with H" when you
want to introduce beginning letters later.

Telling One's Name

Telling One's Age

Telling One's School

Telling One's Grade Level

SUGGESTED ACTIVITIES FOR THE DIFFERENT LANGUAGE SKILLS

SKILLS	ACTIVITIES
Listening	Record each child's voice as he or she tells something about himself or herself. When everyone is done, play back the recording and let the children listen to their voice clips. Pause the recording after each voice clip and have the children guess who is speaking.
Speaking	Play a speaking and listening game! Have the children sit in a circle. Start the game by whispering your name to the child who sits to your left. The child then whispers his or her name to the one who is sitting on his or her left. The game goes clockwise until everybody has finished whispering his or her name. Then have the children recount the names that they have heard. You may also do this in pairs.
Reading	• Put the children's names up everywhere. Label everything up with their names. Use their names in your activities. Put children's names and pictures on a name wall in your classroom. • Write each child's name on a paper plate (the first letter written in red and in bold face). Mount the paper plates in a circular position in a corner of your classroom. Have the children sit on their "name plates" during circle time.
Writing	Using colored glue, write the first letter of each child's name on a sheet of paper. When the glue dries up, have the children trace the beginning letters of their names. After some time, they may complete writing their first names and have them trace their entire names.

<u>Direction</u>: Paste a close-up picture of yourself. Cut out from old magazines pictures of the things you like such as food, pets, toys, games, friends, and places. Paste the pictures around your photo to create a collage. Tell something about yourself and your favorite things in class. *(10 points)*

ACTIVITY 1

SCORE: _______

Supply the answer to each question. Practice saying the dialogues with a classmate. *(5 points)*

Telling One's Name

Telling One's Age

Telling One's School

Telling One's Grade Level

CLASS ACTIVITY 2

Guide: Teach the children how to make puppets using photos of themselves. Have them use these puppets to present themselves in new ways. They may also use the puppets to ask about another person.

Materials:

- face or whole-body photos of each child
- construction paper
- paper plates
- popsicle sticks
- drinking straws or barbeque sticks
- rubber bands
- scissors
- tape or glue

Procedure:

Stick Puppets

1. Mount each face or whole-body photo on construction paper.
2. Cut out the photos of the children.
3. Tape or glue a popsicle stick to the back of each puppet.

<u>Paper Plate Masks</u>

1. Mount enlarged full-face photos on paper plates.
2. Tape or glue a drinking straw or barbecue stick to the back of each puppet. Alternatively, you may punch holes on opposite ends of the paper plate and attach rubber bands to the holes.

(Help the children turn the photos into masks by cutting out eye holes. Invite them to decorate their masks in any way they like using different materials. Encourage the children to roleplay as they wear their masks, then have them exchange masks with their classmates.)

<u>Finger Puppets</u>

1. Mount small photos of faces on construction paper.
2. Attach each photo to a paper ring.

<u>Paper Dolls</u>

1. Mount enlarged whole-body photos on construction paper.
2. Cut out the figures.
3. Tape or glue drinking straws or barbecue sticks to the back. Invite the children to create paper clothes to tape on the puppets.

<u>Guide</u>: Take the children on a tour around your school. Have them meet new friends, schoolmates, and teachers. Teach them the proper way of introducing oneself. Encourage them to talk, ask questions, and socialize with others. Later in class, let them tell the names or the number of persons they met.

My Gender: Boy or Girl

> **Guide:** Ask a boy to go in front of the class. Let him introduce himself and tell things about himself. Call on a girl to go in front and have her do the same thing. Invite the children to compare the two children: their haircuts, the clothes they are wearing, etc. Have the children classify themselves into groups of boys and girls.

ACTIVITY 2 SCORE: ______

Are you a boy or a girl? Color the picture that is the same as you. *(5 points)*

I am a ____________________.

boy

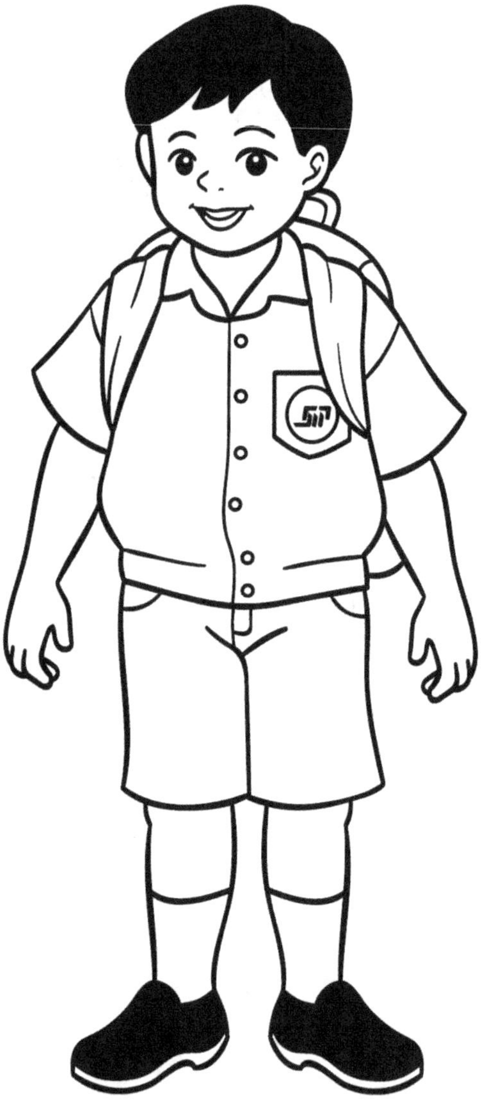

girl

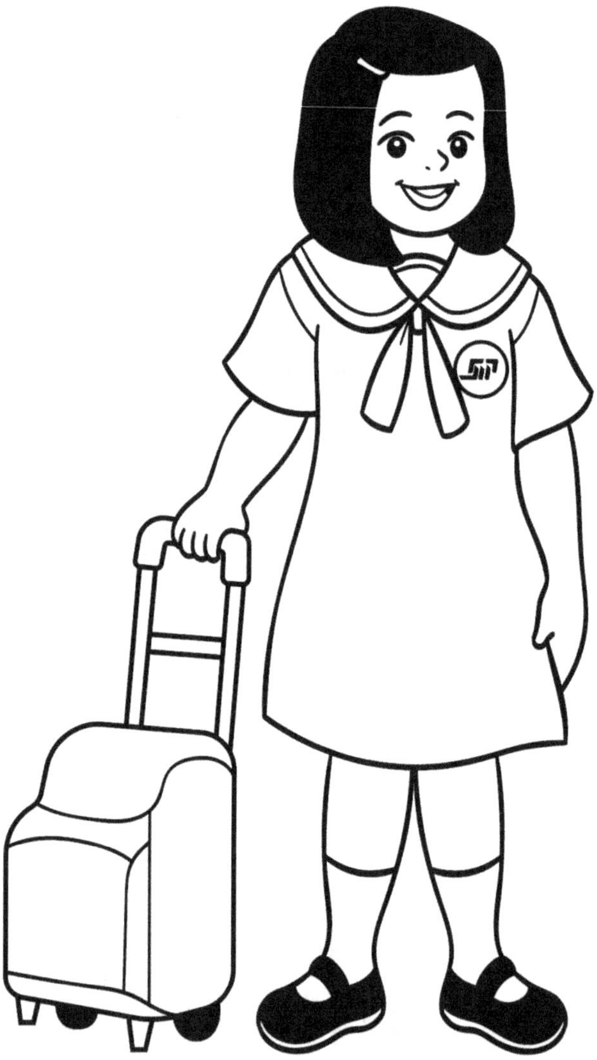

Direction: Paste close-up pictures of the members of your family under the proper column. Count how many are boys and how many are girls. Talk about them in class. *(10 points)*

boys	girls

<u>Direction:</u> Check (✓) all the pictures of girls.
Encircle (◯) all the pictures of boys.

Things I Wear

ACTIVITY 3

SCORE: _______

ACTIVITY 4

SCORE: _______

HOME ACTIVITY 3   SCORE:_______

Direction: Color with blue the boxes before the things that boys wear. Color with red the boxes before the things that girls wear.

1.

2.

3.

4.

5.

6.

7.

8.

9.

10.

QUIZ NO. 2

SCORE: _______

Direction: Connect to the cloud the things that we wear on cold and rainy days. Connect to the sun those that we wear on hot and sunny days.

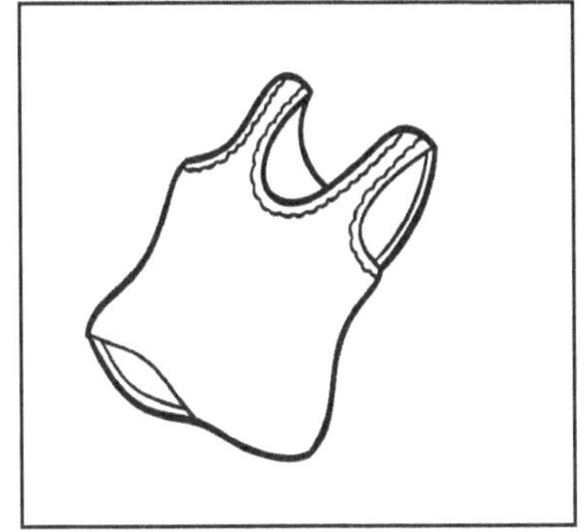

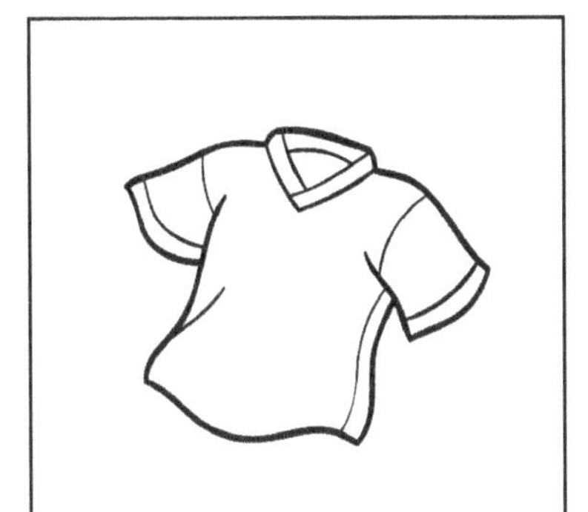

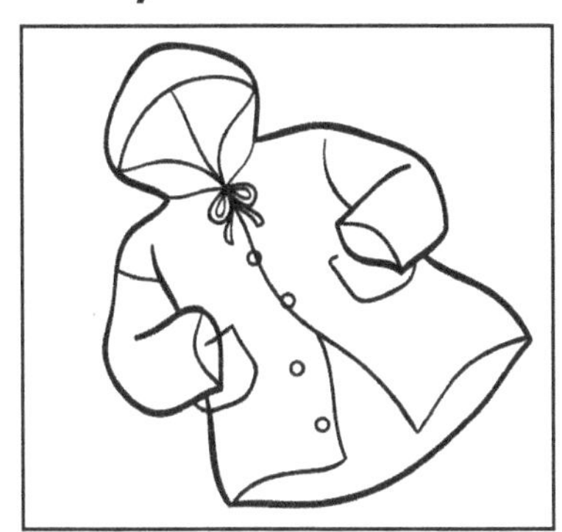

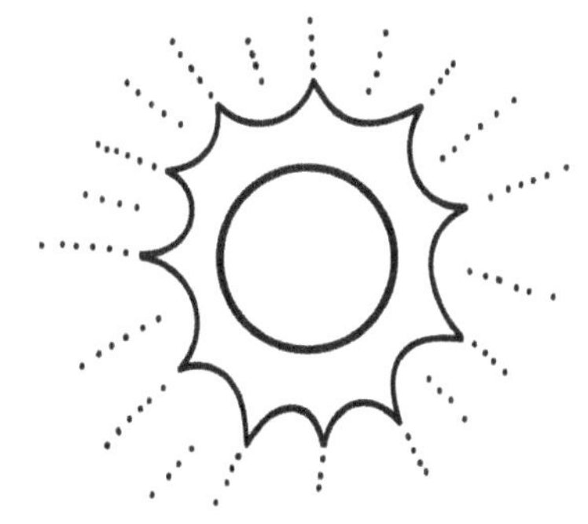

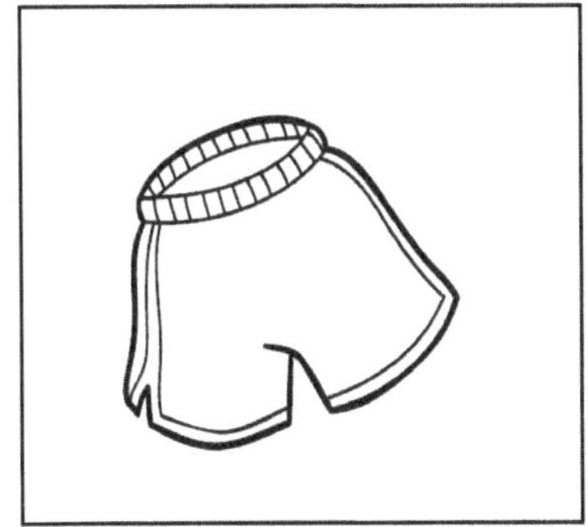

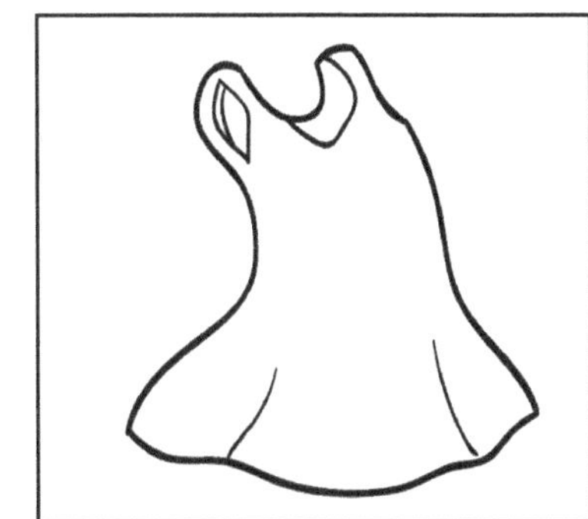

My Body Parts

Guide: Using tag board, make a big human figure. Let the children draw the eyes, nose, mouth, ears, and hair. Cut each part away (head, neck, arms, hands, legs, and feet) like puzzle pieces. Have the pupils identify each part, then form the human puzzle.

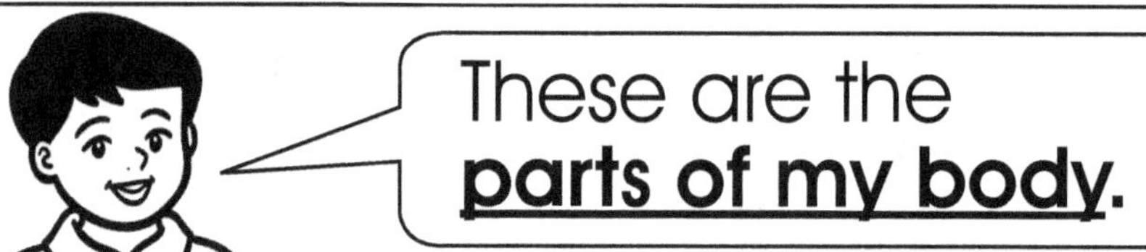

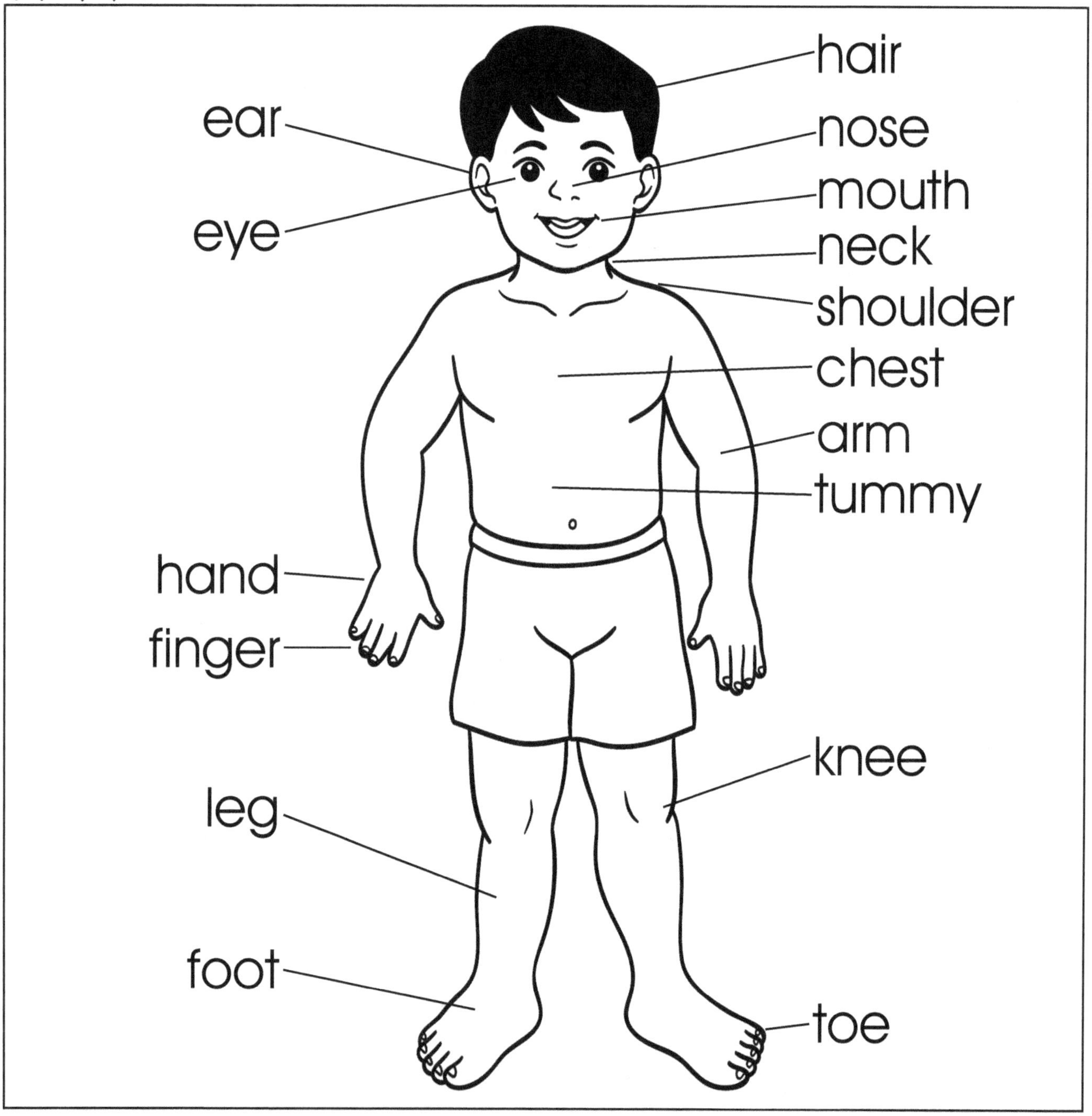

<u>RHYME</u>:

> <u>Guide</u>: Recite the rhyme while pointing to the parts of the body mentioned. Motivate the pupils to do the same.

Can you touch your eyes?

Can you touch your toes?

Can you touch your ears?

Can you touch your nose?

If you can, if you can,

Show me, friend, if you please

And I'll give you a snap,

And a clap, clap, clap!

<u>GAME</u>:

> <u>Guide</u>: Play a different version of "Simon Says" with the children. Together with them, point to any part of your body while saying its name 3 times. Pause for a while, then point to and say the name of another body part. Test the children by pointing to a different body part instead of the name you mentioned. Reward the children who are able to point to the correct body part.

The Body Rap

Teacher: (Intro and Outro)
>   This is the way that we do the Body Rap.
>   Everyone, come, shake your hips and give a clap.
>   This is the way that we do the Body Rap.
>   Everyone, come, shake your hips and give a clap.

Teacher: Can you show me your eyes,
>   Your eyes, eyes, eyes?

Pupils: Teacher, these are my eyes,
>   My eyes, eyes, eyes.

Teacher: Can you show me your nose,
>   Your nose, nose, nose?

Pupils: Teacher, this is my nose,
>   My nose, nose, nose.

Teacher: Can you show me your tongue,
>   Your tongue, tongue, tongue?

Pupils: Teacher, this is my tongue,
>   My tongue, tongue, tongue.

Draw the missing parts of the head that are the same as yours. *(5 points)*

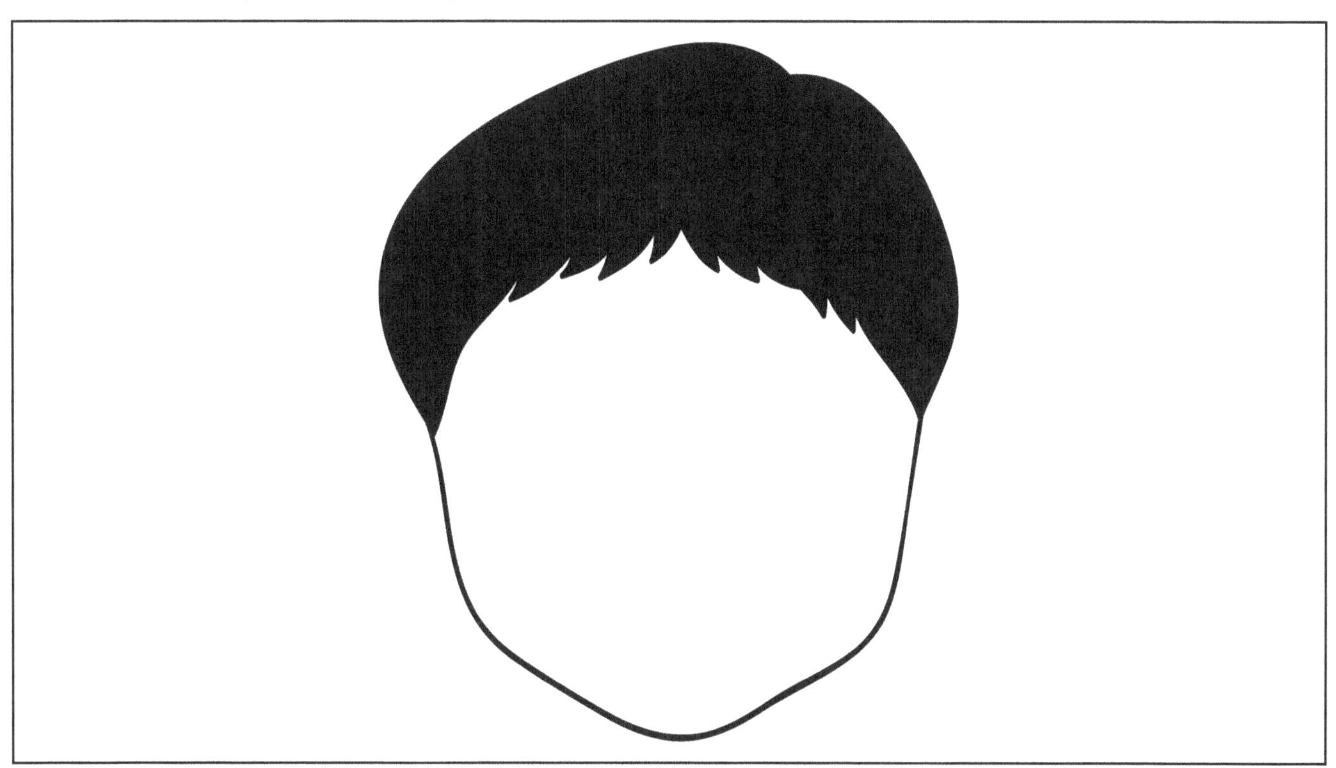

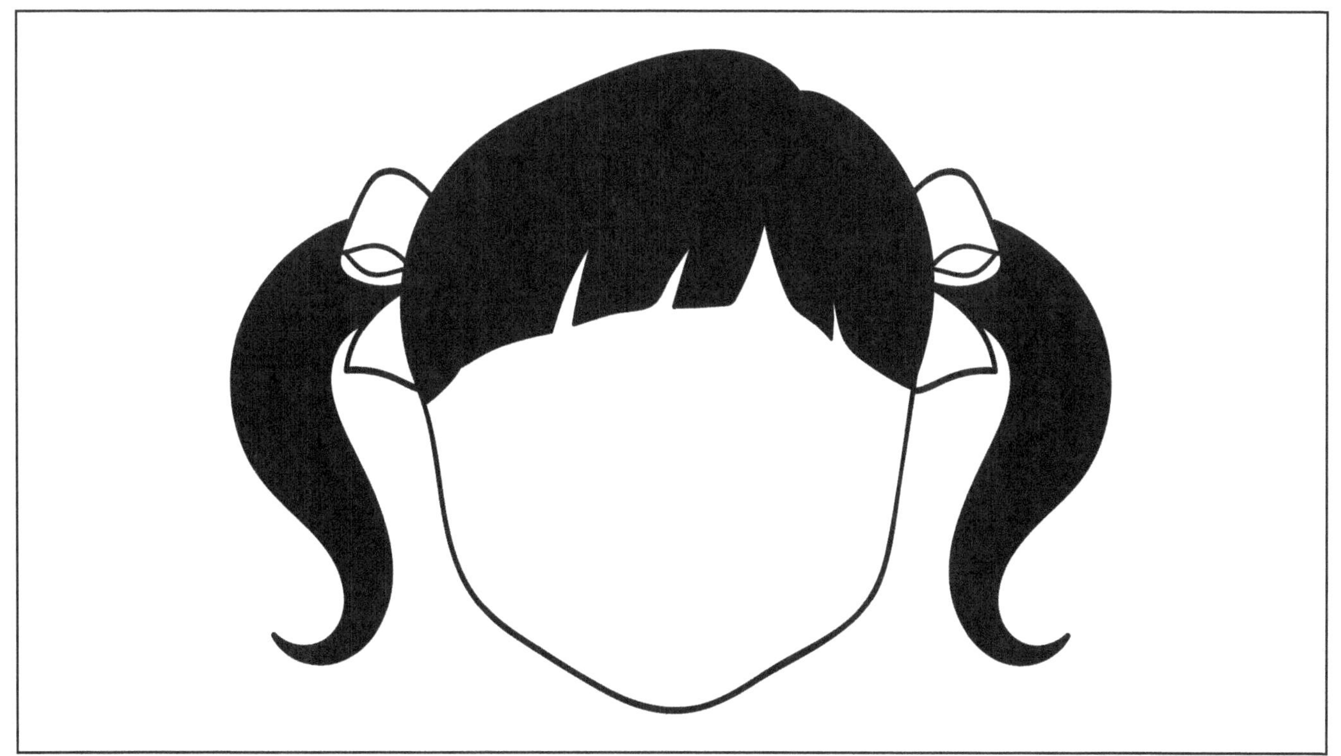

# QUIZ NO. 3

SCORE: ______

Direction: Match the name of each body part with the correct picture by connecting them with a line.

1. ears   •

2. feet   •

3. shoulder •

4. finger   •

5. head   •

6. legs   •

7. arm   •

8. toe   •

QUIZ NO. 4 SCORE: ______

<u>Direction:</u> Encircle the correct picture that matches each body part.

1. knee

2. hand

3. mouth

4. chest

5. neck

6. eyes

7. nose

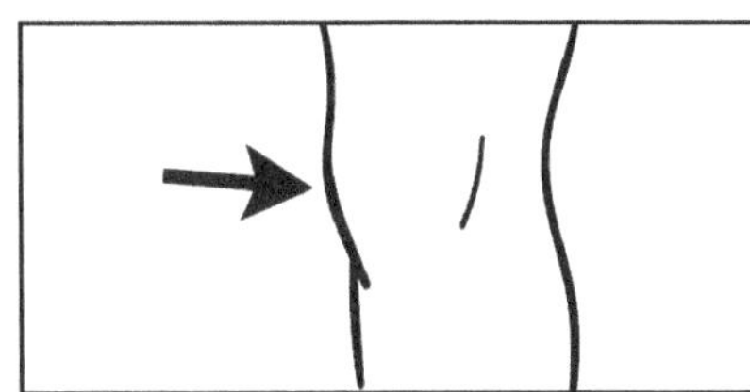
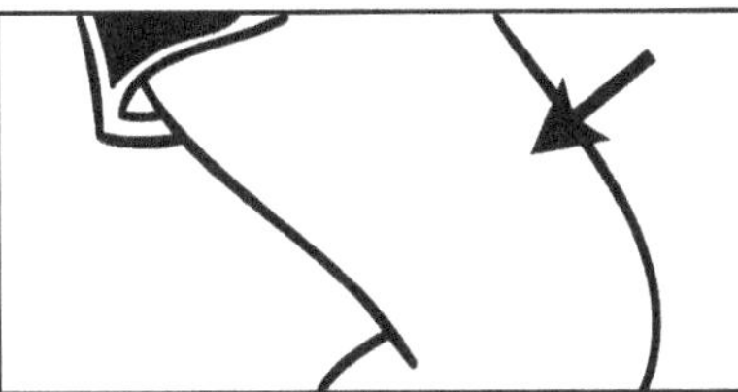
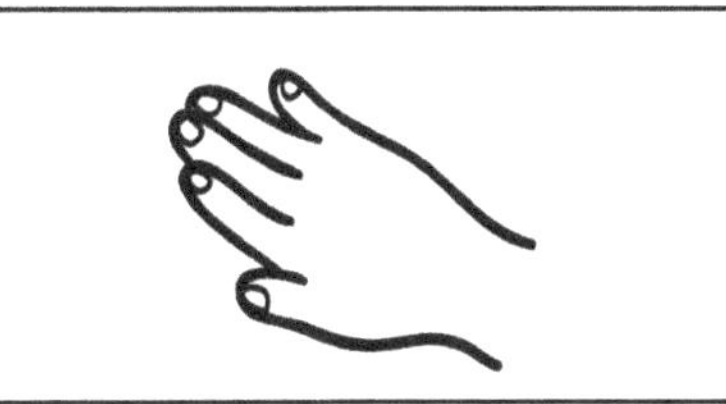

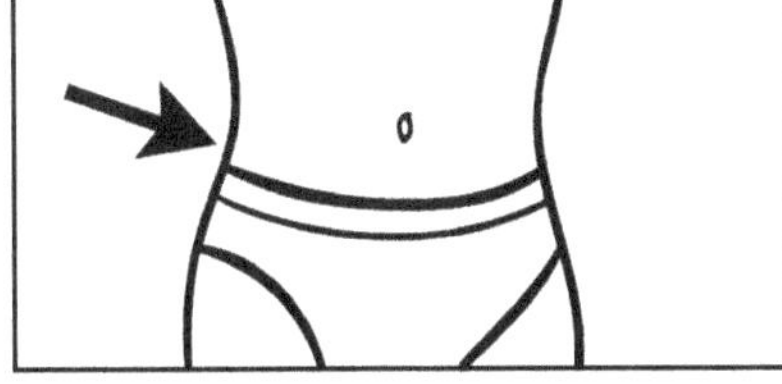
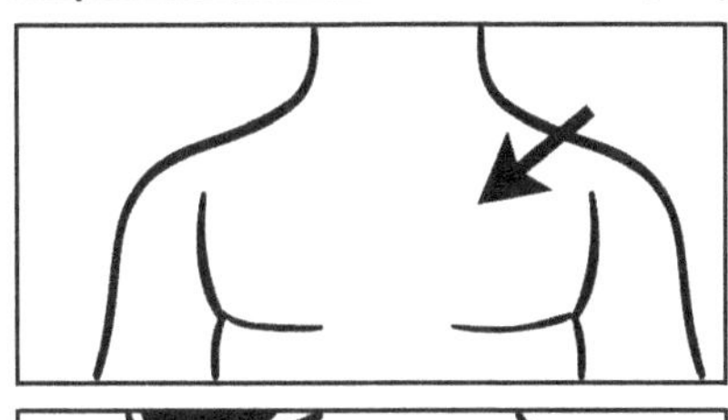

 ## QUIZ NO. 5

SCORE: _______

Direction: What does each body part do? Check the correct picture.

1.     

2.     

3.      

4.      

5.     

Things I Can Do with My Body Parts
My Eyes

My Eyes

I use my eyes for seeing things—
like flowers that bloom,
and butterflies that flutter;
like the rainbow in the sky,
and the sunset from afar.

I use my eyes for seeing things—
like children playing in the street,
and birds flying high above;
like beautiful colored dresses,
and stars that shine so bright.

I use my eyes for seeing things—
yes, many different things!

Direction: Check the two things that are alike in each group.

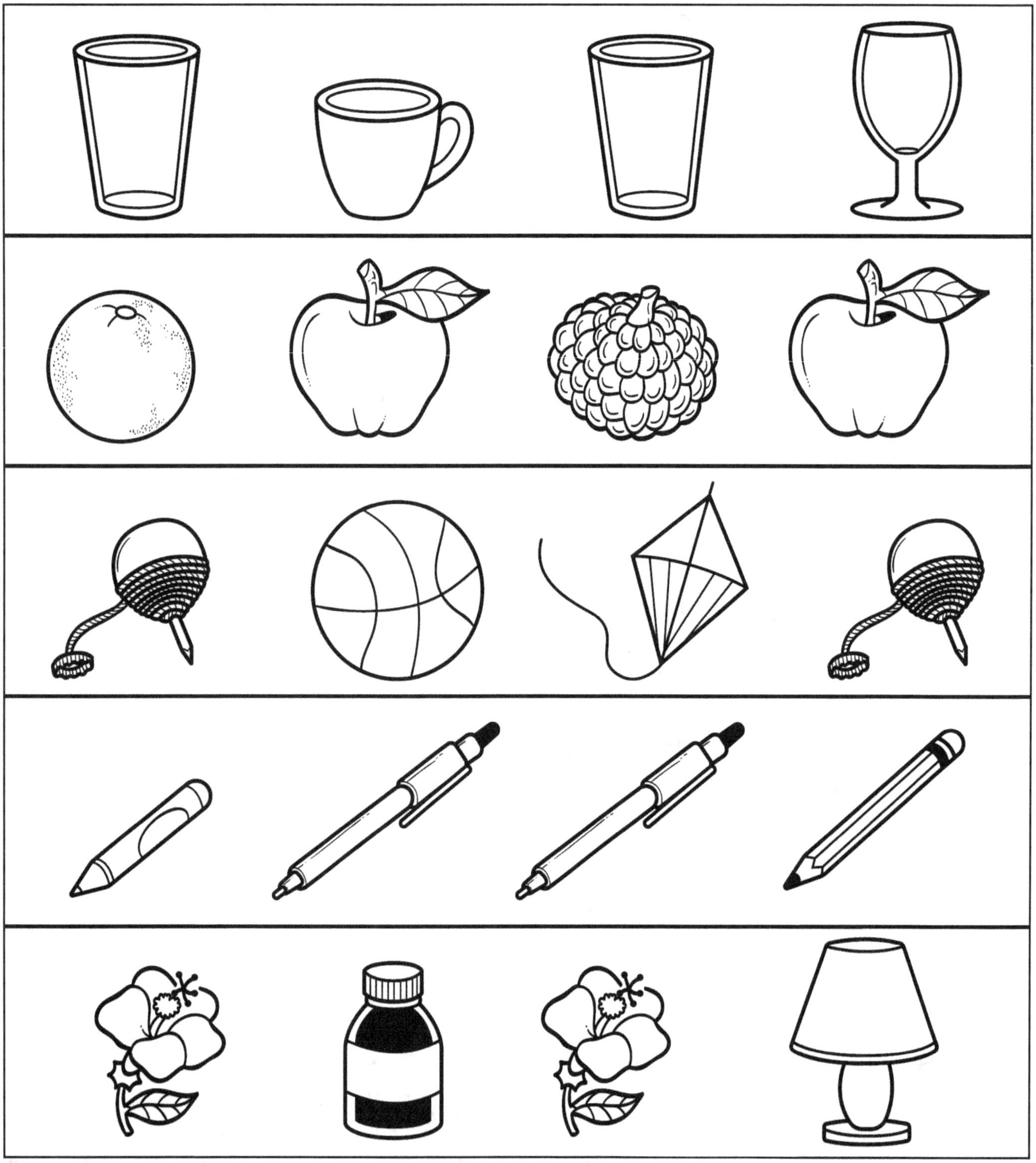

Direction: Encircle (◯) the letter that is different from the others in each group.

D	D	B	D
M	N	N	N
L	I	L	L
O	O	O	C
E	F	E	E

My Hands

My Hands

I use my hands for writing things—
like straight and slant lines,
and curved and broken ones;
like the letters of the alphabet,
and the numerals one to one hundred.

I use my hands for writing things—
like my pet's name,
and other favorite things;
like notes for a friend so dear,
and words that tell how
happy I am.

I use my hands for writing things—
yes, many different things!

ACTIVITY 6

SCORE: _______

Connect the broken lines from the pictures of a boy and a girl to the things that they wear.

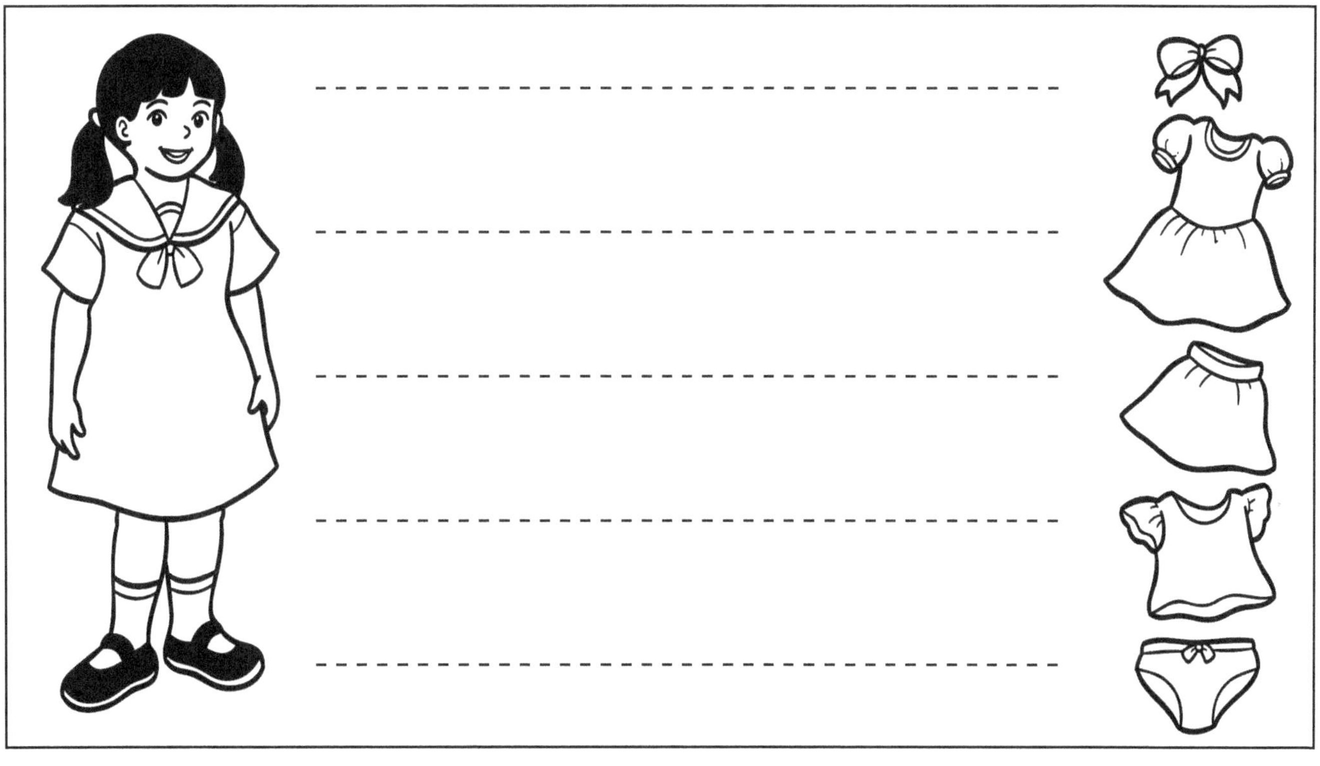

My Ears

My Ears

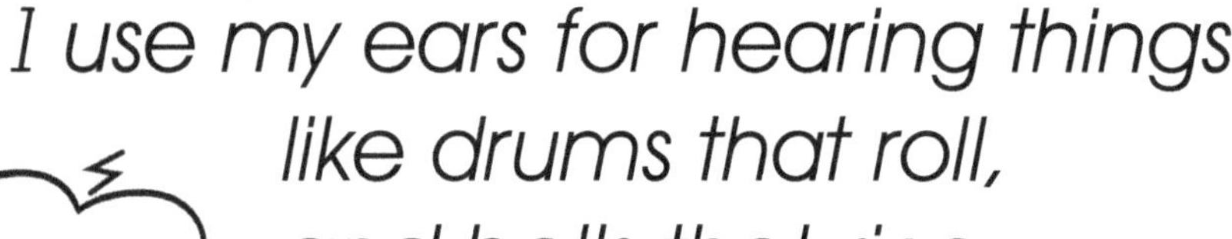

I use my ears for hearing things—
like drums that roll,
and bells that ring;
like clocks that tick,
and forks that ting.

I use my ears for hearing things—
like honking on the street,
and knocking at the door;
like storms loudly thundering,
and children softly singing.

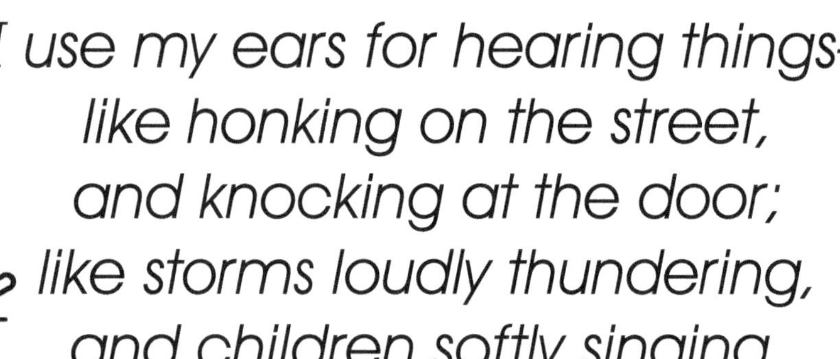

I use my ears for hearing things—
yes, many different things!

Check the things that produce sound. Cross out those that don't produce sound.

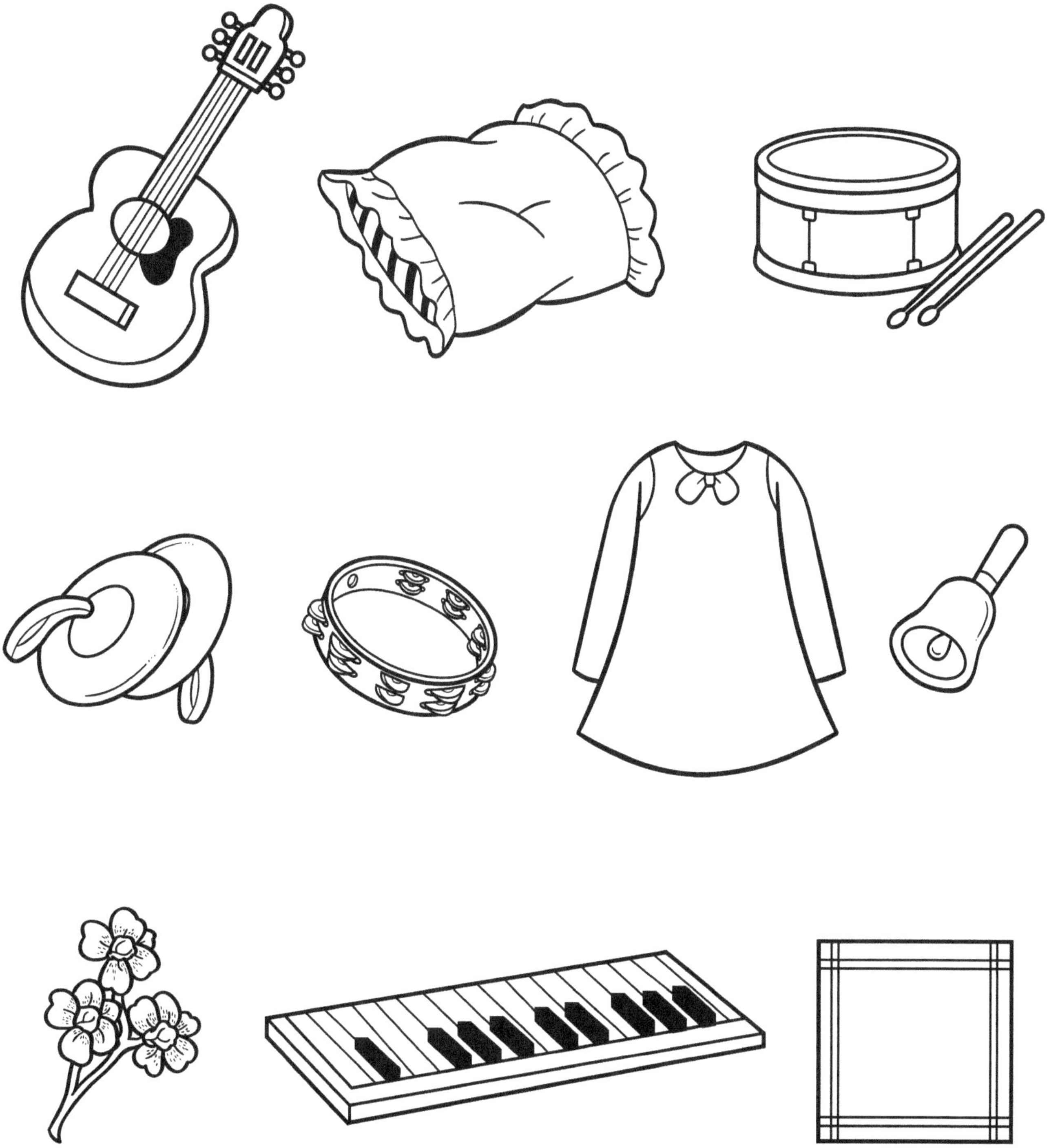

Color with green the animals that make sound. Color with yellow those that don't make sound.

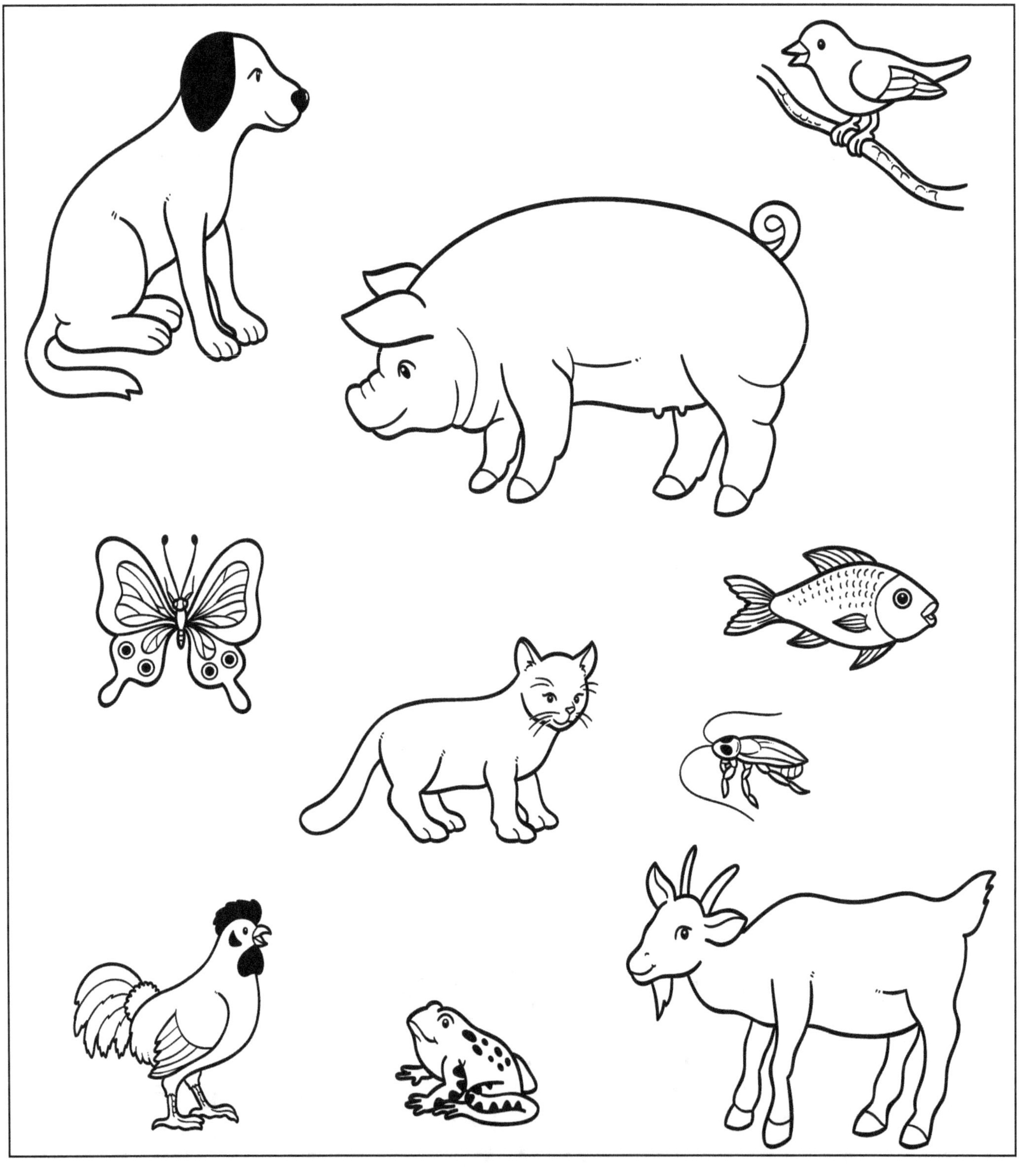

<u>Direction</u>: Connect the sound to the animal.

1. meow •

2. arf •

3. oink •

4. quack •

5. bzzz •

6. hiss •

7. moo •

8. tweet •

SCORE: _______

Direction: Encircle the one which makes a louder sound in each pair.

1. 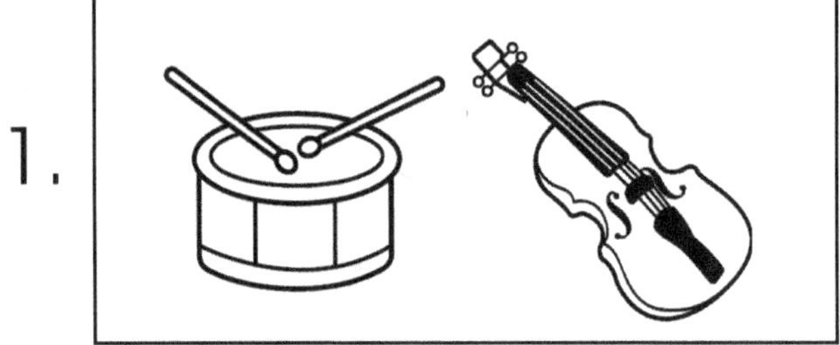

6. 

2. 

7. 

3. 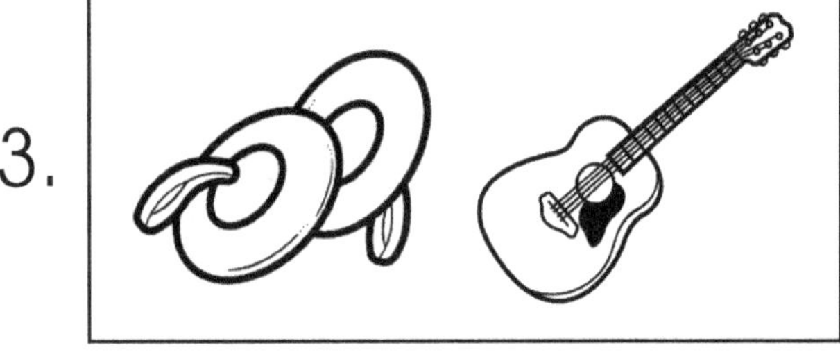

8. 

4. 

9. 

5. 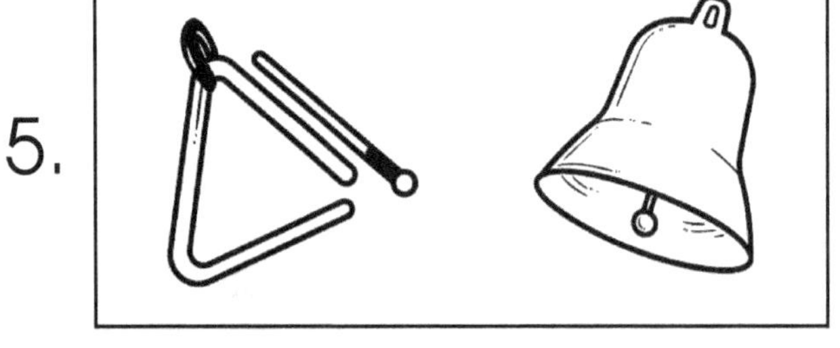

10. 

My Mouth

My Mouth

*I use my mouth for saying things—
like "Good morning" and "Good afternoon,"
and "Good evening" and "Good night";
like "Hi" and "Hello,"
and "Excuse me," "Please," and "I'm sorry."*

*I use my mouth for saying things—
like my name and my grade,
and how old I am;
like telling God "I love you!"
and telling Mom and Dad "Thank you!"*

*I use my mouth for saying things—
yes, many different things!*

Guide: Provide each child with a small mirror. Have each child hold a mirror in front of his or her mouth. Sound out each letter of the alphabet with them. Have them observe their lips, teeth, and tongue closely as they form each letter sound. Next, say some simple three-letter words and have them repeat after you (e.g., "cat," "bed," "pit," "hot," etc.). Have them observe their mouth in the mirror as they say the words. Later, have them look at your face while you say three-letter words without sound. Have them guess each word that you are forming with your mouth.

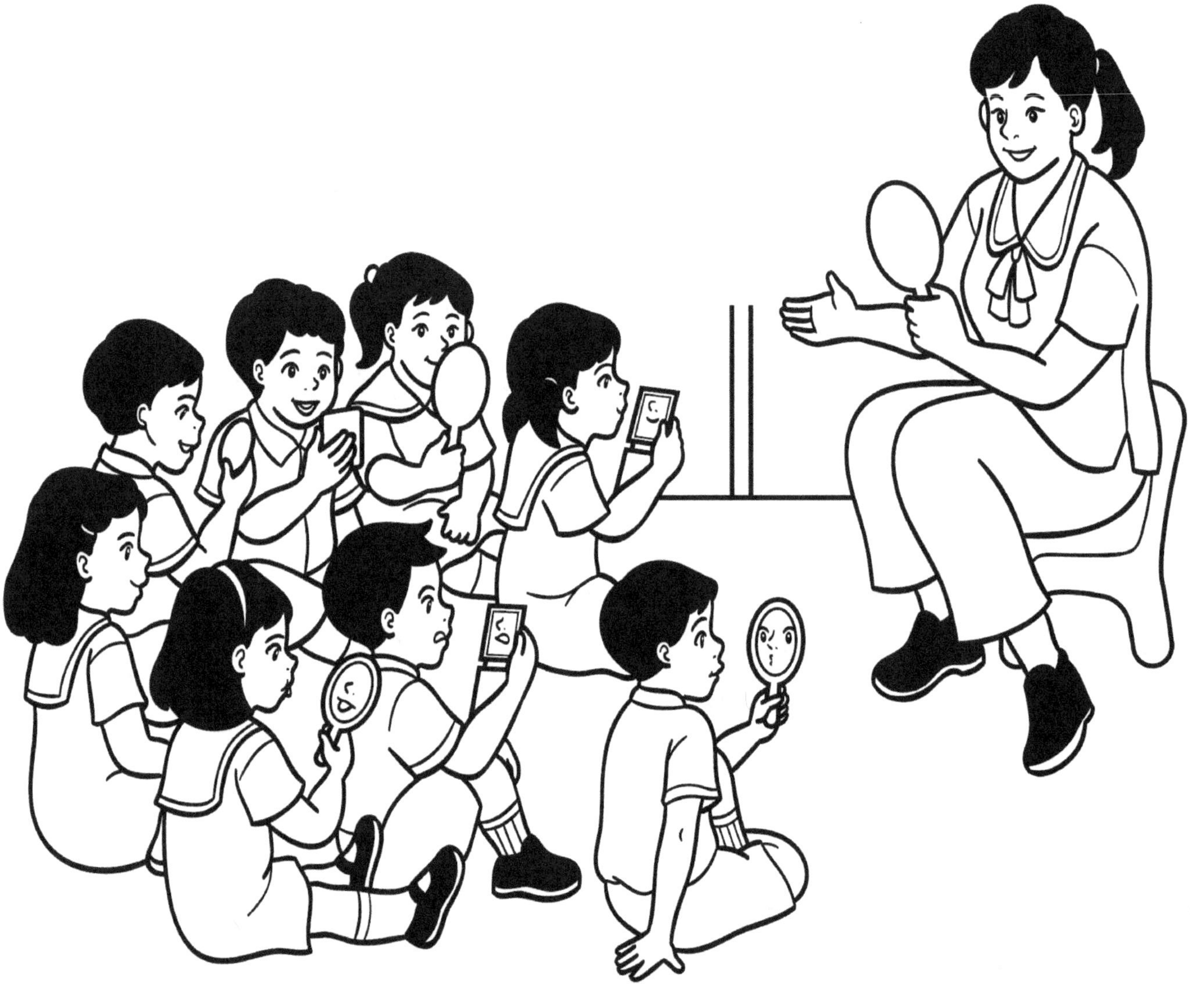

SUGGESTED ACTIVITIES FOR THE DIFFERENT LANGUAGE SKILLS

SKILLS	ACTIVITIES
Listening 	Prepare different sets of small objects (e.g, set of coins, set of shells, set of pencils, etc.). Put each set of objects in a small covered box. Shake each box and have the children listen to the sound that the box makes. Have the children guess what kind of object is inside each box, then reveal the contents.

Speaking 	Choose six letter sounds. Have the children sing _The Alphabet Song_ using the chosen letter sounds, with each sound replacing each line of lyrics in the song.
	For example:
	    1st line - _ah, ah, ah, ah, ah, ah, ah_
	    2nd line - _buh, buh, buh, buh, buh, buh, buh_
	    3rd line - _kuh, kuh, kuh, kuh, kuh, kuh, kuh_
	
	You may later choose a new set of letter sounds for the children to sing.

Reading 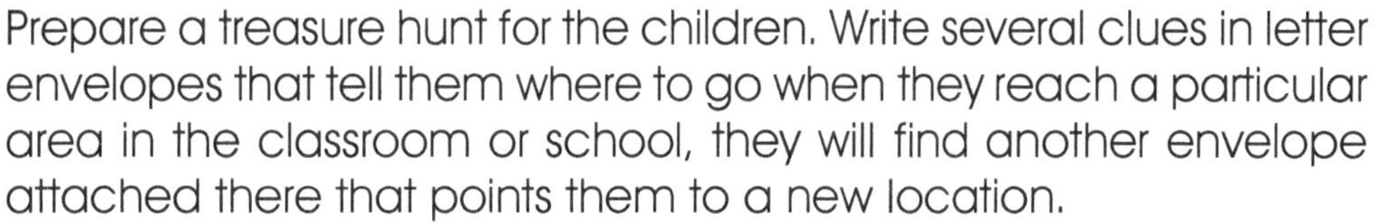	Prepare a treasure hunt for the children. Write several clues in letter envelopes that tell them where to go when they reach a particular area in the classroom or school, they will find another envelope attached there that points them to a new location.
	For example:
	    1st clue - "Go to the door."
	    2nd clue - (attached to the door)
	           "Go to the teacher's table."
	    3rd clue - (attached to the teacher's table)
	           "Go to the biggest window." (and so on)
	
	Prepare five to seven of these clues. You may help them in reading. Your "hidden treasure" may be toys or snacks.

Writing 	Name some objects around the classroom. Have the children "write" the first letter of each object's name using their forefinger in the air. You may visit other parts of the school and name some interesting things there, and have the children trace in the air the first letter of each object's name.

GREETINGS

Guide: Call on a pupil and say the following dialogues with him/her. Ask everybody to get a partner and do the same. Ask the children to color the pictures that show what they say and do.

These are some of the greetings we use every day. Let's practice saying them, pronouncing each greeting properly.

In the Morning

Any Time of the Day

In the Afternoon

When Leaving

In the Evening

Before Going to Bed

 Sing while clapping to the beat. Then invite the children to sing and clap with you.

"Good Morning Song" #1

Good morning, good morning!
We love to say "Good morning."
Good morning, good morning,
Good morning to you all!

"Good Morning Song" #2

Good morning, good morning,
And how do you do?
Good morning, good morning,
I'm fine, how are you?

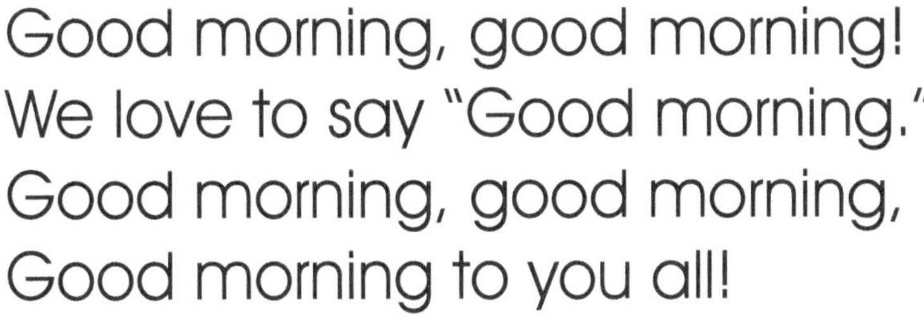

"Hello Song"

Hello, hello, hello,
How are you today?
Hello, hello, hello,
We are fine.
Tra la la la la la la la la…
Tra la la la la la la la la…

"Goodbye Song"

We are going, we are going,
Now goodbye, now goodbye.
See you all tomorrow, see you all tomorrow,
Now goodbye, now goodbye!

SUGGESTED ACTIVITIES FOR THE DIFFERENT LANGUAGE SKILLS

SKILLS	ACTIVITIES
Listening and Speaking	• Say the different greetings to the children, and have them practice replying to you. (For example, say "Good morning, children!" and the kids must answer "Good morning, teacher!") Cycle through the different greetings a few times. Next, reverse your roles; they must be the one to say the greetings first, and you will answer. • Prepare four picture cards that show the time of the day: one card shows a sunrise, one card shows the sun in the sky, one card shows the moon, and one card shows a bed. Show them a card at random and they must greet you depending on the picture shown. You may turn this activity into a game.
Reading and Writing	Write the different greetings on big flashcards. Provide the children with blank flashcards and sharpies of their own. Show them a greeting at random, and they must write the appropriate response on a blank flashcard. Continue doing this until all the greetings have been answered and the blank flashcards have been filled up. For the next few days, instead of greeting the children verbally, you hold up a card and show it to them; the children must choose the appropriate response from the flashcards they made and show it to you.

QUIZ NO. 10

SCORE: _______

Direction: Connect the greetings to the correct pictures. *(Your teacher will read them for you.)*

Good night. •

Hi! •

Goodbye. •

Good afternoon.

Good morning.

Good evening.

POLITE EXPRESSIONS

When Receiving Something

When Someone Thanks Us

After Hurting Someone or Doing Something Wrong

When Asking for Help or Favor

When Getting Someone's Attention

When Borrowing Something

When Leaving the Room or When Asking Permission

SUGGESTED ACTIVITIES FOR THE DIFFERENT LANGUAGE SKILLS

SKILLS	ACTIVITIES
Listening and Speaking	**Reminder Bracelets** **Materials:** - old watch straps or wide ribbon lace - plastic cover - strips of paper to write on - tape - Sharpie marker - scissors **Procedure:** 1. Write different polite expressions on the strips of paper. 2. On a few of them, write "I am polite!" 3. Cover the strips of paper in plastic. 4. Attach each strip securely to the watch straps or wide ribbon lace. If you're using lace, cut them to an appropriate length. 5. You now have reminder bracelets. Whenever a child forgets to use a polite expression, wrap the appropriate bracelet on his or her wrist to remind the child to use the correct expression when the situation calls for it. Whenever a child practices using polite expressions, have him or her wear the "I am polite!" bracelet as a reward. The children wear these for the rest of the day.
Reading and Writing	Choose a short story for the children, but modify it so that the characters use more polite expressions. Read your modified story to the children; then have them read the story themselves. After discussing the story with them, have them write down the polite expressions used in that story.

Direction: Connect the polite expressions to the correct pictures. *(Your teacher will read them for you.)*

Can you please help me? •

Thank you. •

Excuse me, may I pass? •

May I go out?

May I borrow
your toy?

I'm sorry.

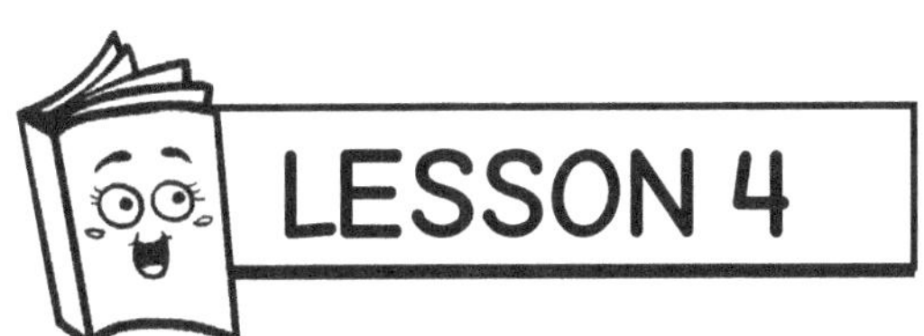

BODY LANGUAGE
Facial Expressions

Guide: Express different emotions using just your face and have the children identify each emotion being expressed. Then have the children take turns acting out different facial expressions while the rest of the class identify each emotion.

happy

sad

mad

afraid

tired

sleepy

QUIZ NO. 12   SCORE: _______

Direction: Connect the word to the correct facial expression.

1. afraid •

2. mad •

3. happy •

4. sleepy •

5. sad •

Gestures

Guide: Demonstrate different gestures to the children and have them mimic you. During the next class break, you and the class play "The Quiet Game." Challenge the children to go about their usual routine without speaking, using only gestures to communicate.

We use **gestures** to express ourselves without using words. We also use gestures while speaking to express ourselves more clearly. Here are some examples.

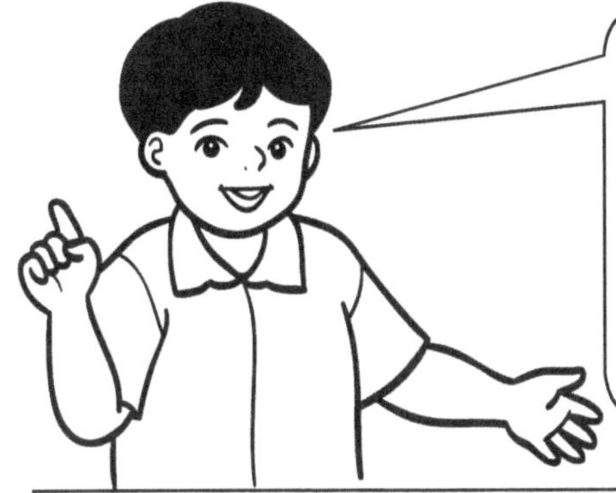

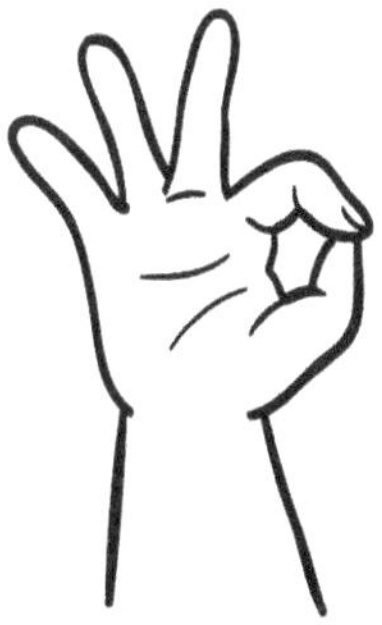

okay

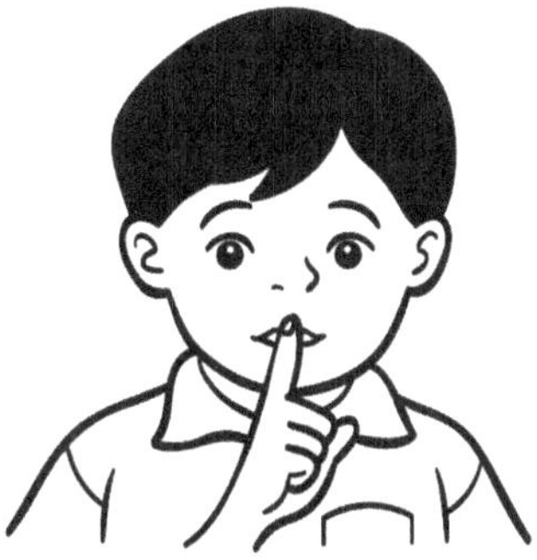

shush

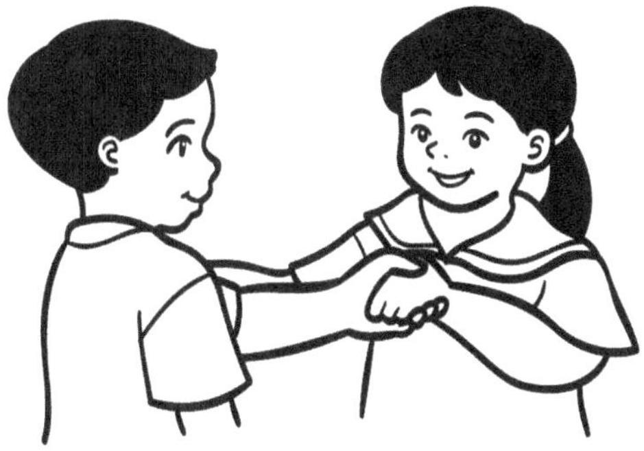

handshake

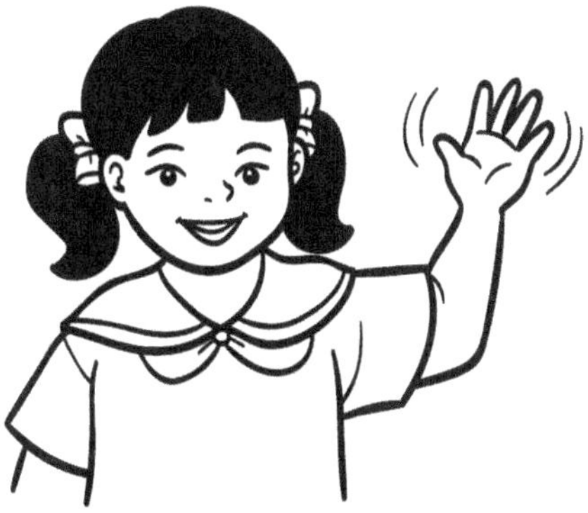

wave

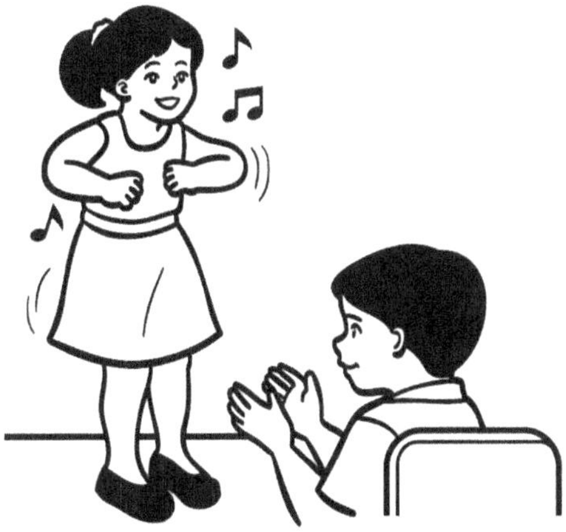

clap

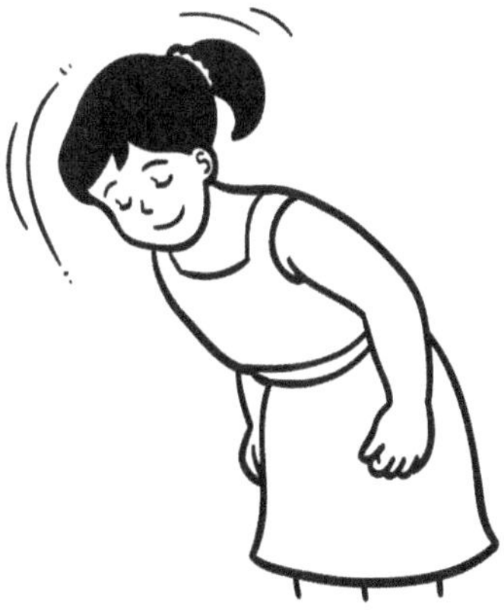

bow

QUIZ NO. 13

SCORE: _______

<u>Direction:</u> Color the correct picture for each gesture.

1. wave

2. bow

3. shush

4. clap

5. okay

<u>SUGGESTED ACTIVITIES FOR THE DIFFERENT LANGUAGE SKILLS</u>

SKILLS	ACTIVITIES
Listening and Speaking	Demonstrate the different facial expressions to the children. Preface each expression by saying "I am happy!" "I am sad!" "I am mad!" and so on, Exaggerate your expressions. Next, have the children play charades. Call on one of them to act. Whisper an emotion to the chosen actor, and he or she must demonstrate it using only his or her face and body. The other children must guess the emotion by saying "He is sad!" "She is happy!" "He is afraid!" etc.
Reading and Writing	Search Youtube Kids for an animated short film for children. There are many of these that usually do not have any spoken language. Watch the video once for enjoyment. Then watch it again, this time pausing the video whenever a character on-screen shows an interesting facial expression or gesture. Have the children mimic the expression or gesture, then ask them what it signifies. Discuss the actions on-screen with the children, making sure that they are able to follow the story even with no dialogue.

HE AND <u>SHE</u>

<u>**Guide:**</u> Make two flashcards: one with the word *he* and the other one with the word *she*. Instruct the boys to stand up when you show the flashcard with the word *he*, and the girls to do the same when you show the flashcard with the word *she*. You may turn this into a game, changing the instruction from standing up to clapping, dancing, waving hands, etc.

Bradley is a boy.

He is a handsome boy.

Aya is a girl.

She is a pretty girl.

<u>Remember</u>:

- We use <u>**he**</u> for a boy.
- We use <u>**she**</u> for a girl.

ACTIVITY 9

SCORE: _______

Connect to the triangle the pictures that use <u>he</u>.

Connect to the heart the pictures that use <u>she</u>.

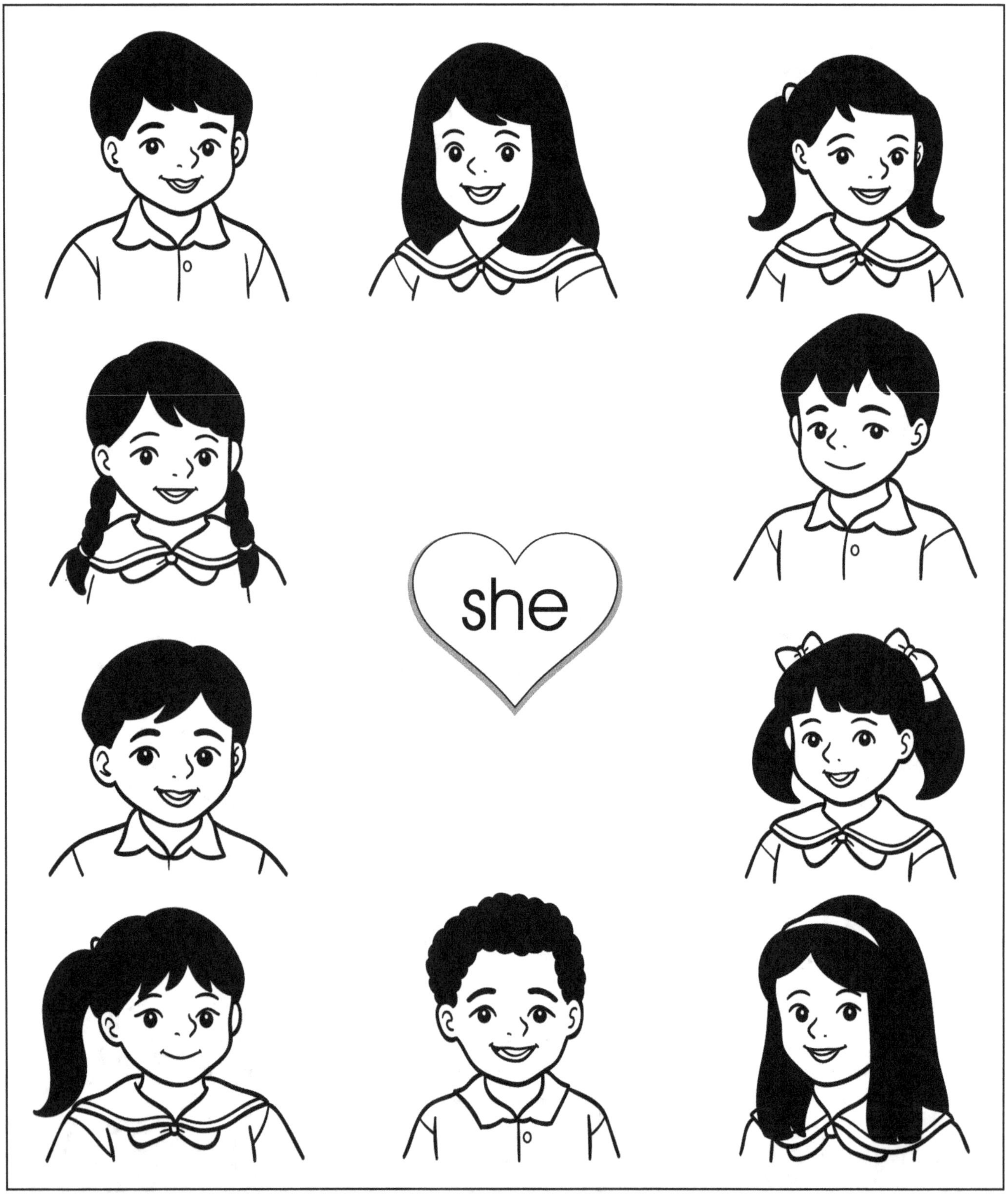

QUIZ NO. 14

SCORE: _______

Direction: Encircle the correct word for each picture.

1.  he she	6.  he she
2.  he she	7.  he she
3.  he she	8.  he she
4.  he she	9. he she
5.  he she	10. he she

FIRST QUARTERLY TEST

Name: _______________________________________ **Score:** ____________

Level: _______________ **Date:** ____________

I. Color the box of the correct picture that matches each body part.

1. feet

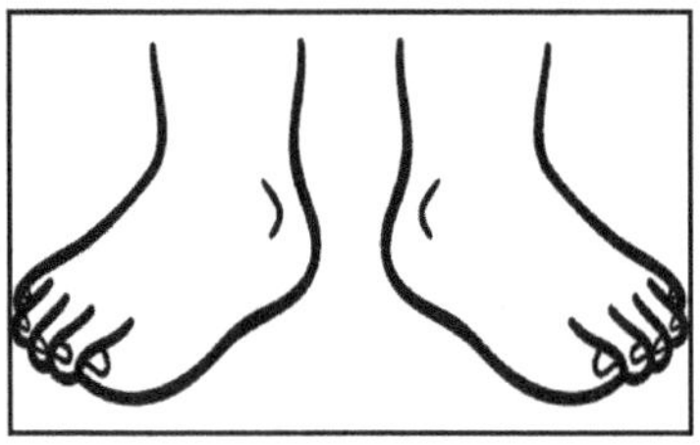

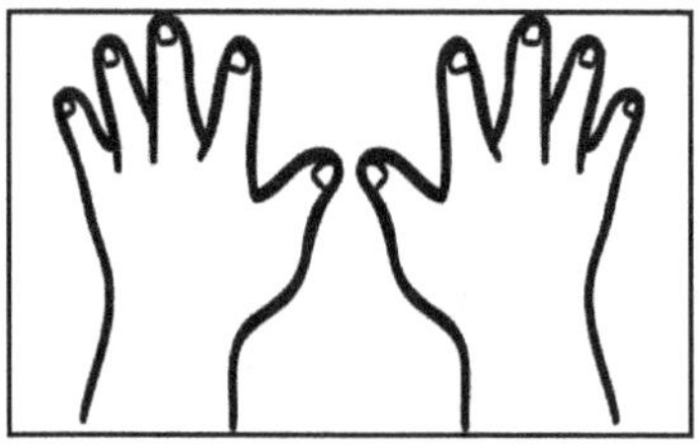

2. knee

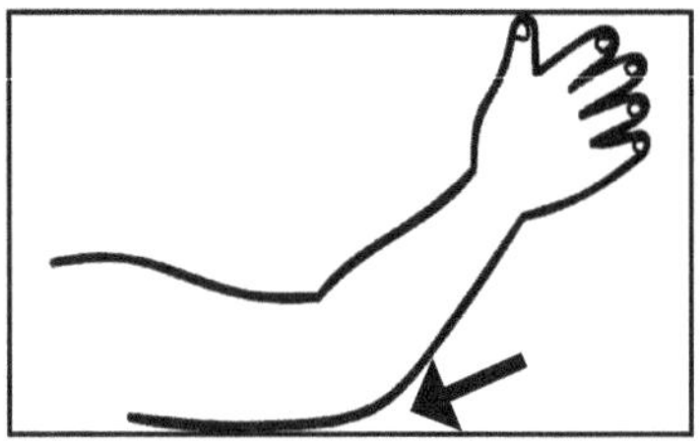

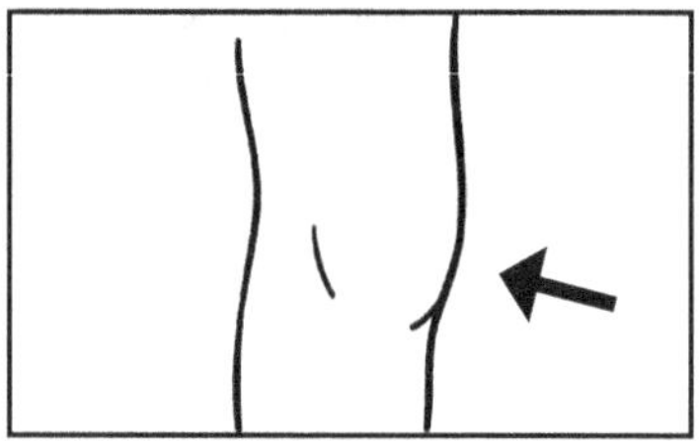

3. shoulder

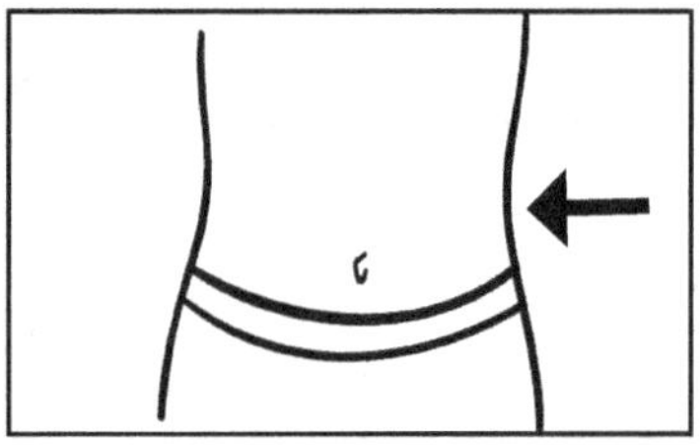

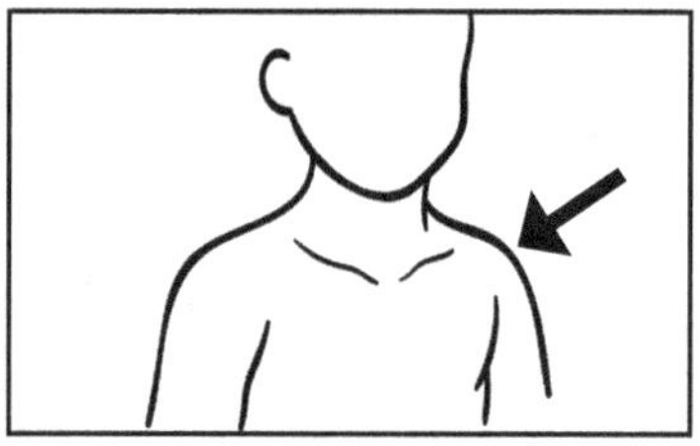

4. mouth

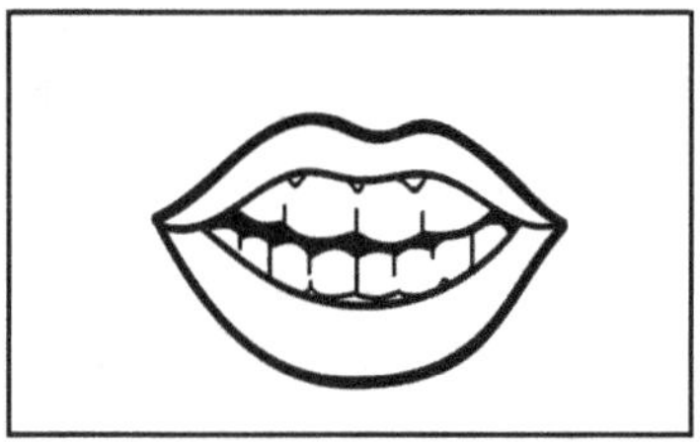

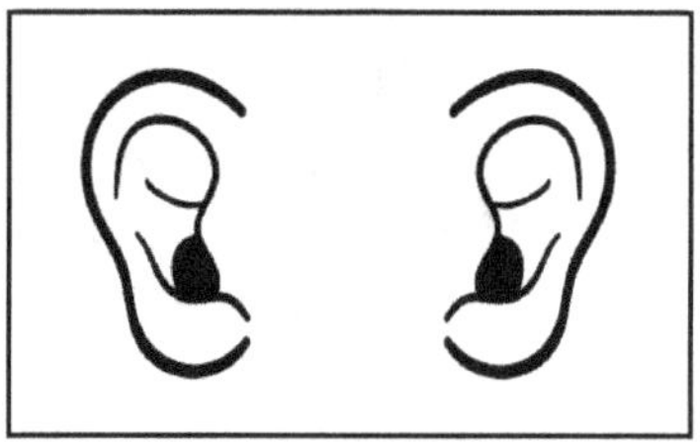

5. chest

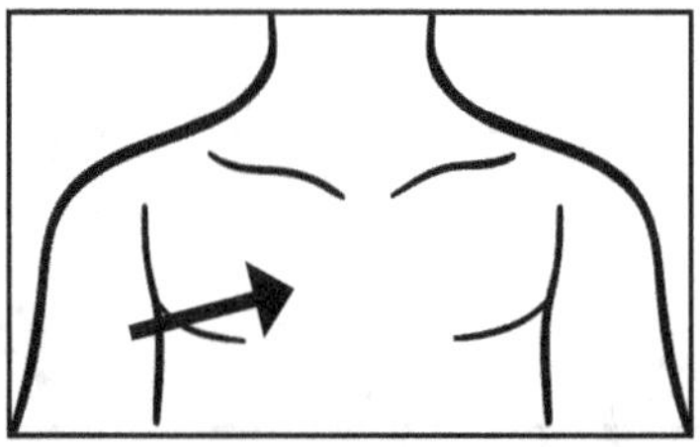

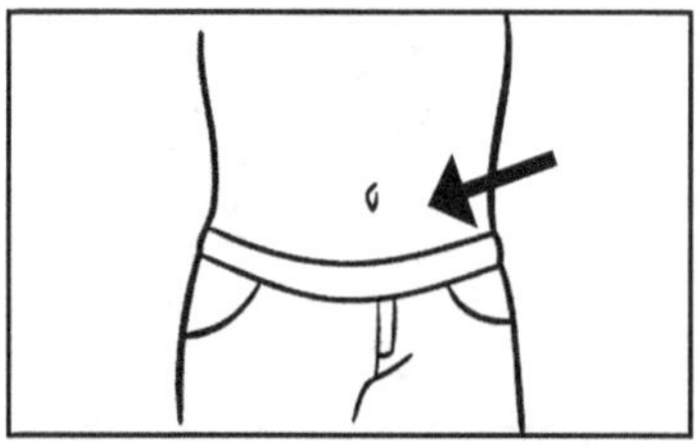

II. Encircle the part of the body that does each activity.

1. 

2.

3.

4.

5.

III. Check the correct facial expression for each
     word.

1. mad

2. sad

3. tired

4. afraid

5. happy

IV. Connect the word to the correct gesture.

1. wave

2. okay

3. clap

4. handshake

5. shush

V. Write **B** before the pictures of boys.
Write **G** before the pictures of girls.

______ 1.

______ 2.

______ 3.

______ 4.

______ 5.

______ 6.

______ 7.

______ 8.

______ 9.

______ 10.

VI. Cross out the correct picture for each word.

1. she

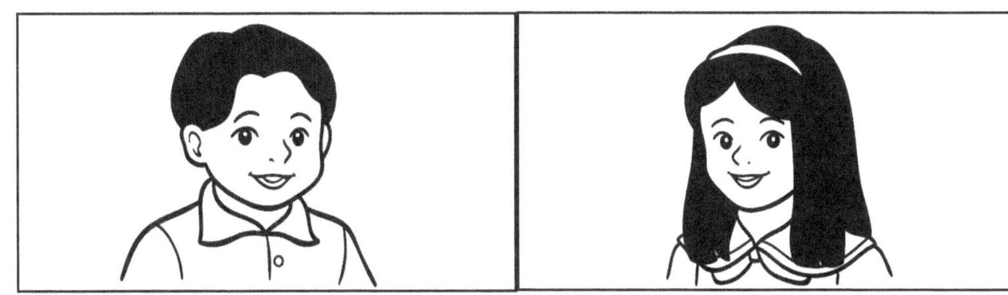

2. he

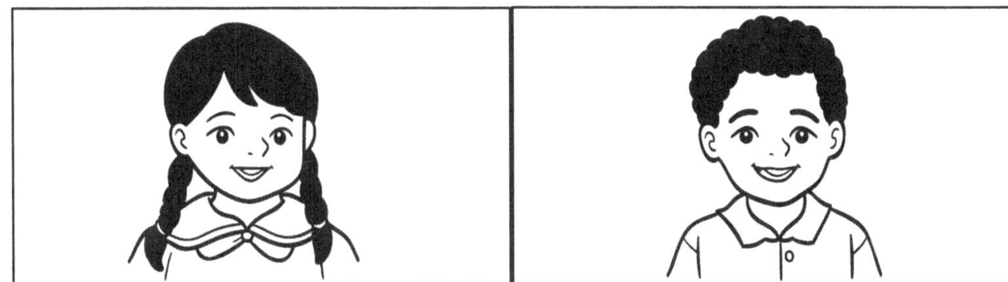

3. she

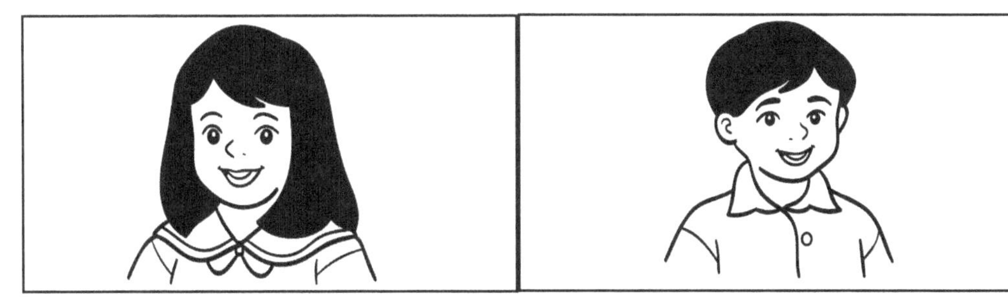

4. she

5. he

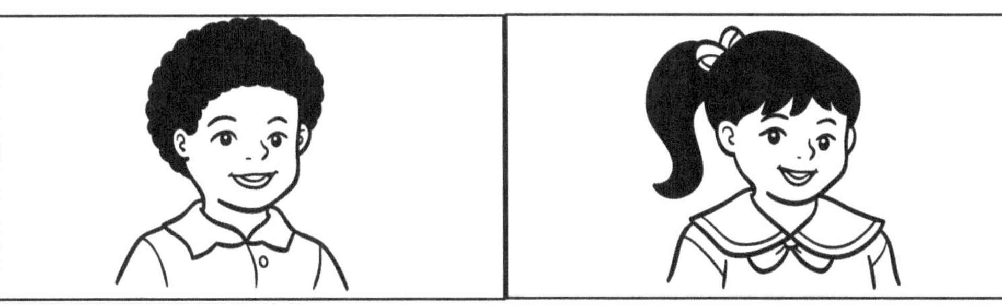

PROGRESS CHART
FIRST QUARTER

Name: _________________________________   Level: _____________

ACTIVITY	No. of Items	My Score	HOME ACTIVITY	No. of Items	My Score	QUIZ	No. of Items	My Score
1	5		1	10		1	10	
2	5		2	10		2	10	
3	10		3	10		3	8	
4	10					4	7	
5	5					5	5	
6	10					6	5	
7	10					7	5	
8	10					8	8	
9	10					9	10	
10	10					10	6	
						11	6	
						12	5	
						13	5	
						14	10	
TOTAL	85		TOTAL	30		TOTAL	100	

_______________________________   _______________________________
Parent's/Guardian's Signature   Teacher's Signature

SECOND QUARTER
MY FAMILY, MY HOME, MY SCHOOL AND MY FRIENDS

Teacher's Objectives and Student Evaluation

Lesson	*At the end of the activities, the child should be able to:*	NI	S	E
1	1. recognize and name the members of the family			
	2. tell the names of the family members			
	3. name the other members of an extended family			
	4. know the differences of families			
	5. love and appreciate one's family			
	6. show respect for family members			
2	7. tell the different parts of a house			
	8. identify the rooms in a house			
	9. understand the importance of having a house			
	10. love and respect the people living in one's house			
	11. thank God for the gift of a happy home			
3	12. tell the different places in school			
	13. enumerate some of the things found in a classroom			
	14. tell the things that are used in school and know the importance of these things			
	15. love, respect, and take care of the things in school			
4	16. identify naming words for persons, animals, things, and places			
	17. increase vocabulary words			
	18. improve sensory-motor skills through drills			
5	19. tell the difference between one and many			
	20. differentiate between is and are			
	21. differentiate it from they			
	22. use this and that properly			
	23. tell when to use has and have			
	24. use is and are, it and they, this and that, and has and have in sentences			
	25. use the words learned in day-to-day communication			

Legend:

NI — Needs Improvement   S — Satisfactory   E — Excellent

LESSON 1

MY FAMILY

Guide: Show the children a picture of your family. Tell them something about the members of your family. Explain to the children that not all families are the same (e.g., one or two members may be absent, family members may have different roles, etc.). Encourage the children to tell something about their families.

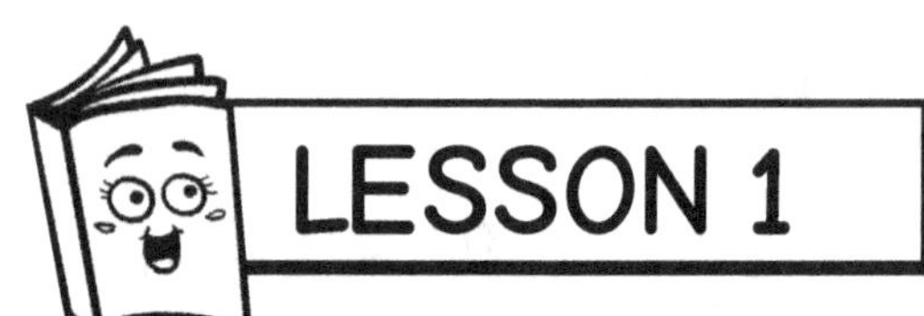

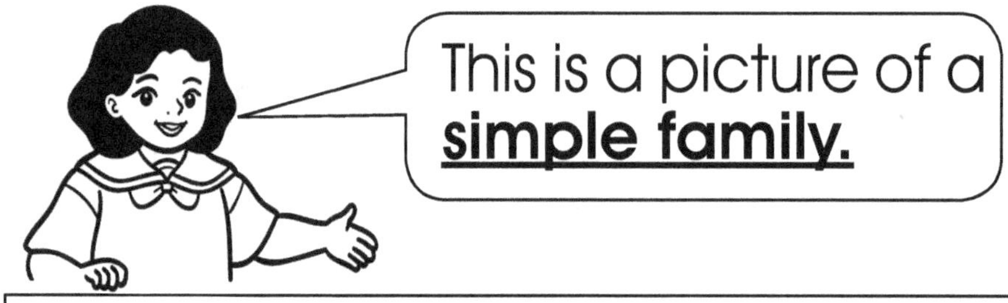

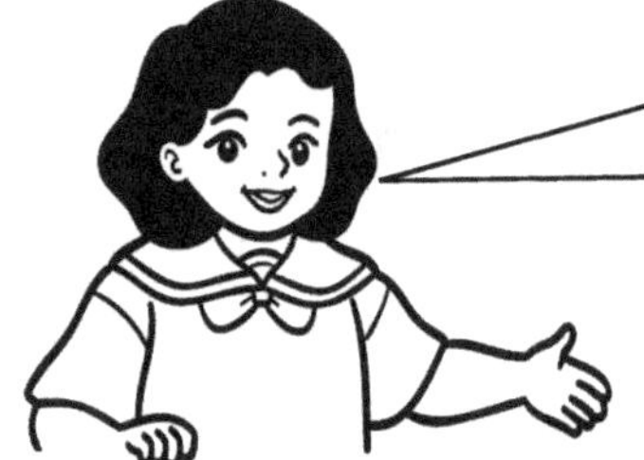

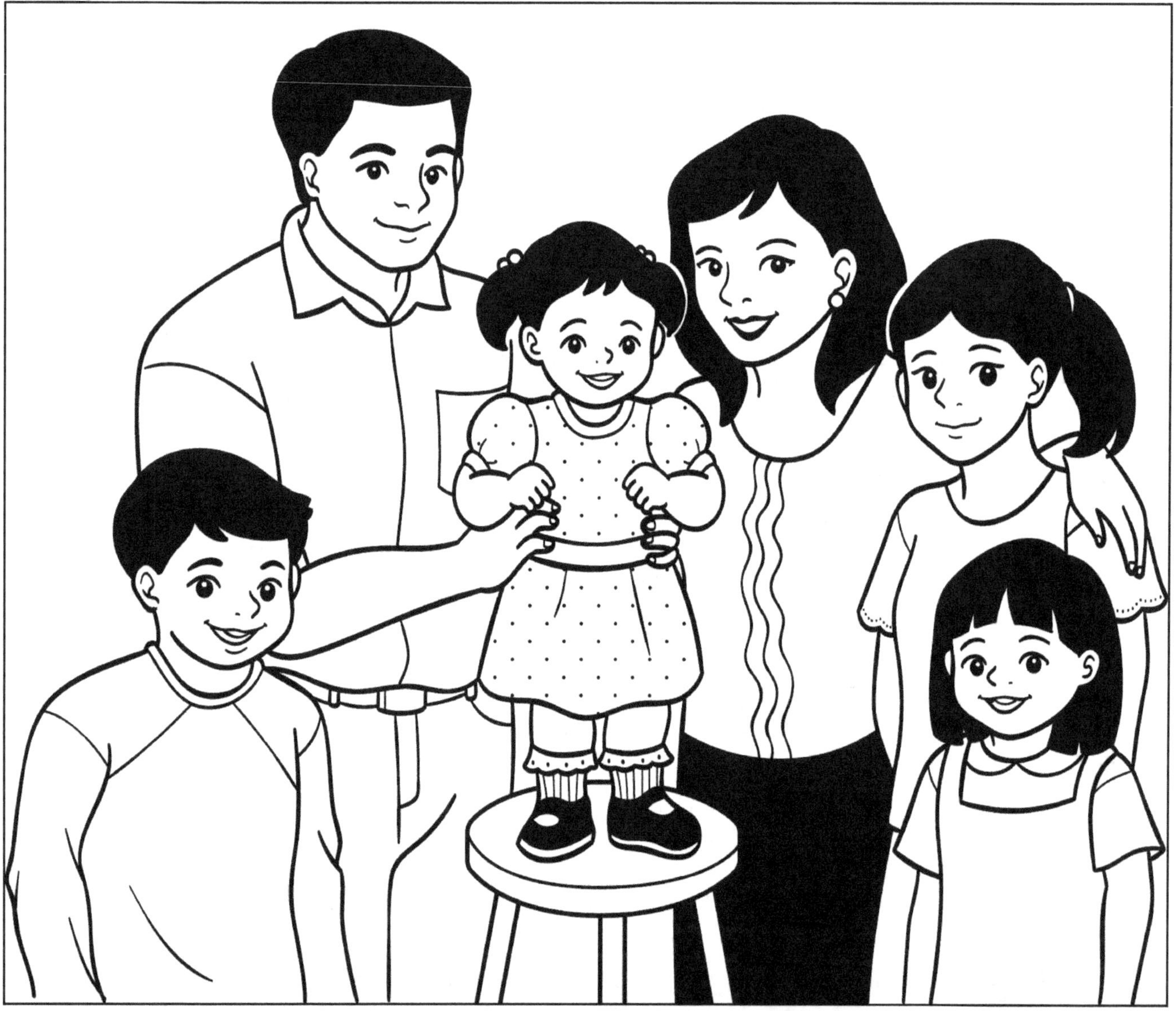

father

mother

brother

sister

baby

Color the pictures of other people who live with your family.

grandfather

grandmother

uncle

aunt

cousins

SUGGESTED ACTIVITIES FOR THE DIFFERENT LANGUAGE SKILLS

SKILLS	ACTIVITIES
Listening and Speaking  	In advance, cut out many little people shapes. Prepare a large chart that has the children's names in the left hand column. Ask each child who is in their family. As the child answers, he or she tapes a person shape next to his or her name (one person shape for each family number; e.g., Mom, Me, Grandpa). Print the names below their little people after they tape it. This can be used throughout the year to compare families during circle time for some math activities. Ask questions like: 1. Who has the greatest/least number of family members? 2. How many have brothers/sisters? 3. How many have babies? 4. How many brothers and sisters in all? 5. Who has a bigger family, Sol or Giona? 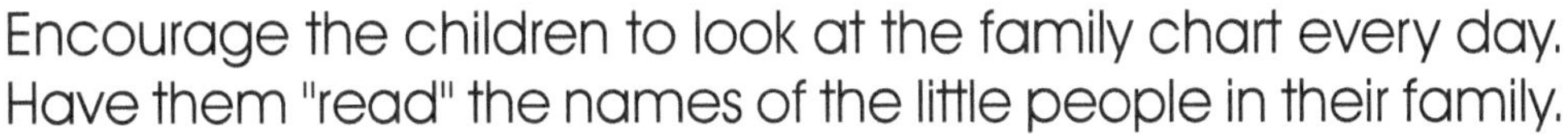
Reading and Writing  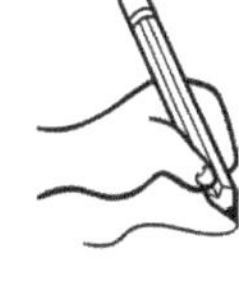	Encourage the children to look at the family chart every day. Have them "read" the names of the little people in their family.

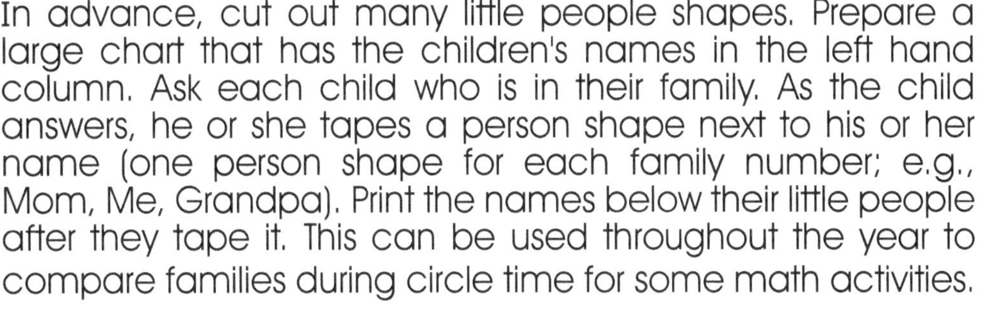

CLASS ACTIVITY 1

Guide: Gather the children in a circle. Discuss and roleplay the different family members and the things they do. Then sing the song together with the children, each pupil acting out what each member does.

SONG

Tune: "Where is Thumbman?"

Teacher: Where is Father? Where is Father?

Pupils: Here I am. Here I am.

    (Standing up and acting out what Father does.)

Teacher: How are you today?

Pupils: Very well, I thank you.

Teacher: Now, sit down. Now, sit down.

(Change *Father* to *Mother, Brother, Sister,* and *Baby.* You may include *Grandfather, Grandmother, Uncle, Aunt,* and *Cousin.*)

ART ACTIVITY

Family Puppets

Materials: crayons, popsicle sticks or drinking straw, glue, tape, scissors

Procedure:

1. Color the shapes (which will be used for the body) on the next page.
2. Cut out the templates and the shapes. (They may be glued to a thin cardboard to make them sturdier.)
3. Tape the shapes and family templates to popsicle sticks or drinking straws.

<u>Templates:</u>

Direction: Paste a picture of your family in the frame. Tell something about each member of your family during class. Also, tell your classmates what you do together as a family. *(10 points)*

My Family Picture

QUIZ NO. 1   SCORE:______

<u>Direction:</u> Check the correct picture for each name.

1. mother  

2. grandfather  

3. father  

4. brother  

5. grandmother  

6. baby  

7. sister  

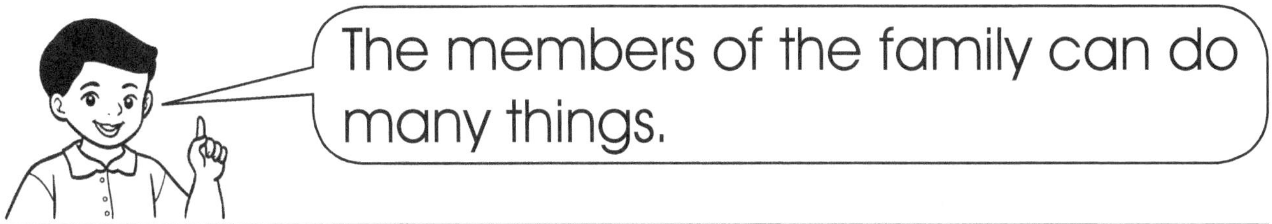

Father is the head of the family. He works for the family. He helps Mother in raising the family. He also helps in household chores. *(To the teacher: Explain to the children that not all fathers do the same thing and that fathers differ in their roles.)*

Color the pictures that show what your father does.

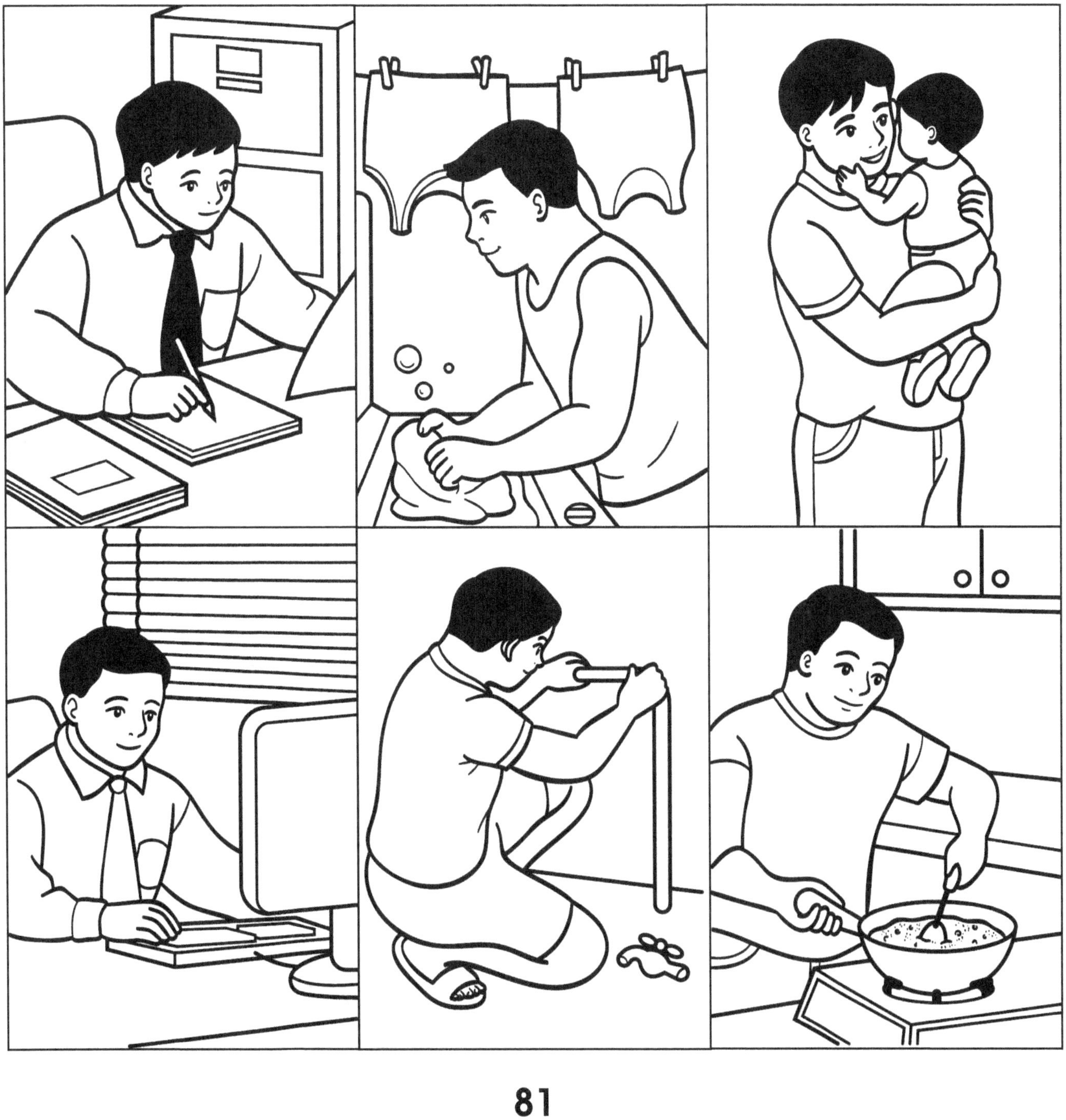

Encircle the pictures that show what your mother does.

Box the pictures that show what your brother does, or what you do if you are the brother in the family.

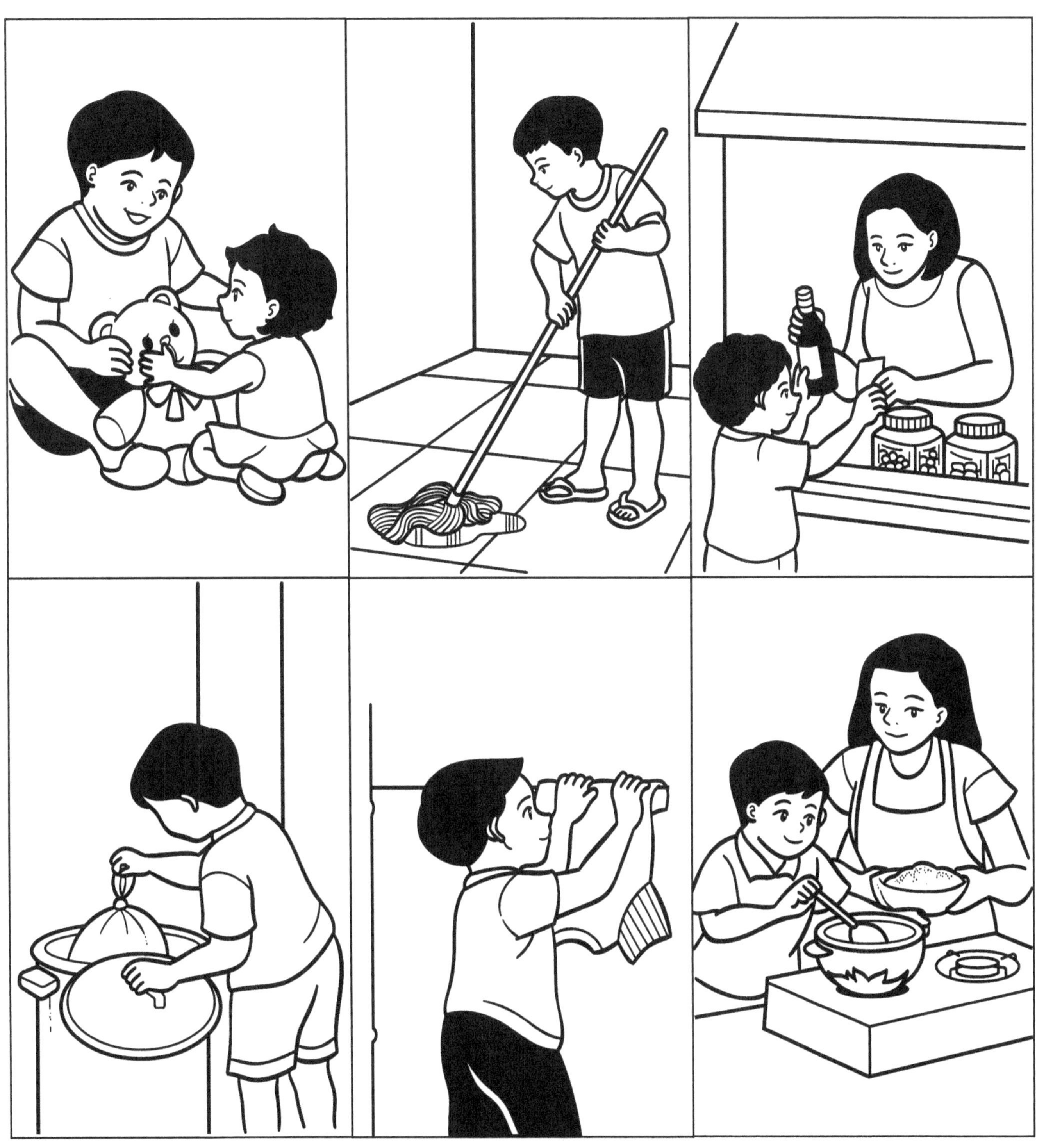

Check the pictures that show what your sister does or what you do if you are the sister in the family.

Cross out the pictures that show what the baby in your family does.

ACTIVITY 1

SCORE: _______

Look at the pictures. Connect to the happy face (☺) those that show what your family should do together. Connect to the sad face (☹) those that show what the family should not do.

QUIZ NO. 2   SCORE: _______

<u>Direction:</u> Check the activity that each family member does.

1. sister

2. baby

 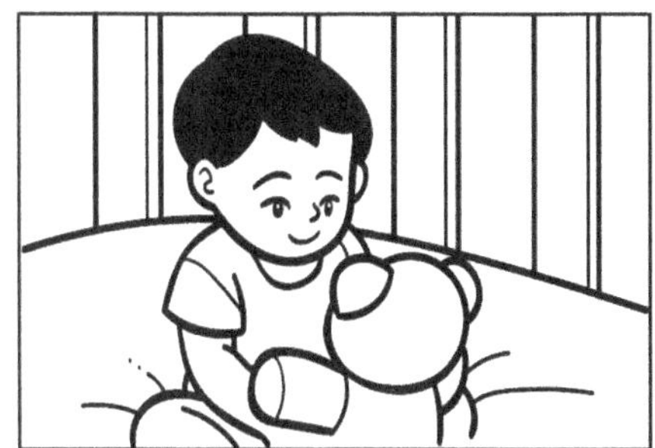

3. father

4. mother

5. brother

QUIZ NO. 3

SCORE: _______

Direction: Cross out the correct picture.

1. Who is the youngest member of the family?

2. Who usually takes care of the family?

3. Who runs errands for the family?

4. Who helps with the work at home?

5. Who usually works for the family?

OUR HOUSE

Guide: Using cardboard, make two sets of cut-outs of the different parts of a house. Scatter the pieces on the floor. Divide the children into two groups; let each group pick up some parts and assemble them to make a "house." Let the children identify the parts. Discuss with them the different rooms in a house and invite them to tell something about their respective houses.

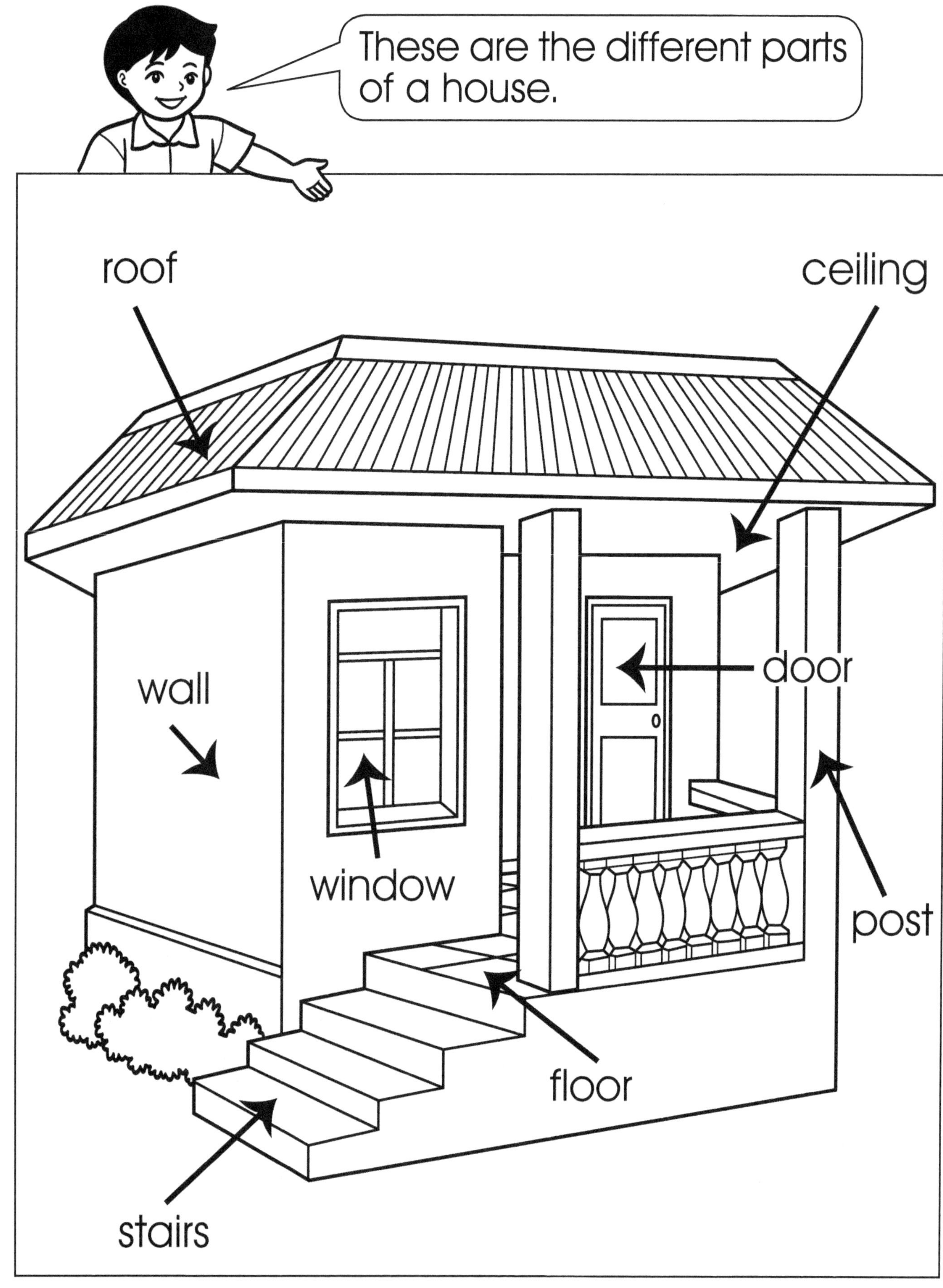

These are the different parts of a house.
roof
ceiling
wall
door
window
post
floor
stairs

CLASS ACTIVITY 2

Materials:

1. square sheet of cartolina (9 inches on each side)
2. art paper scraps
3. colored marking pens
4. scissors
5. glue

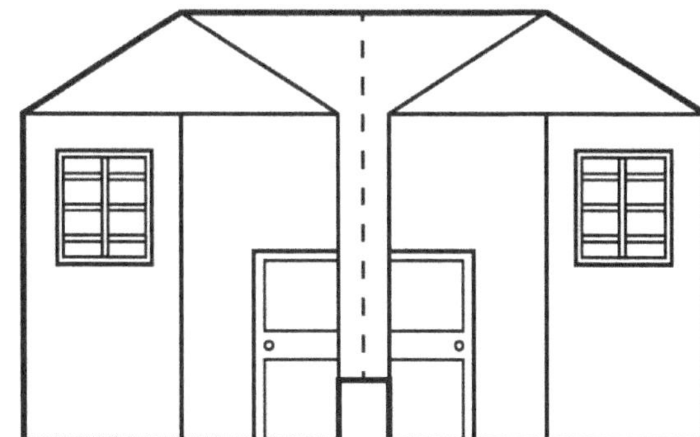

Procedure:

1. Fold the cartolina.

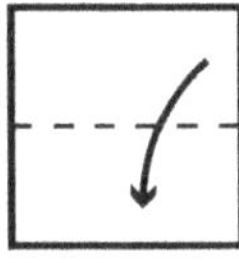 a.  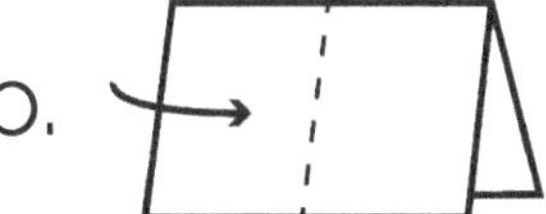 b.  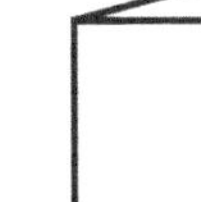 c. 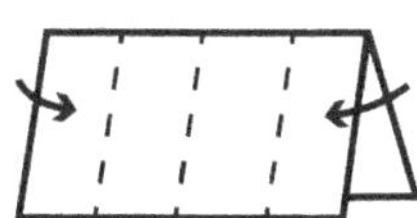

 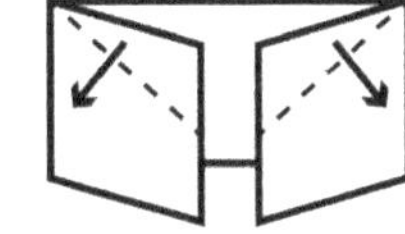 d.   e. 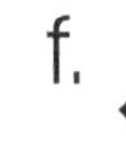 f. 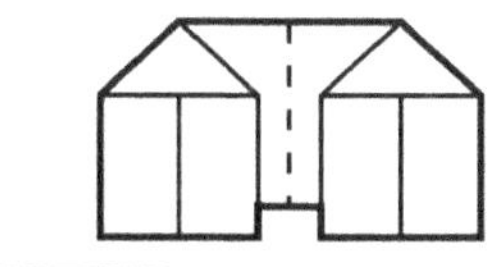

2. Add details using art paper
   scraps or marking pens.

3. Decorate the inside of the house.

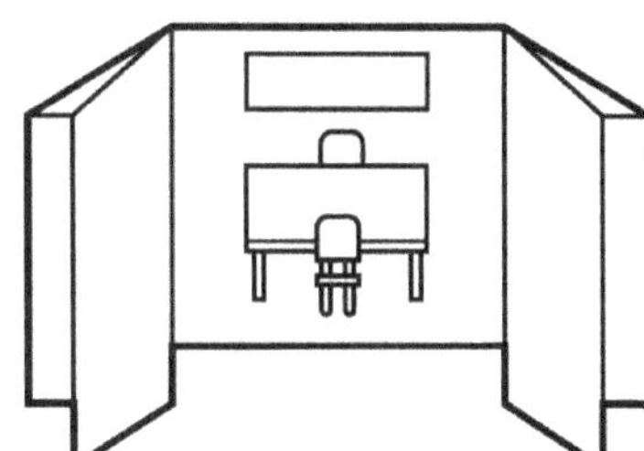

Suggested Activities:

1. Let the children lift the flaps and draw their families inside
   the houses.
2. Pin the completed model houses to a bulletin board to
   create a model neighborhood or community.

<u>SUGGESTED ACTIVITIES FOR THE DIFFERENT LANGUAGE SKILLS</u>

SKILLS	ACTIVITIES
Listening and Speaking	• Transform your circle or sharing time into a collective story. Ask each child to tell a story about something that happened in their home. Encourage children to tell something about their houses, too. Jot down everything they say. Read their collective story to them once they all have had a chance to speak. They may illustrate their story and display it on the wall. They may also take turns retelling their collective story. • Go for a walk with the children. Show them different types of houses: single family houses, apartment buildings, town houses, etc. Ask the children to show you a house which looks like their own. Encourage them to talk more about their homes.
Reading and Writing	• Have each child bring a storybook from home and exchange with another child. Let the children bring the books home with them. This will encourage parents to read to their child. • Read stories about houses to the children. Stories like "The Three Little Pigs" and "Princesses in Castles" are excellent choices. Have the children browse over the pages for them to get acquainted with picture reading. • Display picture books showing different types of houses. • Make word flashcards representing the parts of a house. • Provide dotted outline of a house for tracing.

ACTIVITY 2

SCORE: _______

Color the parts of a house as indicated.

roof	– red	stairs	– orange
windows	– green	wall	– yellow
door	– violet	floor	– blue

QUIZ NO. 4

SCORE: _______

Direction: Connect the names to the correct parts of the house.

stairs •

• door

roof •

• wall

window •

• floor

This is our **living room**. We receive our visitors here. We also gather here to have some fun.

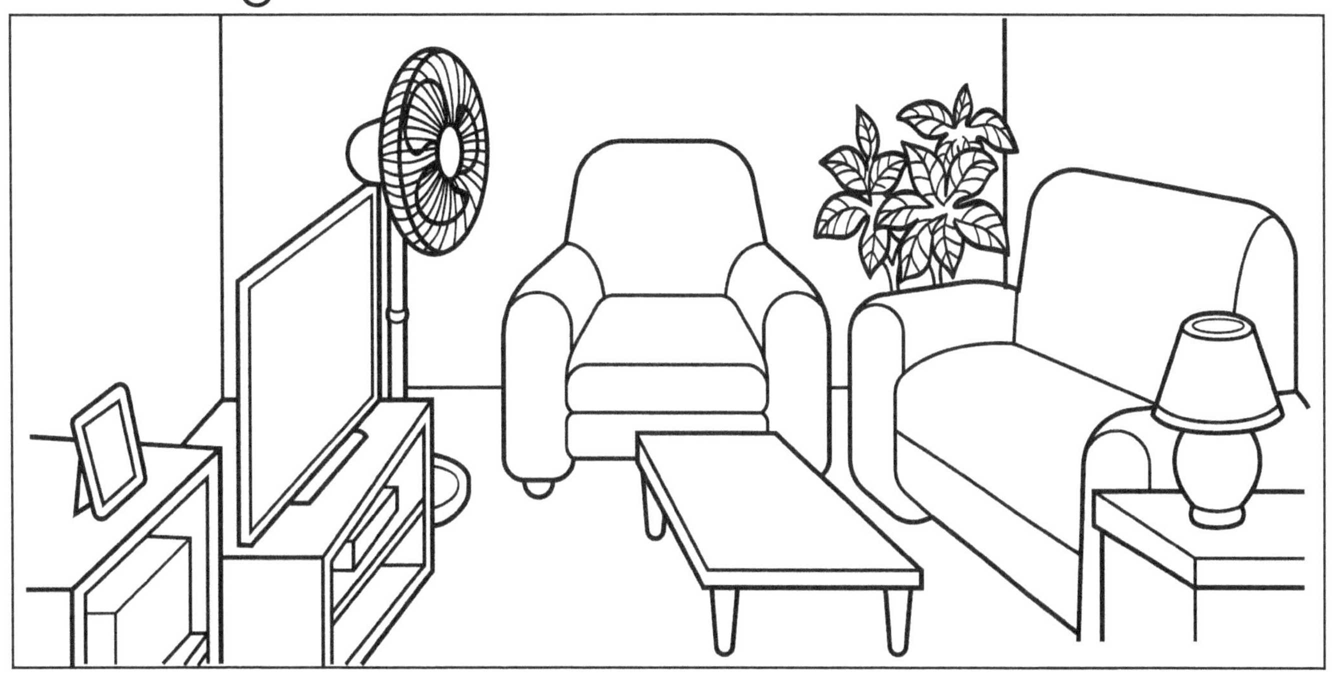

This is our **bedroom**. We sleep or rest here.

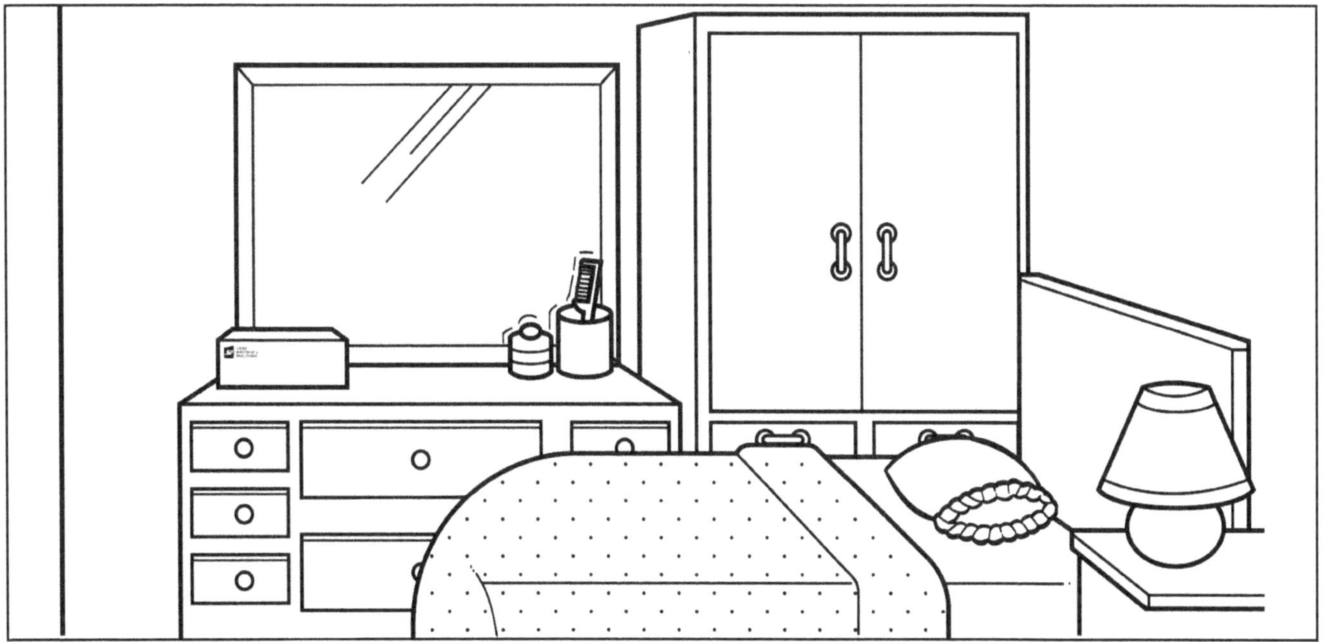

This is our **dining room**.
We eat our meals and
snacks here.

This is our **kitchen**.
We prepare and cook
our food here.

This is our **bathroom**.
We take a bath, wash
up, or relieve ourselves
here.

Where do we find the things on the left? Connect these things to their correct place on the right.

QUIZ NO. 5   SCORE: _______

Direction: Where do we do these activities? Color the box of the correct answer.

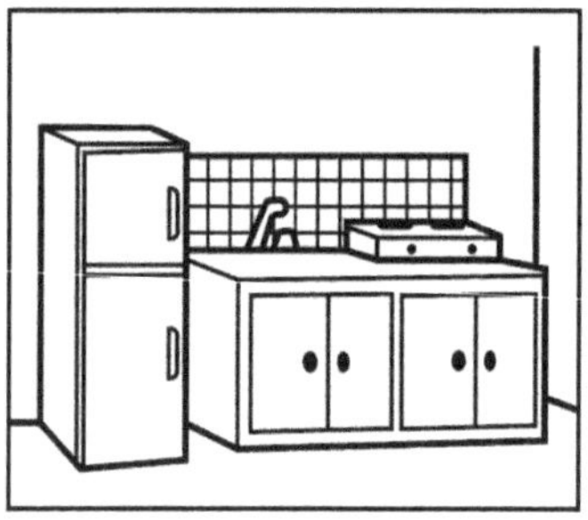

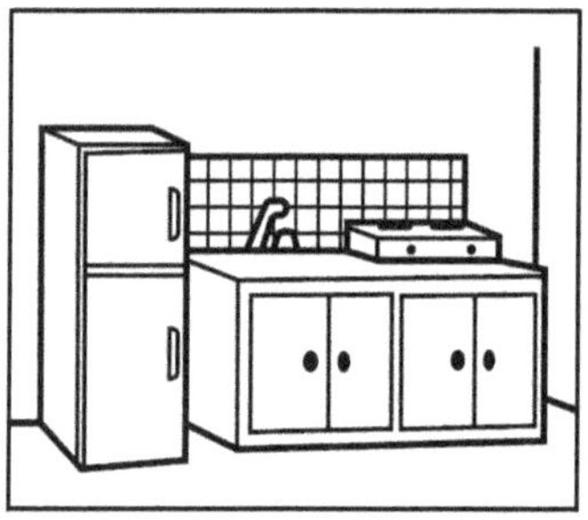

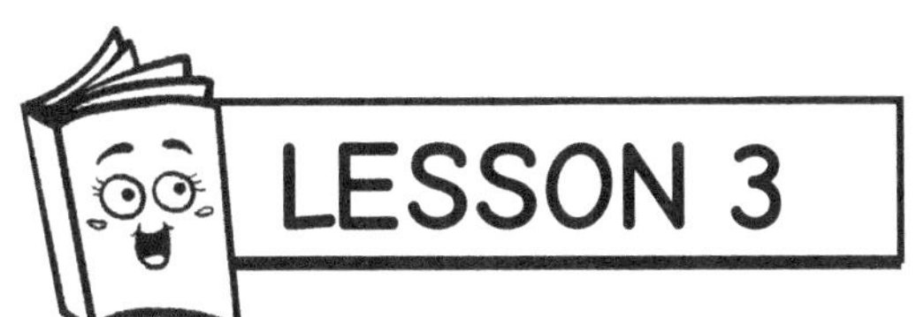

LESSON 3

MY SCHOOL

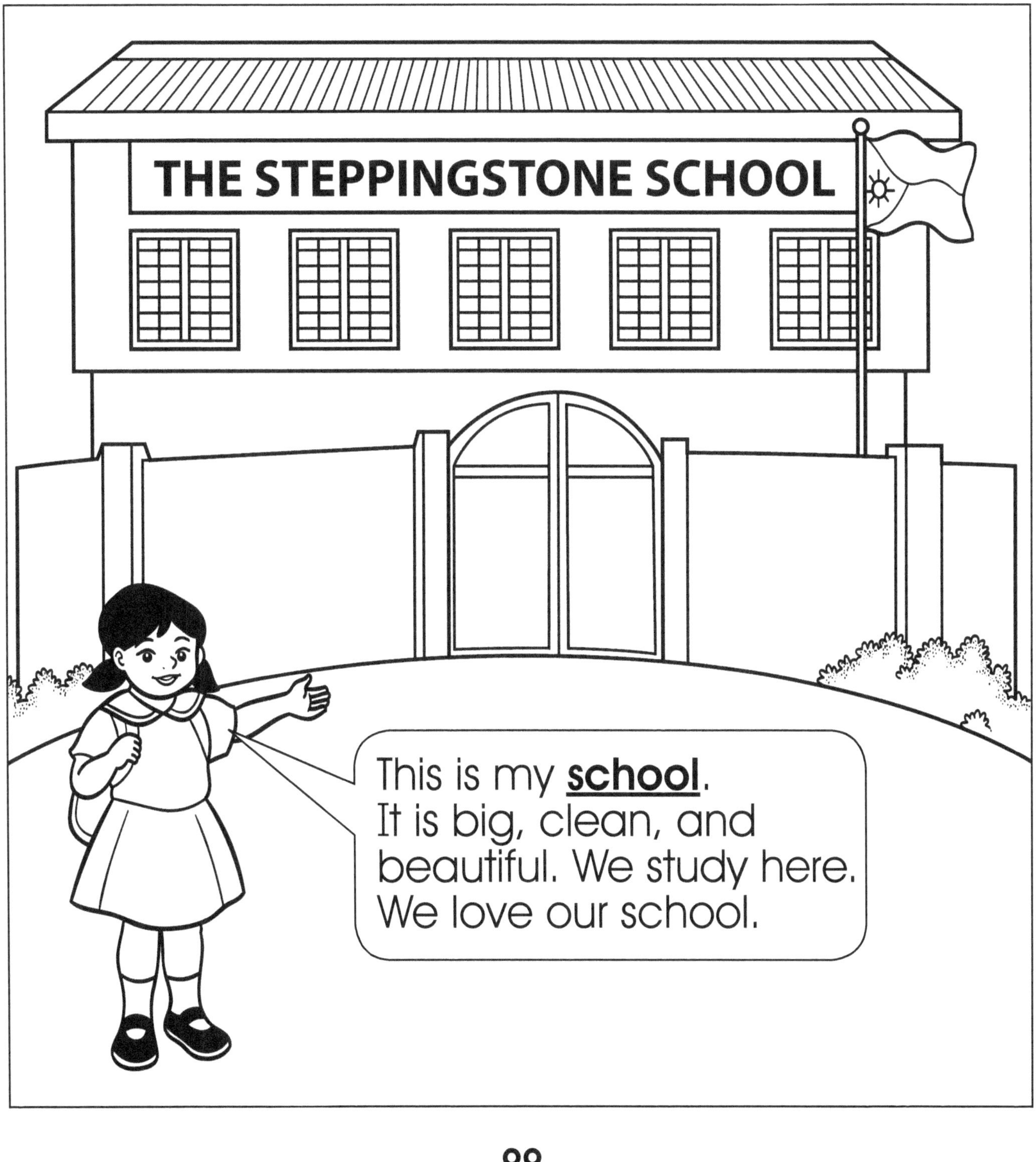

This is a picture of a classroom.
These are some of the things
we see and use in school.

ACTIVITY 4

SCORE: _______

Check the things that we do in school.
Cross out those that we should not do.

HOME ACTIVITY 2   SCORE:______

Parent's/Guardian's Guide:

Play a pretend game with your child. Below is a picture of a messy room. Tell your child that you are going out for ice cream or pizza, but he or she needs to put the things back in their proper places before you go out. The things needed in school must go on the shelf, and the toys go into the big box.

Direction: Draw a line from each object on the floor to the place where it belongs. Color with yellow the things that you use in school. Color with green the things that you play with. *(10 points)*

CLASS ACTIVITY 3

Guide: Pretend that you are at a school shop. Have the following things ready: play money, paper or plastic bags, different school materials like pencils, crayons, erasers, pad papers, sharpeners, etc. Place all the school materials on the table. Distribute paper or plastic bags to the children. Invite them to "shop" for school supplies with them paying with play money. Act as the saleslady/cashier. After the children have finished "shopping," have them bring out what they "bought" and let them identify each item.

To the teacher:

At the start of the second quarter, you must have already done computing your pupils' grades during the first quarter. This delightful bulletin board with a night scene will motivate pupils to improve their behavior and study habits. As children gain high grades and improve behavior, reward them with a star. Glue each child's picture onto the star or write his or her name on it and pin it to the bulletin board.

WHO ARE SHINING IN NURSERY?

School Bus Activity Sheet

Guide: Have the children color the school bus (yellow for the body, black for the wheels, and red for the door). Have them draw themselves and their friends riding in the bus.

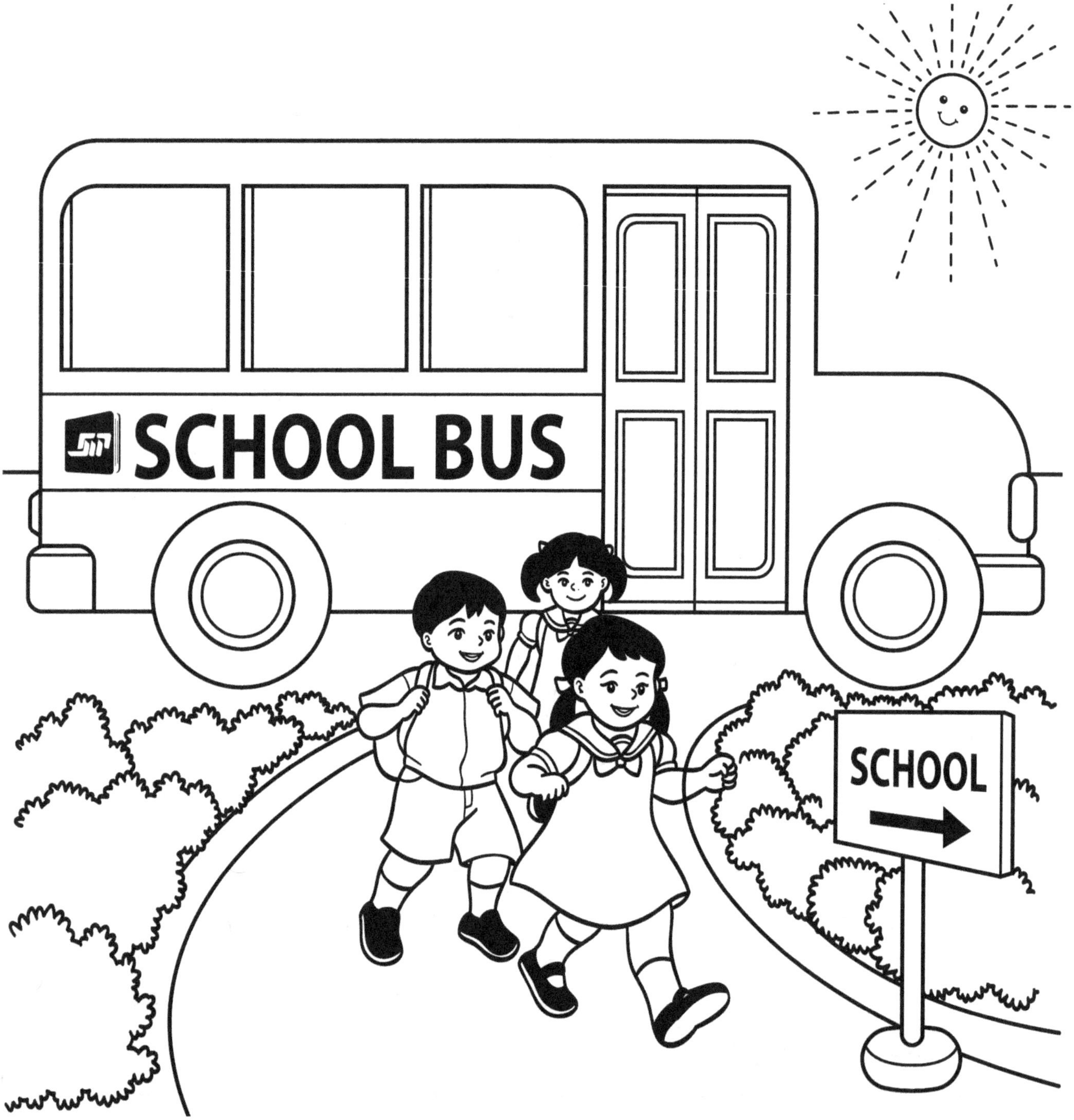

Direction: Draw a square (□) before the things that we use in school. Draw a circle (○) before those that we don't use in school.

_______ 1. 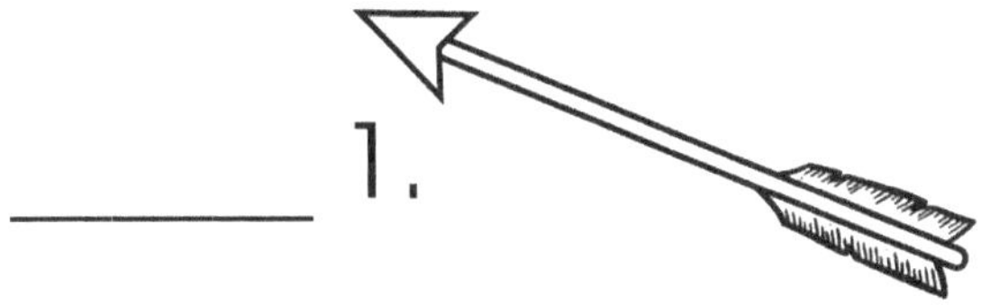

_______ 6. 

_______ 2.

_______ 7. 

_______ 3. 

_______ 8. 

_______ 4.

_______ 9. 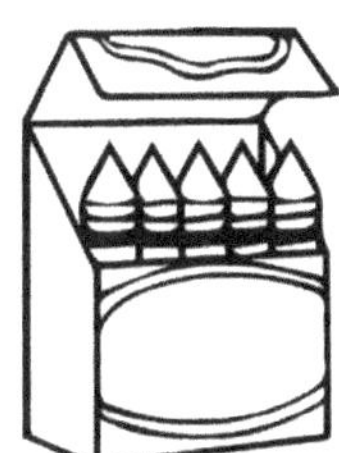

_______ 5. 

_______ 10. 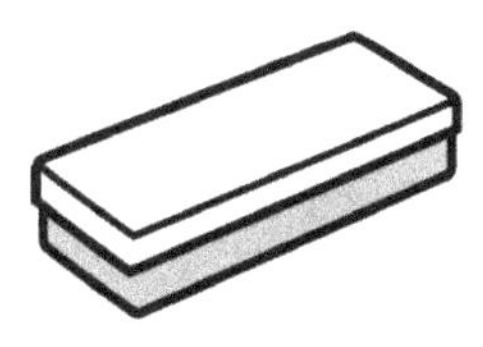

principal's office

classroom

library

canteen

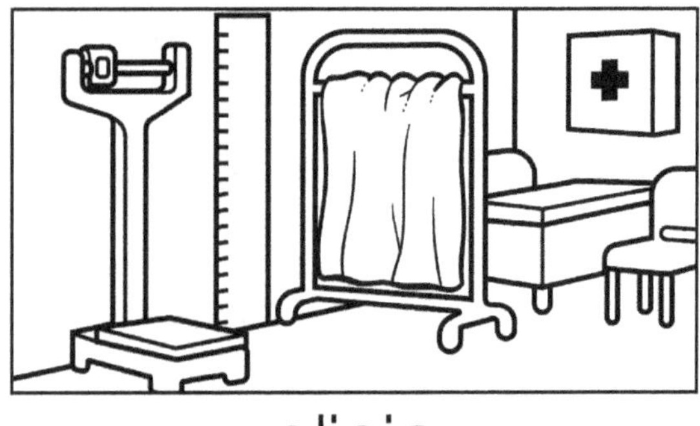

clinic

comfort room

playground

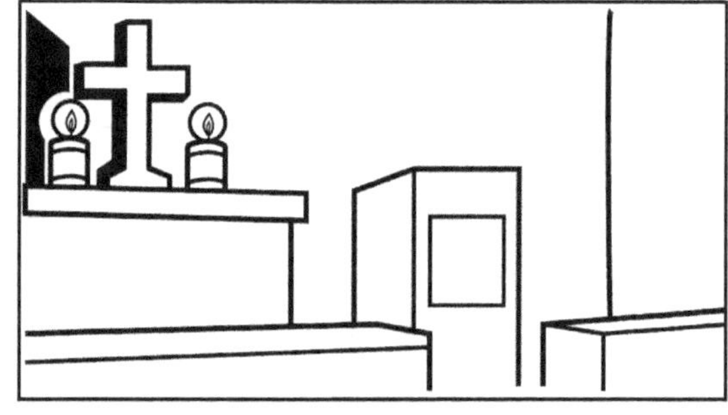

prayer room

(Note: One or more of these may not be found in some schools.)

Direction: Where do we do the following activities? For each activity, write on the blank the shape beside the correct place.

_______ 1.    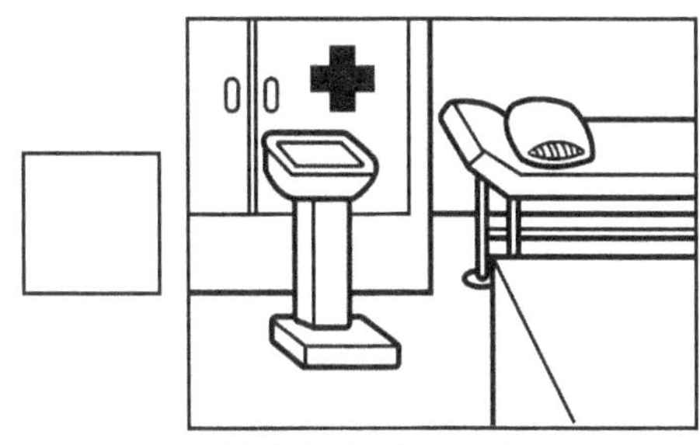

_______ 2. 

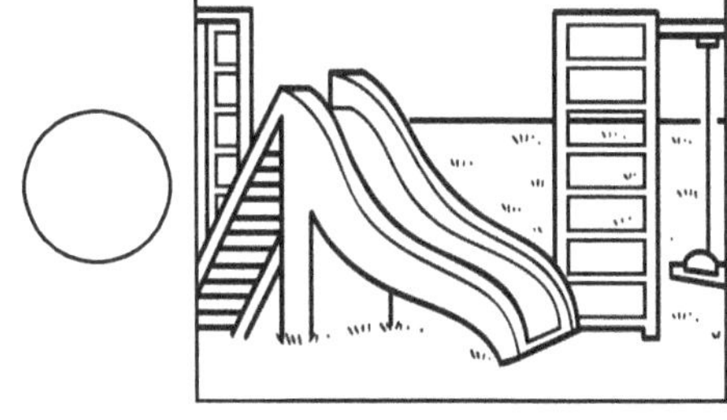

_______ 3.    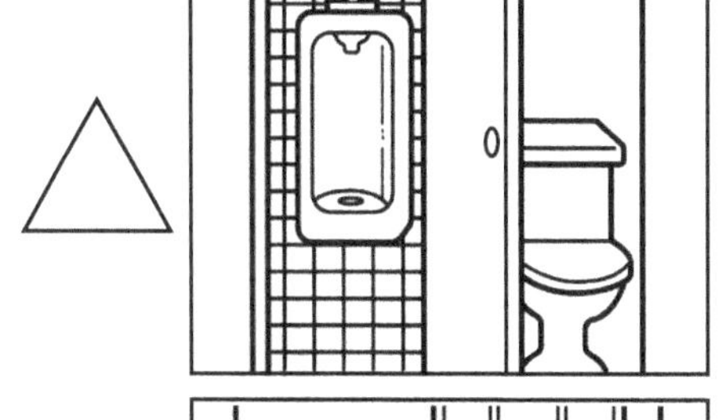

_______ 4.    

_______ 5.    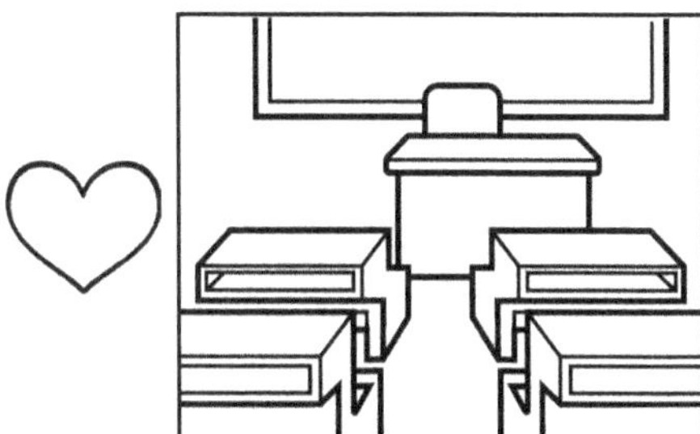

Our Special Friends in School

director
– the head of the school

school principal
– leads the teachers

teacher
– helps the children to read, write, and count

teacher aide
– helps the teacher with her work

school doctor

– takes charge of the
children's health

school dentist

– helps the children take
care of their teeth

school nurse

– takes care of sick
children in school

janitor

– cleans the school

security guard

– protects the children in school

school bus driver

– drives the school bus or school service

food server

– serves food in the canteen

classmates

– help other children learn many things

(Note: One or more of these people may not be present in some schools.)

ACTIVITY 5

SCORE: _______

Connect our friends in school to the things they do.

1. 

2. 

3. 

4. 

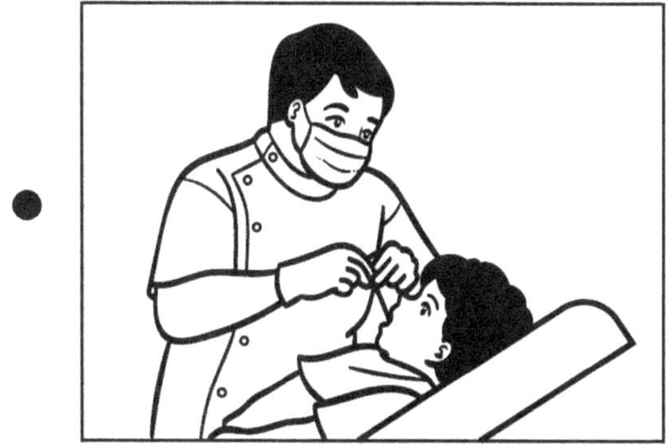

5.    •   • 

6.    •   • 

7.    •   • 

8.    •   • 

9.

10.

11.

12.

SUGGESTED ACTIVITIES FOR THE DIFFERENT LANGUAGE SKILLS

SKILLS	ACTIVITIES
Listening and Speaking  	Make a School Friends Bingo! Create a table with three (3) rows and four (4) columns (depending on the number of teachers and staff in your school). Glue close-up photos of yourself and other teachers and staff in your school onto the cells. Add photos of some children also. Scan the Bingo cards and laminate them. Also, make a set of "calling cards" – photo cards (with the name) that the "caller" (you or the children) can use to call out names during the game. Use inch cubes or blocks as bingo markers.
Reading and Writing  	Hang the School Friends Bingo cards in a visible place where children can see them every day. Occasionally, ask the children to identify the persons in the bingo cards. Have them read the "calling cards" and match them with the pictures. School Friends Bingo Card Calling Cards 1  Calling Cards 2 teacher nurse

QUIZ NO. 8   SCORE:______

<u>Direction:</u> Connect the names to the pictures.

1. school driver •

2. nurse •   •

3. director •   •

4. security guard •   •

5. classmates •   • 

6. teacher •   • 

7. doctor •   • 

8. janitor •   • 

9. food server •

10. dentist •

11. principal •

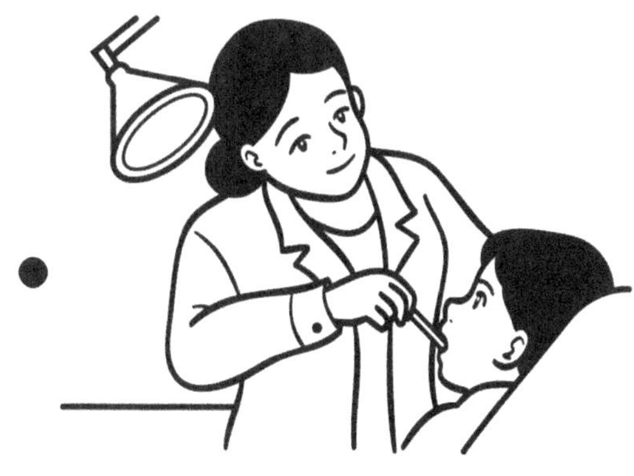

12. teacher aide •

NAMING WORDS

Naming Words for Persons

(Cross out (✗) the pictures of persons you have already met.)

Naming Words for Animals

(Check (✓) the pictures of animals you have already seen.)

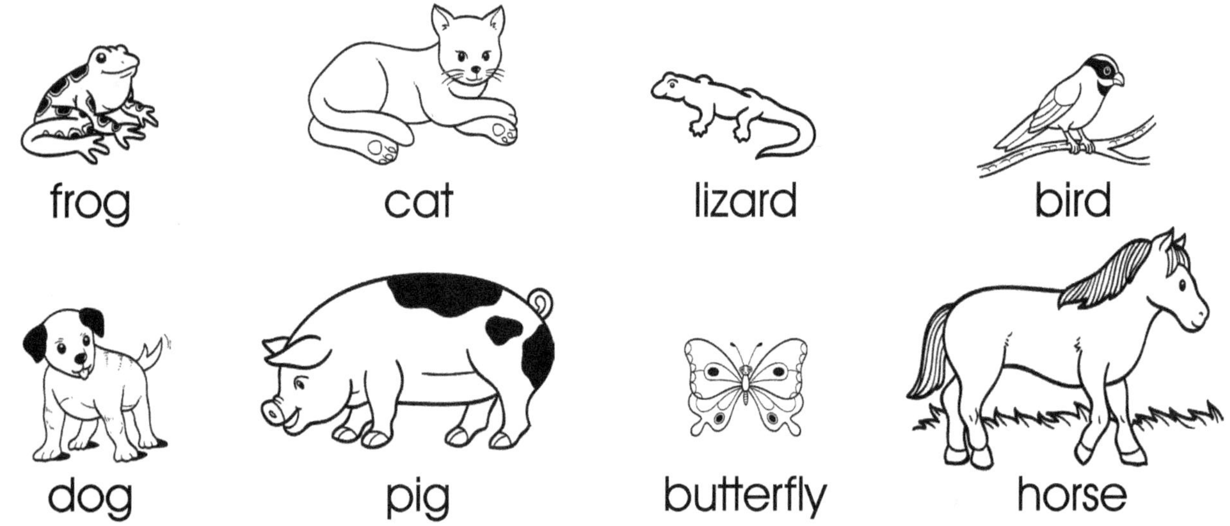

Naming Words for Things

(Color the pictures of the things you have already used.)

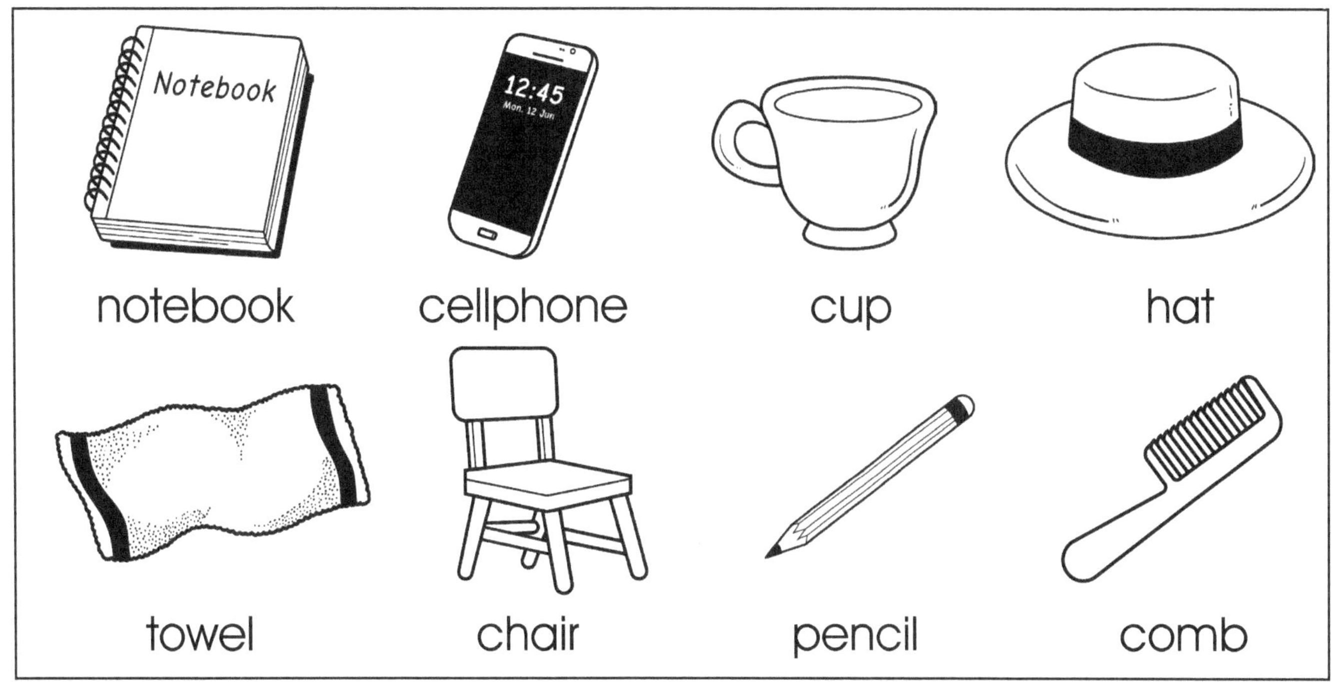

notebook	cellphone	cup	hat
towel	chair	pencil	comb

Naming Words for Places

(Encircle the pictures of places you have already gone to.)

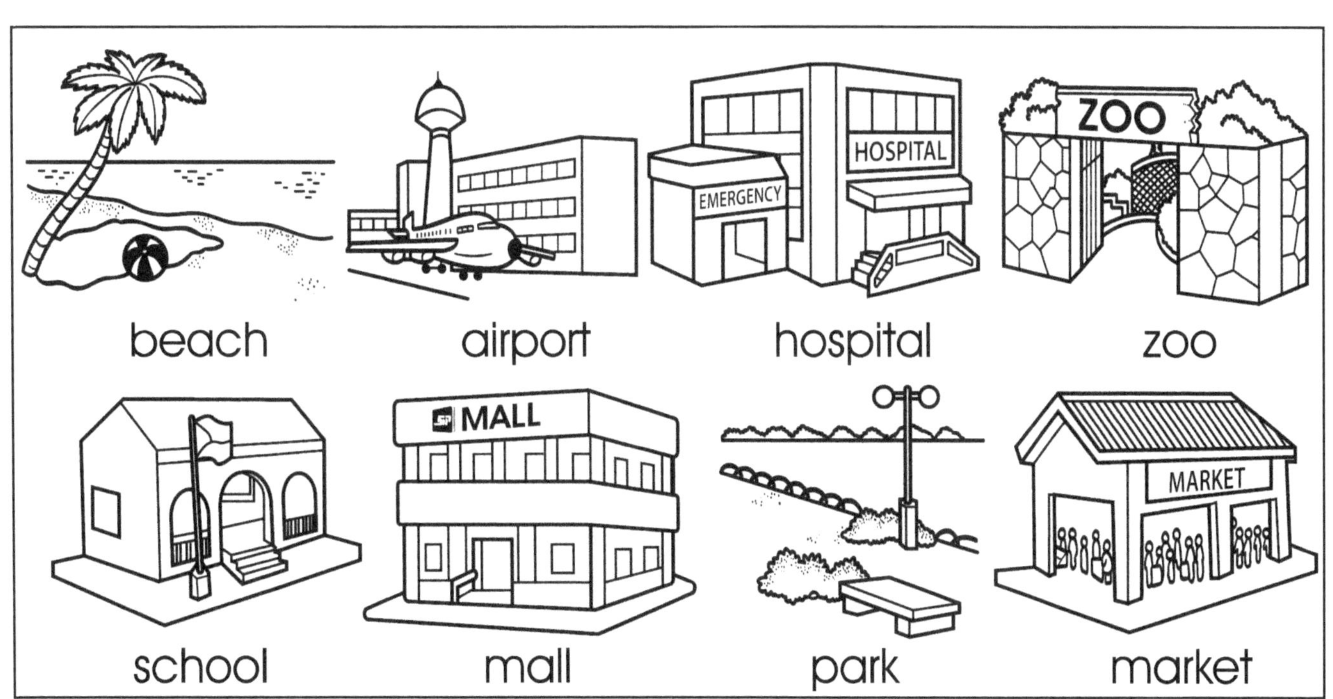

beach	airport	hospital	zoo
school	mall	park	market

POEM

Guide: Recite the poem together with the children while teaching them the actions to the words.

God made the earth,

And God made the sky.

God made the fish,

And the birds that fly.

Animals, flowers, trees so tall.

God made everything,

Big and small.

God made all that I can see.

God made you,

And God made me.

CLASS ACTIVITY 4

Guide: Using the same set of pictures you used to introduce the lesson earlier, play a "classify them" game with the children. Distribute the pictures to the children. Make sure that you have enough for each child. Let them identify the picture they are holding. Have them group themselves together according to the picture they have. The first group to complete the task wins.

SUGGESTED ACTIVITIES FOR THE DIFFERENT LANGUAGE SKILLS

SKILLS	ACTIVITIES
Listening and Speaking	Play a "Guess That Sound" game! Record the following: – different voices of people (e.g., a baby crying, an old man speaking, or a girl singing) – sounds of different places like a busy street, waves of the sea, or a noisy marketplace – sounds of different animals like bees buzzing, dogs barking, or rats squeaking – sounds of different musical instruments Have the children guess each sound. Have them name where the sound is coming from. Then have them identify whether the word names a person, a place, a thing, or an animal.
Reading and Writing	• Make naming word flashcards. The flashcards should have both pictures and names. Have four boxes ready. Label each of the four boxes accordingly: person, place, thing, and animal. Have the children take turns reading the naming word flashcards and putting them in the correct box. • Make a naming word community mural. Have the children cut from old magazines pictures of different places in a community. Help them glue the places onto a sheet of manila paper. Let the children add pictures of people, animals, and things. Label each picture. Hang the mural in a visible area of the classroom. Encourage the children to read the labels and share ideas about what they see in the mural.

ACTIVITY 6

SCORE: _______

Check (✓) the names of persons. Cross out (✗) those that are not names of persons. *[10 points]*

friend

turtle

father

Jean

market

doctor

queen

fork

boy

pencil

ACTIVITY 7　　　　SCORE: _______

Encircle (O) the names of animals. Underline (__) those that are not names of animals. *(10 points)*

school	snake	frog
bee	fish	sister
bell	rat	dog	baby

Check (✓) the names of things. Encircle (O) those that are not names of things. *(10 points)*

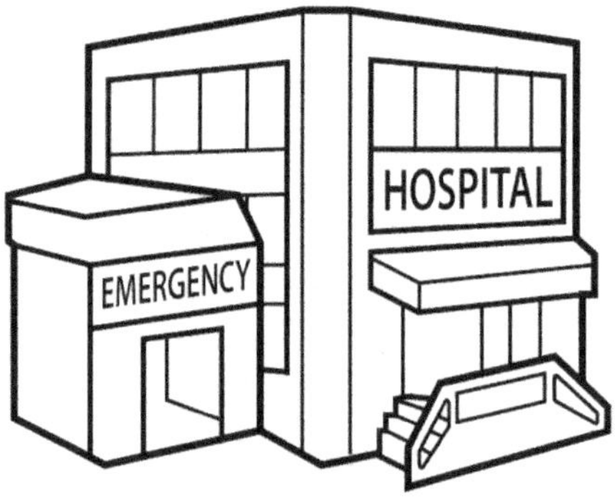

hospital

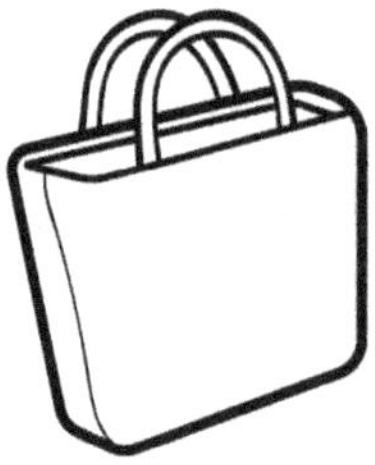

bag

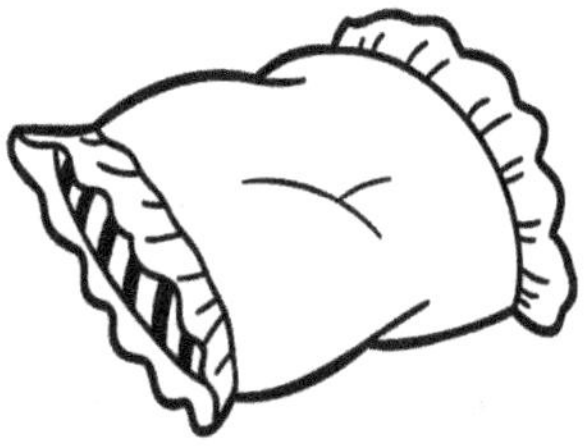

pillow

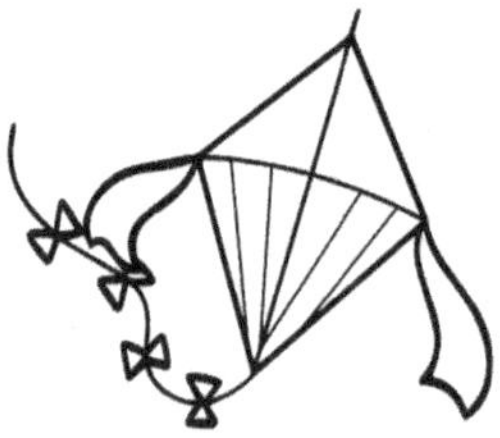

kite

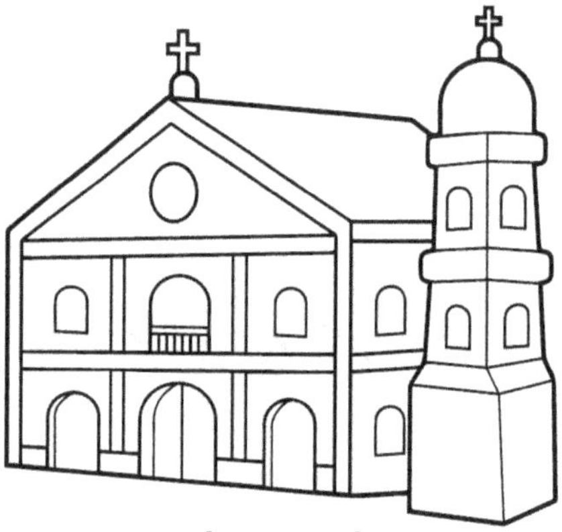

church

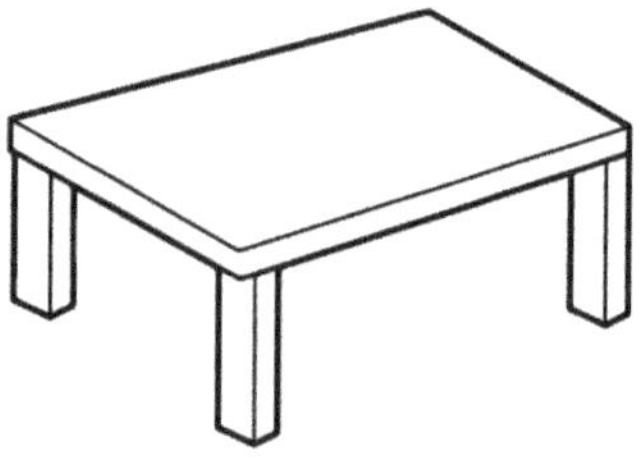

table

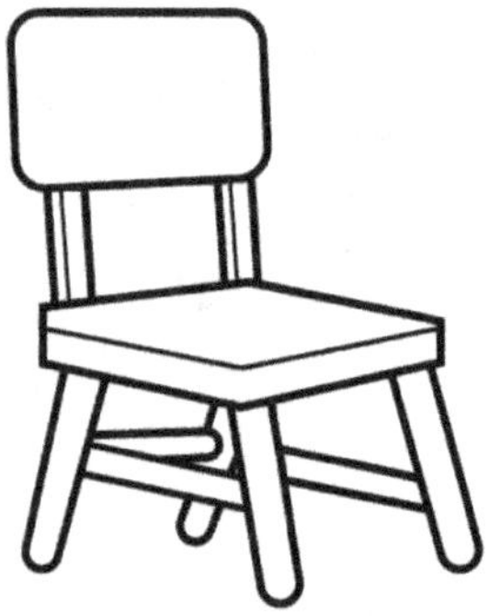

chair

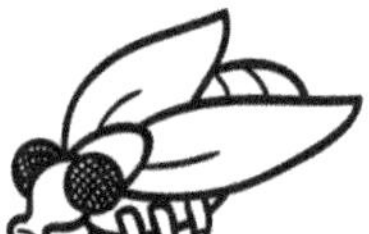

fly

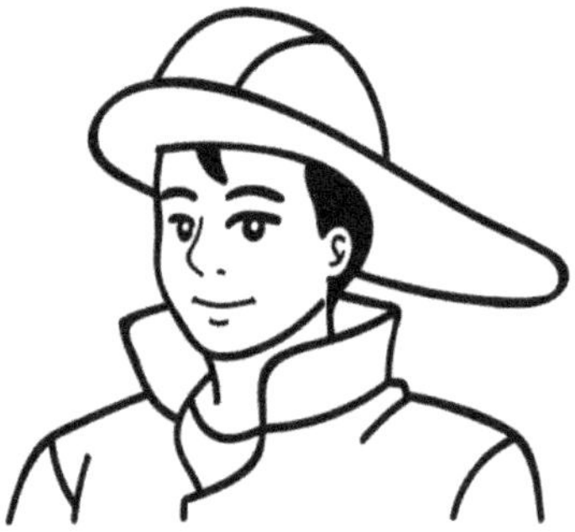

fireman

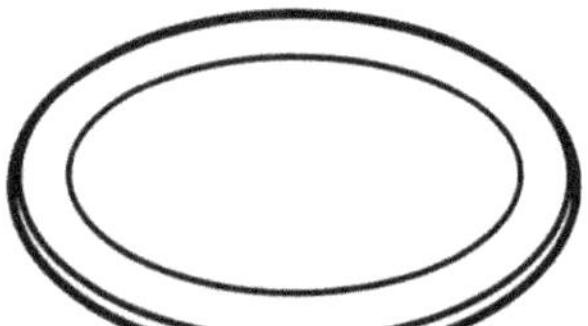

plate

ACTIVITY 9

SCORE: _______

Color with orange the boxes before the names of places. Color with violet those that are not names of places. *(10 points)*

☐ beach

☐ ball

☐ hospital

☐ driver

☐ mall

☐ park

☐ airport

☐ bird

☐ farm

☐ chick

Direction: From old magazines cut out two (2) pictures each of the following. Paste them under the proper column. *(10 points)*

persons   **animals**

things   **places**

Direction: Color the circles beside each naming word as indicated:

red   - naming words for persons
blue   - naming words for things
yellow   - naming words for animals
orange   - naming words for places

1. ◯ flower 

2. ◯ mosquito 

3. ◯ classmate 

4. ◯ glass 

5. ◯ king 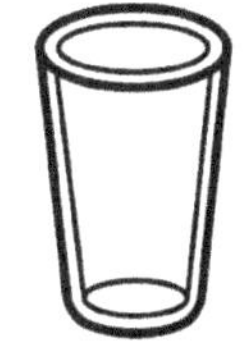

6. ◯ Luneta Park 

7. ◯ beach 

8. ◯ Doris 

9. ◯ ruler 

10. ◯ lizard 

11. ◯ frog 

12. ◯ kitchen 

ONE AND MANY
Use of <u>s</u> to Mean <u>Many</u>

<u>Guide</u>: Show the children one pencil and say, "I have one pencil." Show them three pencils and say, "I have three pencils." Explain to them that we add the letter **s** if we mean <u>many</u>. Show them more examples and let them repeat what you say.

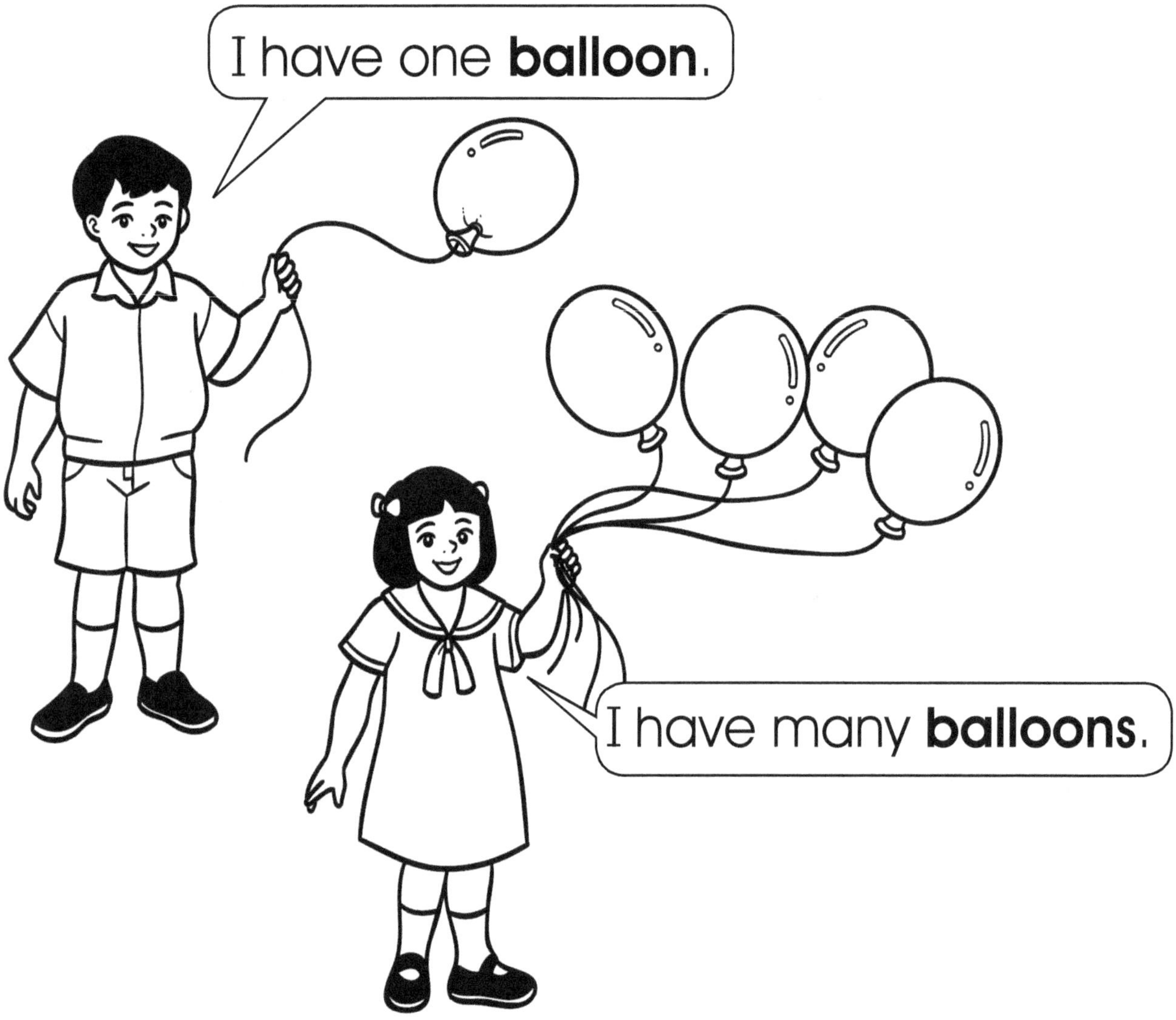

<u>Remember:</u>

- We add <u>s</u> to the word to mean **many** or more than one.

ACTIVITY 10 SCORE: ______

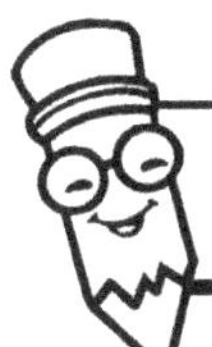

Color the mango with yellow if there is only one object.
Color it with green if there are many objects.

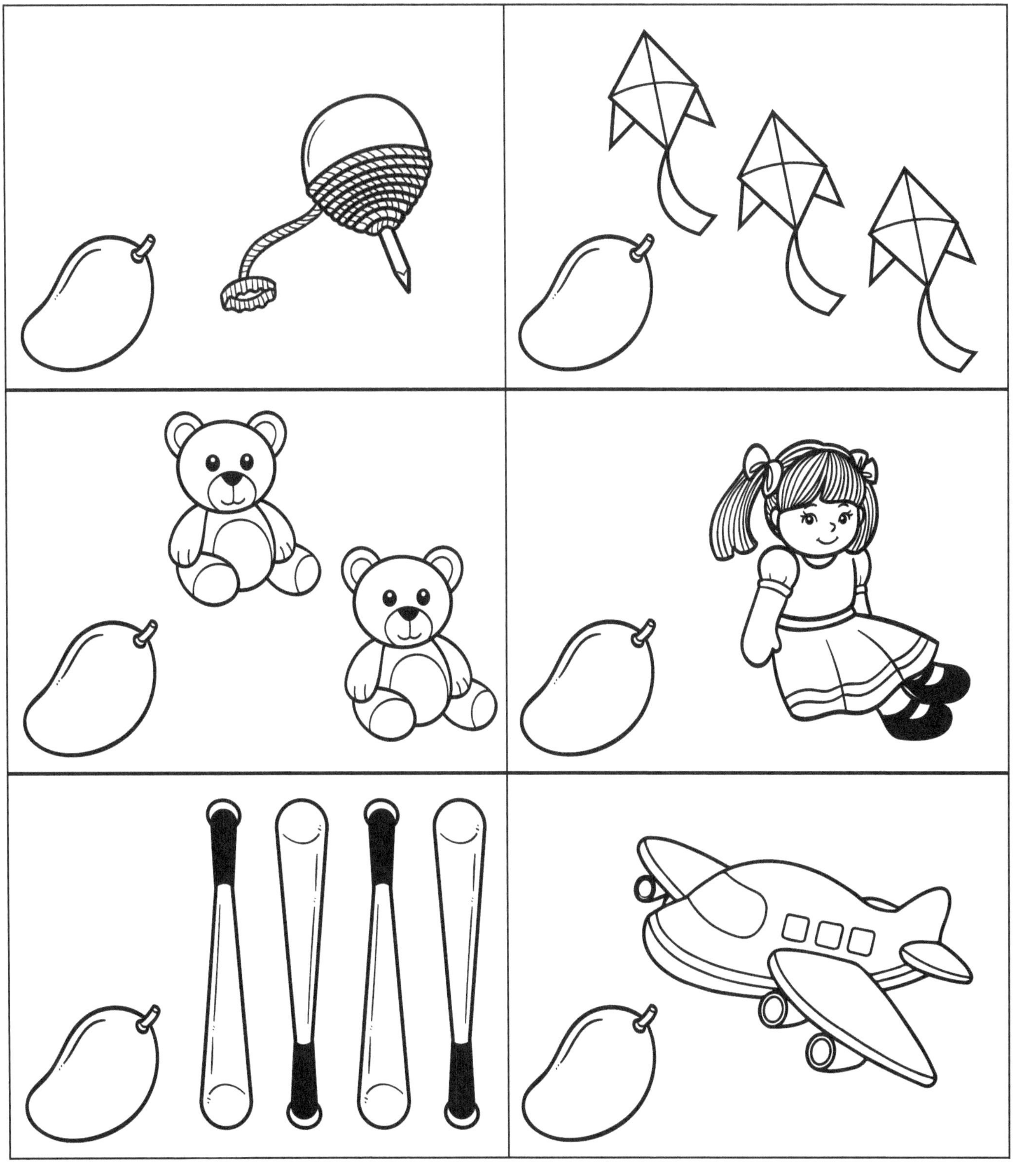

QUIZ NO. 10

SCORE:______

Direction: Connect the words to the correct pictures.

cup •	• 
cups •	• 
fan •	• 
fans •	• 
bug •	• 
bugs •	• 
ant •	• 
ants •	• 

<u>SUGGESTED ACTIVITIES FOR THE DIFFERENT LANGUAGE SKILLS</u>

SKILLS	ACTIVITIES
Listening	Have a list of singular and plural nouns ready (e.g. book, pencils, cats, ring, sister). Read out each noun randomly. Instruct the children to clap once when they hear a singular noun, and to clap many times when they hear a plural noun.
Speaking	Using the same list of singular and plural nouns, read out each noun randomly. This time, have the children say the plural noun for each singular noun that you read and vice versa.
Reading and Writing	Cut out pictures from old magazines or newspapers and have the children glue them onto a notebook and label them with the singular and plural forms. For example, the children might paste one picture of a cat and write the singular noun, and then paste several pictures of different cats and write the plural form. Work on C-V-C words first. In case the children are not reading by this time, tell them to simply classify the pictures into <u>one</u> and <u>more than one</u>.

Is and Are

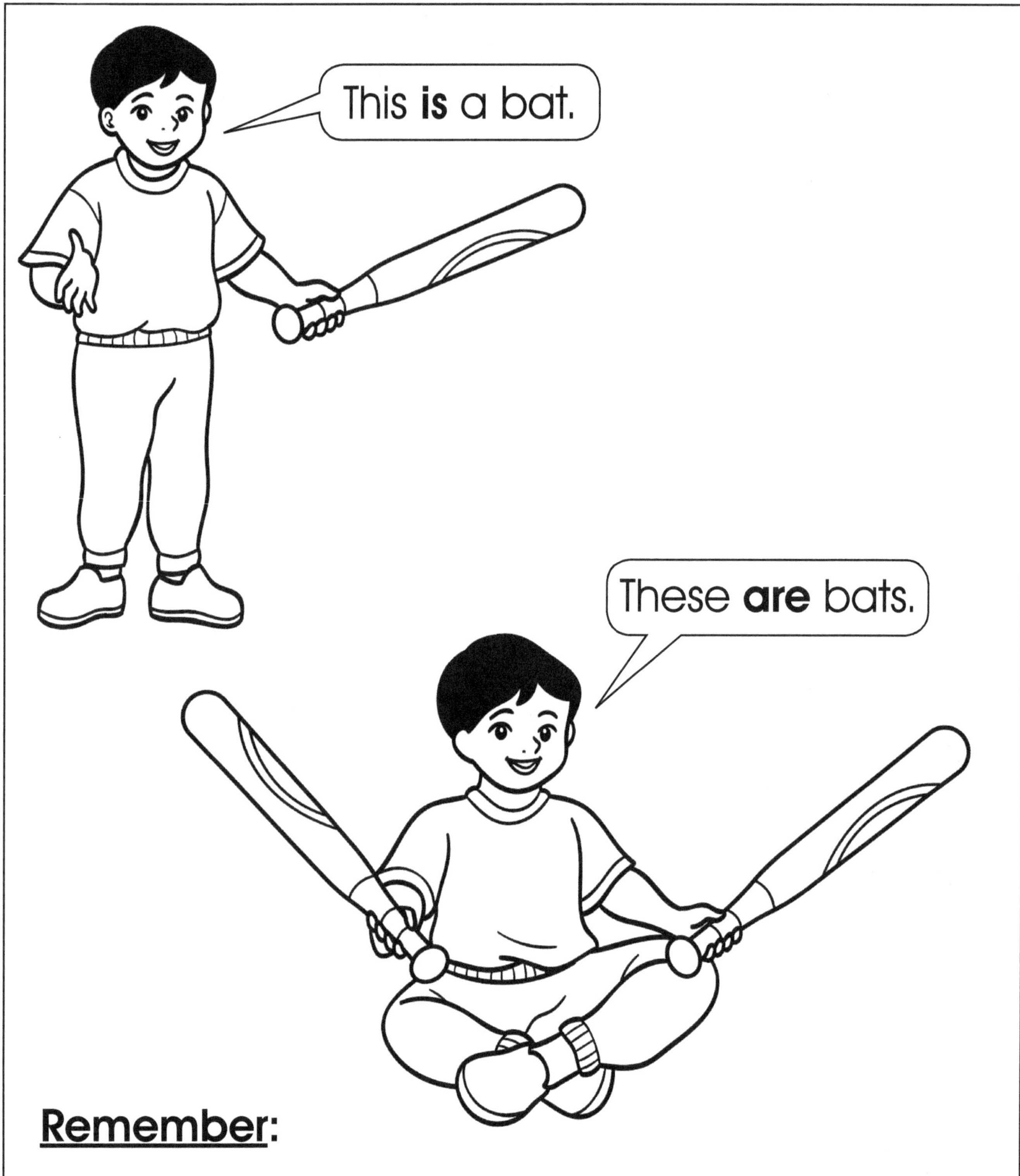

Remember:

- We use **is** when referring to only **one** thing.
- We use **are** when referring to **many** things.

Connect to the triangle the pictures that show the meaning of **is**.

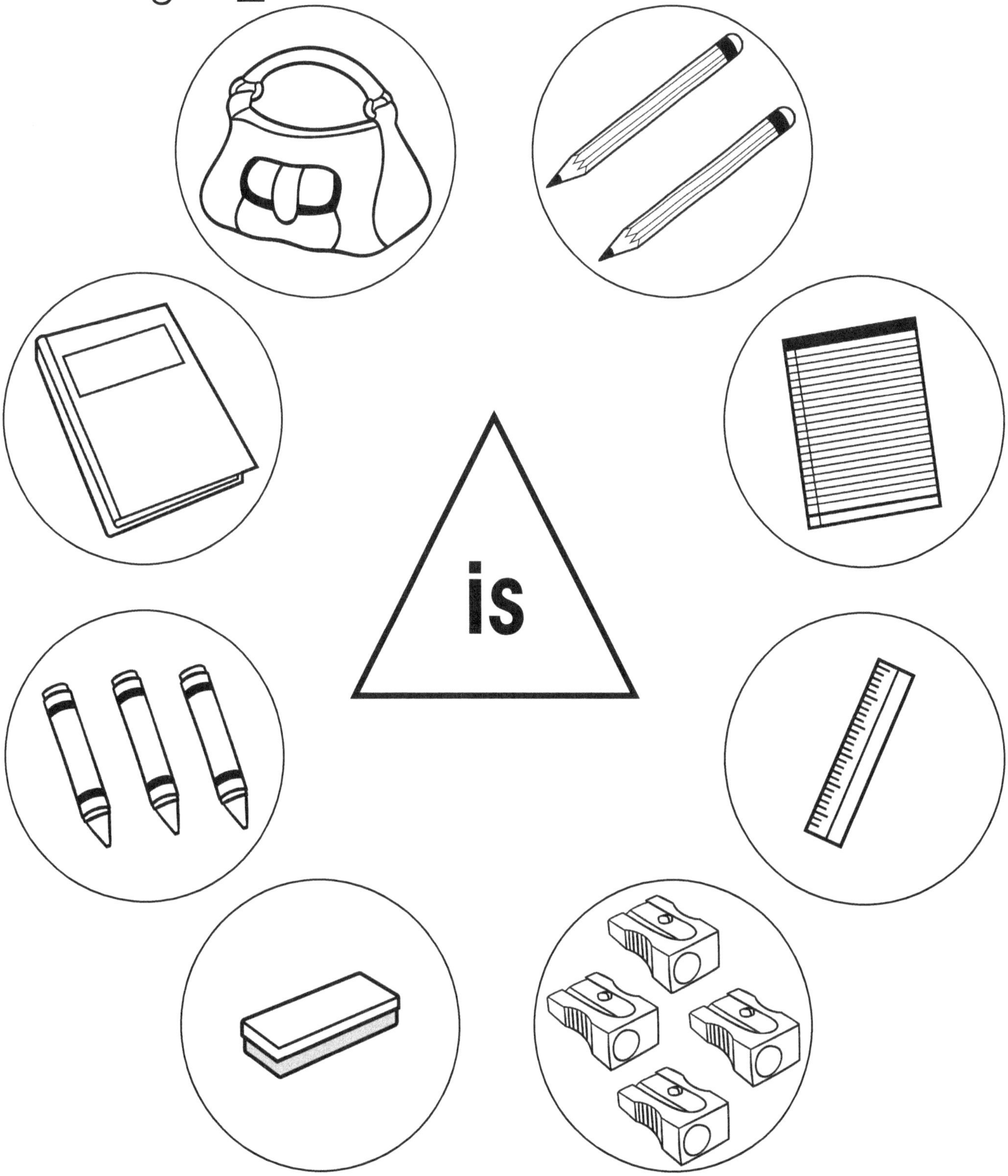

is

ACTIVITY 12

SCORE: _______

Connect to the heart the pictures that show the meaning of **are**.

HOME ACTIVITY 4   SCORE:_______

Direction: Connect the pictures to the word that matches with them.

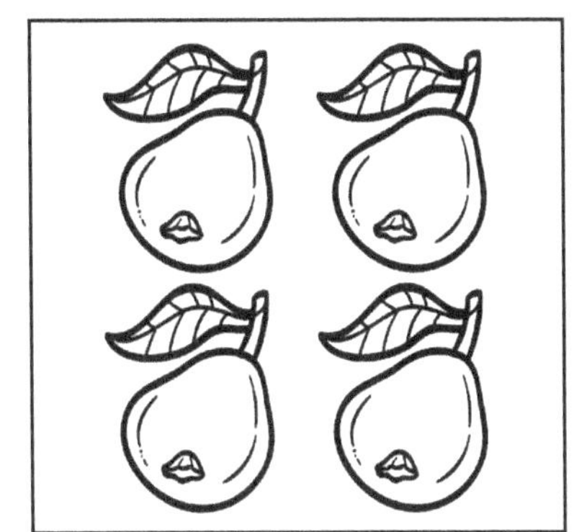

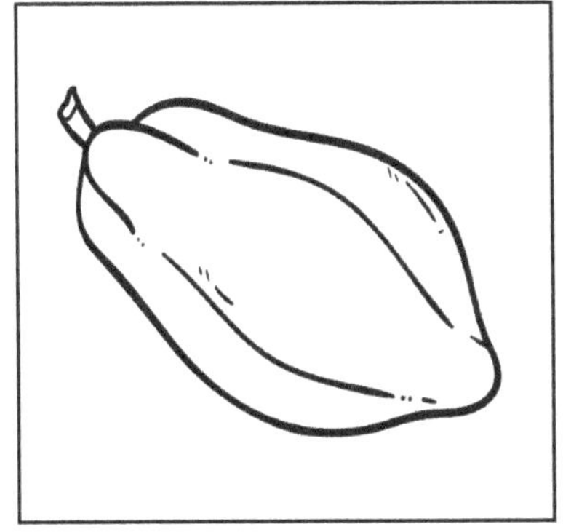

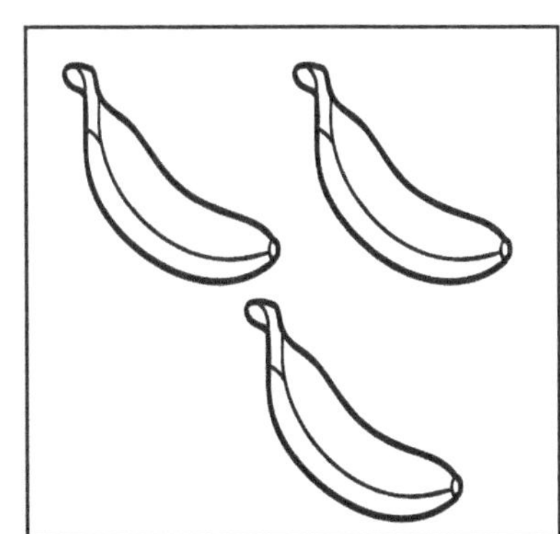

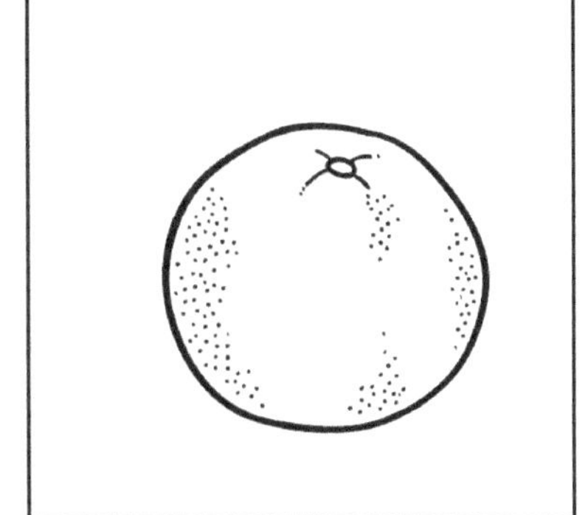

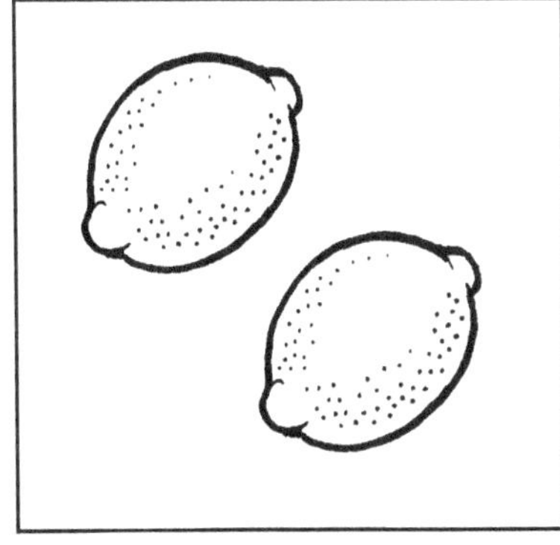

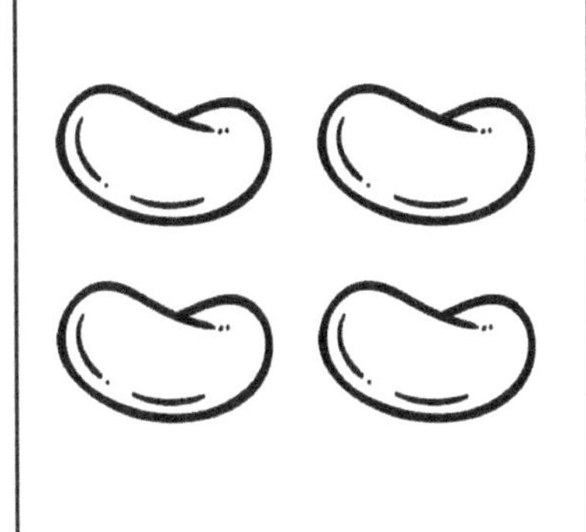

Direction: Color the box of the correct word for each picture.

1. 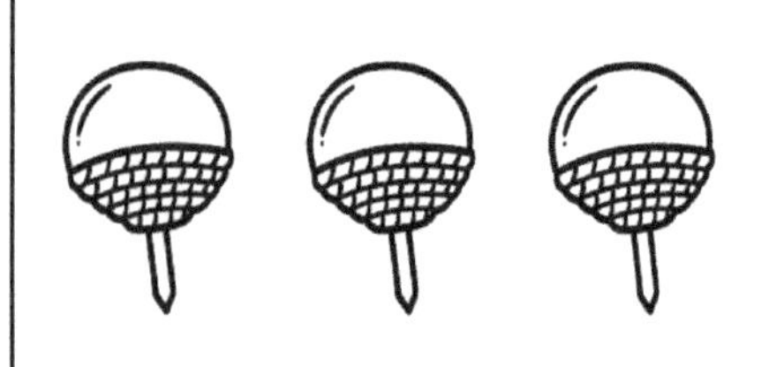 ☐ is ☐ are

2. 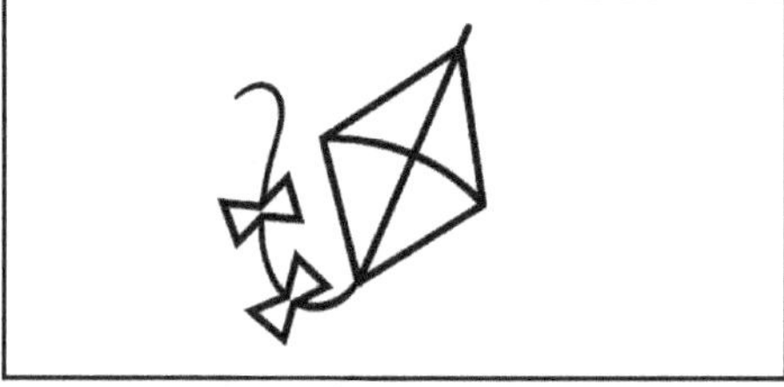 ☐ is ☐ are

3.  ☐ is ☐ are

4.  ☐ is ☐ are

5.  ☐ is ☐ are

6. 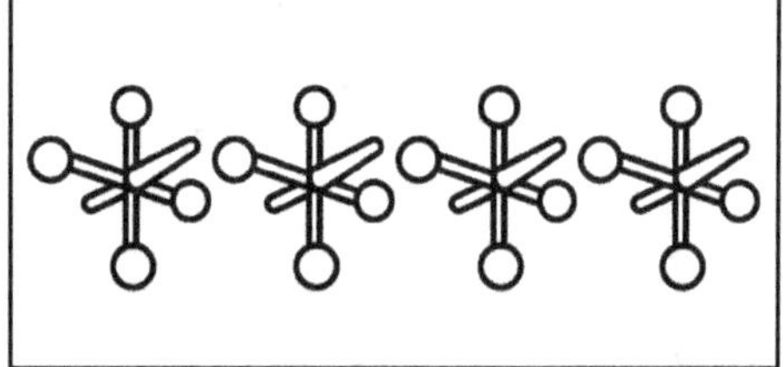 ☐ is ☐ are

<u>It</u> and <u>They</u>

<u>Remember</u>:

- We use <u>**it**</u> when referring to only **one** object or animal.
- We use <u>**they**</u> when referring to **many** objects or animals.

ACTIVITY 13

SCORE: _______

Check (✓) the pictures that show the meaning of <u>it</u>.
Cross out (✗) the pictures that show the meaning of <u>they</u>.

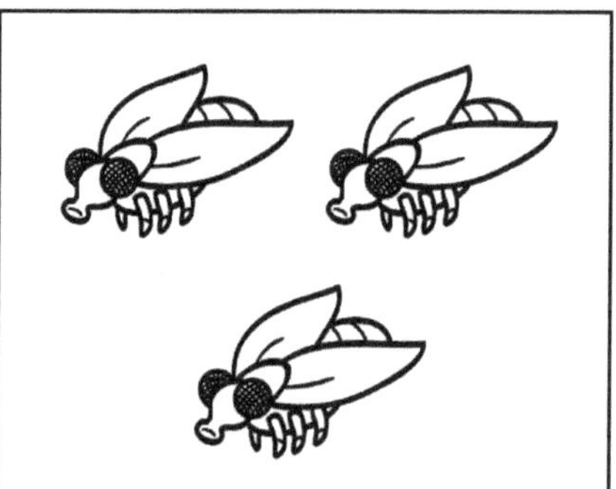

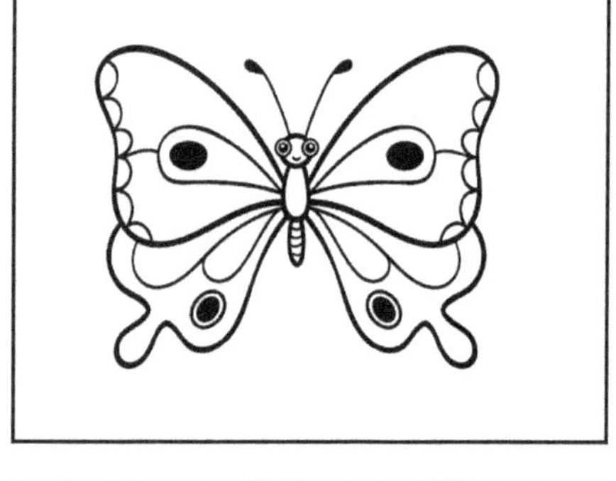

QUIZ NO. 12

SCORE: _______

Direction: Color the correct picture for each word.

 1. they

2. it

3. it

4. they

5. it

 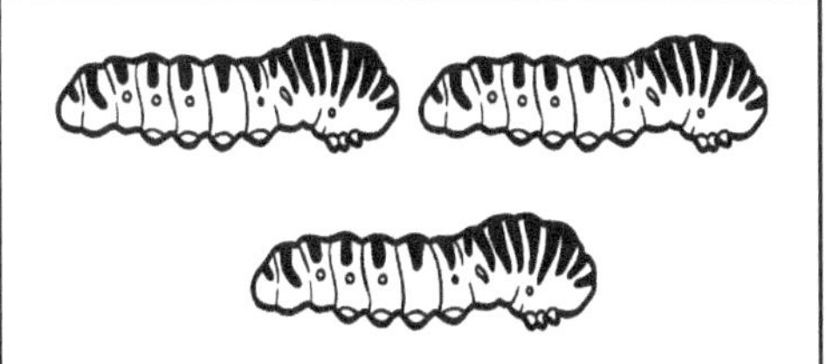

6. they

This and That

Remember:

- We use **this** when referring to only one object **near** the speaker.
- We use **that** when referring to only one object **far** from the speaker.

ACTIVITY 14

SCORE: _______

Draw a moon (🌙) on the pictures that show the meaning of <u>this</u>. *(8 points)*

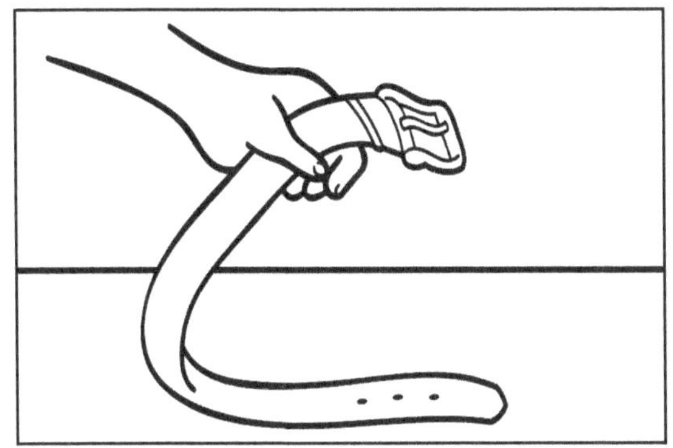

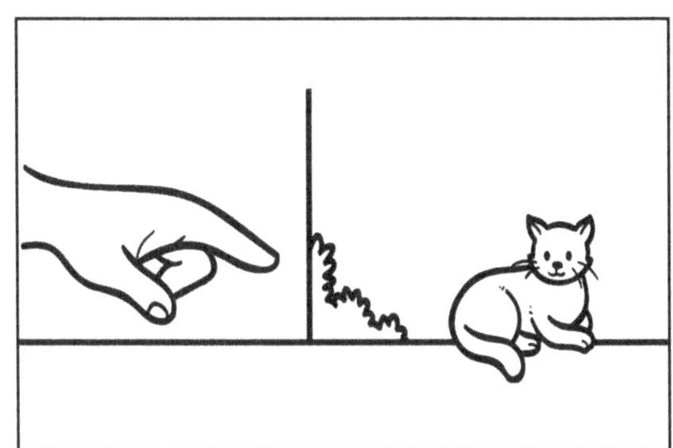

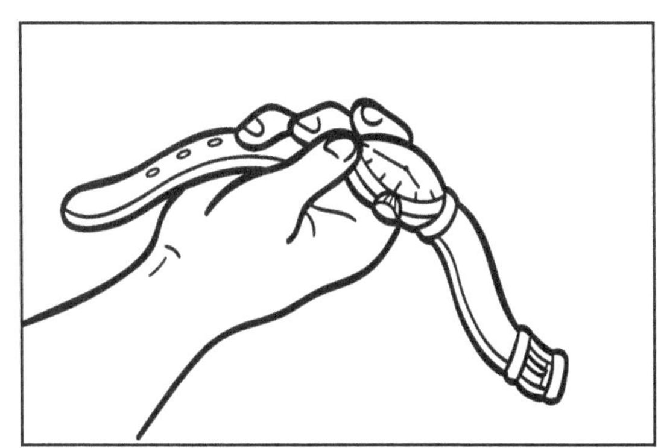

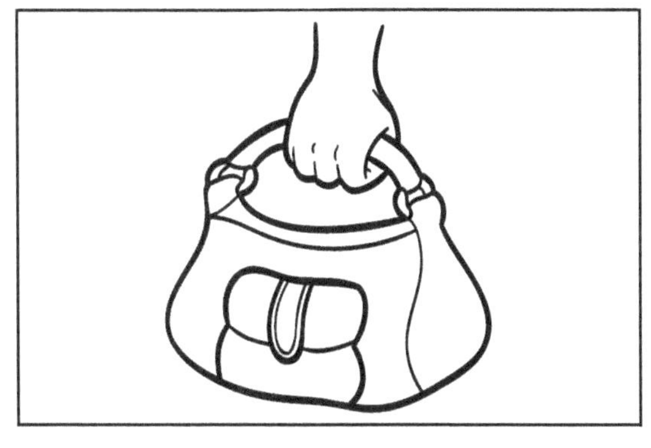

ACTIVITY 15

SCORE: _______

Draw a star (☆) on the pictures that show the meaning of **that**. *(8 points)*

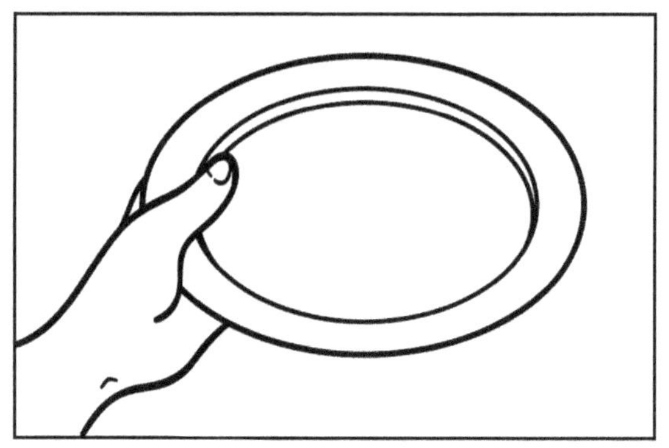

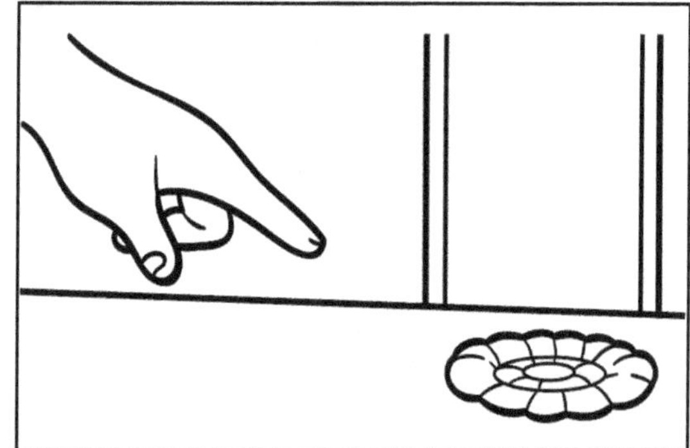

Direction: Connect each picture to the correct word.

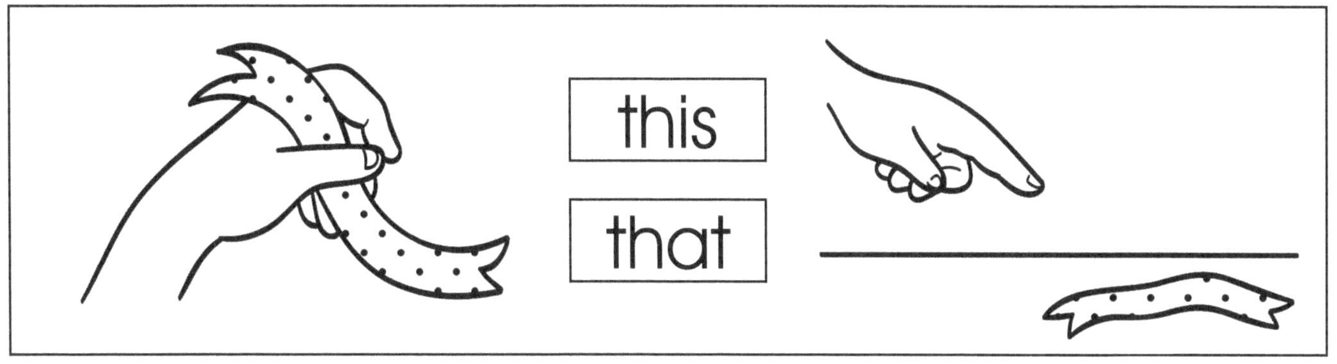

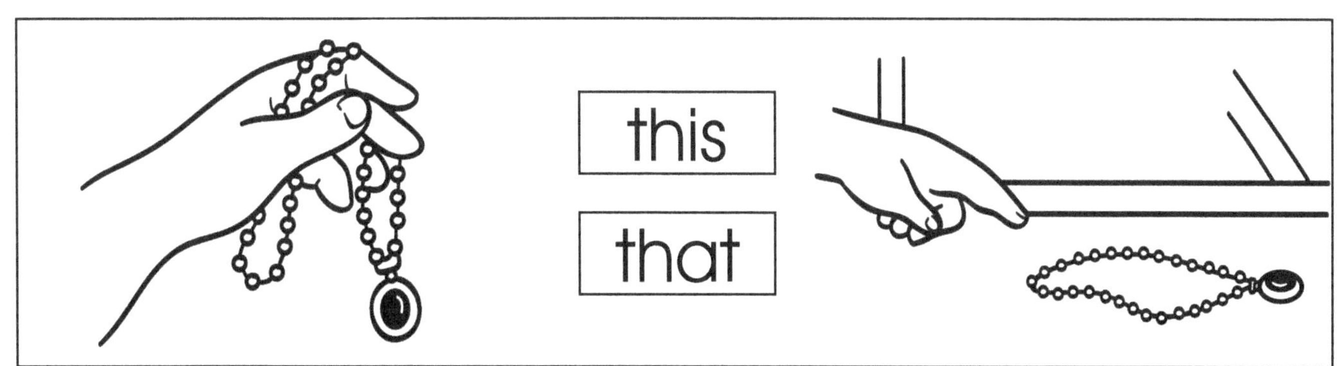

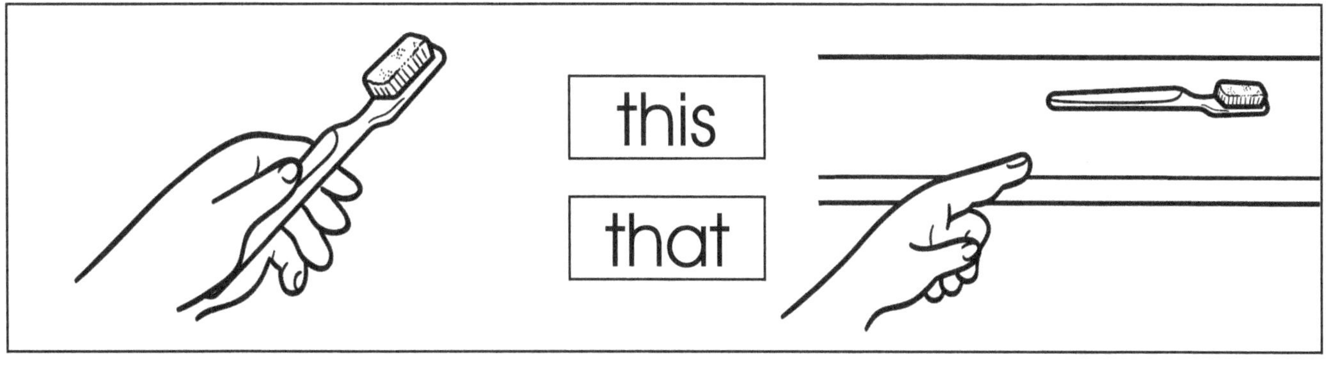

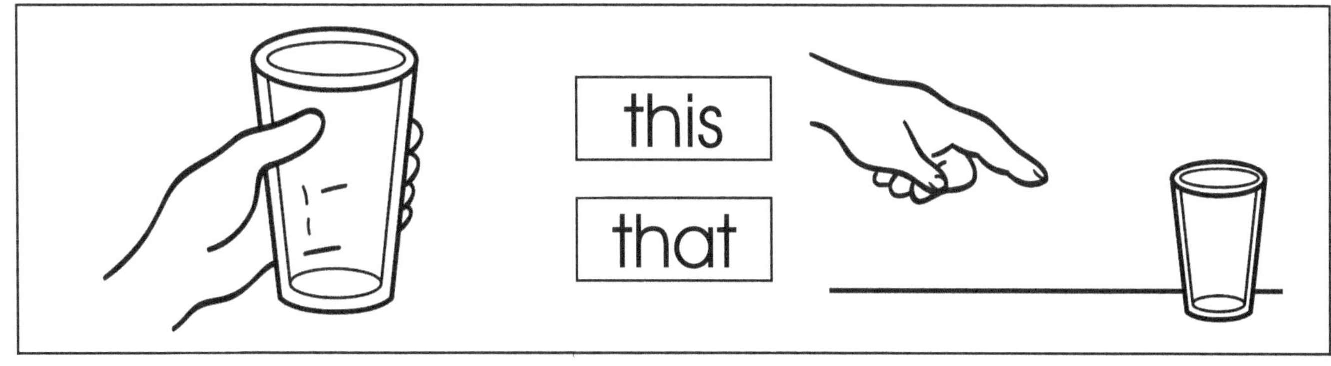

Has and Have

Remember:

- We use **has** when referring to only **one** owner.
- We use **have** when referring to **many** owners.

Connect each picture to the correct word.

QUIZ NO. 14

SCORE: _______

Direction: Underline (___) the correct word for each picture.

1. 

has   have

2. 

has   have

3. 

has   have

4. 

has   have

5. 

has   have

SECOND QUARTERLY TEST

Name: _______________________________ **Score:** _________

Level: _____________ **Date:** _____________

I. Draw a circle (O) before the things that we use in school. Draw a square (□) before those that we do not use in school.

_____________ 1.

_____________ 2.

_____________ 3.

_____________ 4.

_____________ 5.

II. Where do we do the following activities? Draw the shape of the correct picture on the blank.

_____________ 1.

_____________ 2.

_____________ 3.

_____________ 4.

_____________ 5.

III. Connect the names to the pictures.

1. janitor .

2. teacher .

3. principal .

4. security guard .

5. classmates .

IV. Draw the correct shape before each naming word to indicate one of the following:

☐ – animal   ◯ – thing

△ – person   ♡ – place

_____ 1. horse

_____ 2. playground

_____ 3. vendor

_____ 4. rice cooker

_____ 5. Ronron

V. Color the box before the correct word for each picture.

1. □ is   □ are

2. □ is   □ are

3. □ is   □ are

4. □ is   □ are

5. □ is   □ are

VI. Underline (____) the correct word for each picture.

1. it   they

2. it   they

3. it   they

4. it   they

5. it   they

150

VII. Check (✓) the correct picture for each word.

1. that 

2. this 

3. this

4. that

5. this

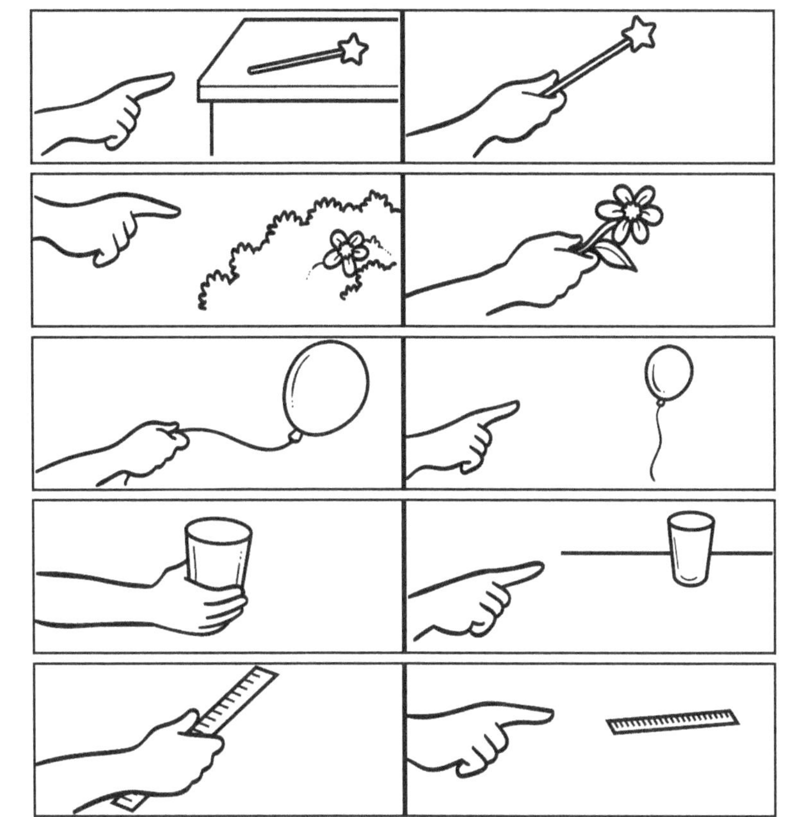

VIII. Connect the pictures to the correct word.

PROGRESS CHART
SECOND QUARTER

Name: _________________________________ Level: _____________

Activity	No. of Items	My Score	HOME ACTIVITY	No. of Items	My Score	QUIZ	No. of Items	My Score
1	10		1	10		1	7	
2	6		2	10		2	5	
3	5		3	10		3	5	
4	8		4	10		4	6	
5	12					5	5	
6	10					6	10	
7	10					7	5	
8	10					8	12	
9	10					9	12	
10	6					10	8	
11	8					11	6	
12	8					12	6	
13	10					13	8	
14	8					14	5	
15	8							
16	6							
TOTAL	135		TOTAL	40		TOTAL	100	

_________________________ _________________________
Parent's/Guardian's Signature   Teacher's Signature

THIRD QUARTER
MY COMMUNITY

Teacher's Objectives and Student Evaluation				
Lesson	*At the end of the activities, the child should be able to:*	NI	S	E
1	1. identify the different places in a community			
	2. know the function of each place			
	3. learn how to take care of our community			
2	4. identify the people who help us in the community			
	5. identify the things these helpers use and the clothes they wear			
	6. understand how these people help us			
	7. respect the community helpers and appreciate their importance in the community			
3	8. recognize the correct usage of <u>in</u>, <u>on</u>, and <u>under</u>			
	9. distinguish the difference between <u>up</u> and <u>down</u>			
	10. know the concepts of <u>over</u> and <u>below</u>			
	11. differentiate <u>left</u> from <u>right</u>			
4	12. understand the concepts of <u>inside</u> and <u>outside</u>			
	13. apply the words learned in day-to-day conversation			

Legend:
NI — Needs Improvement   S — Satisfactory   E — Excellent

LESSON 1

MY COMMUNITY

Guide: Take the children on a short field trip through your community. (You may visit the nearest grocery, vulcanizing shop, bakery, etc.) Introduce them to different people. Have them observe what they see and what goes on in each place you visit. It is also advisable to let the children experience buying from the grocery or the bakery.

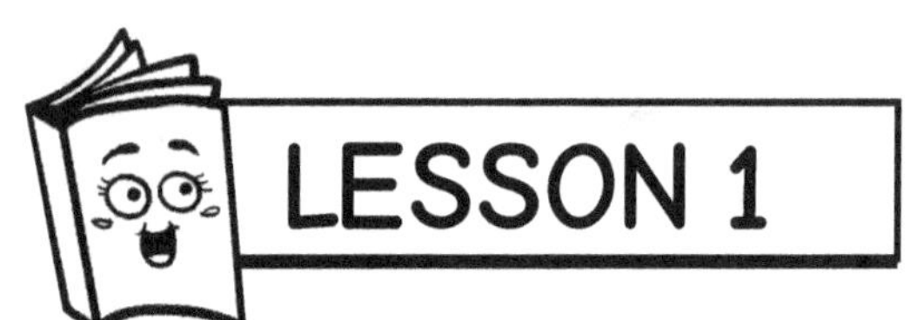

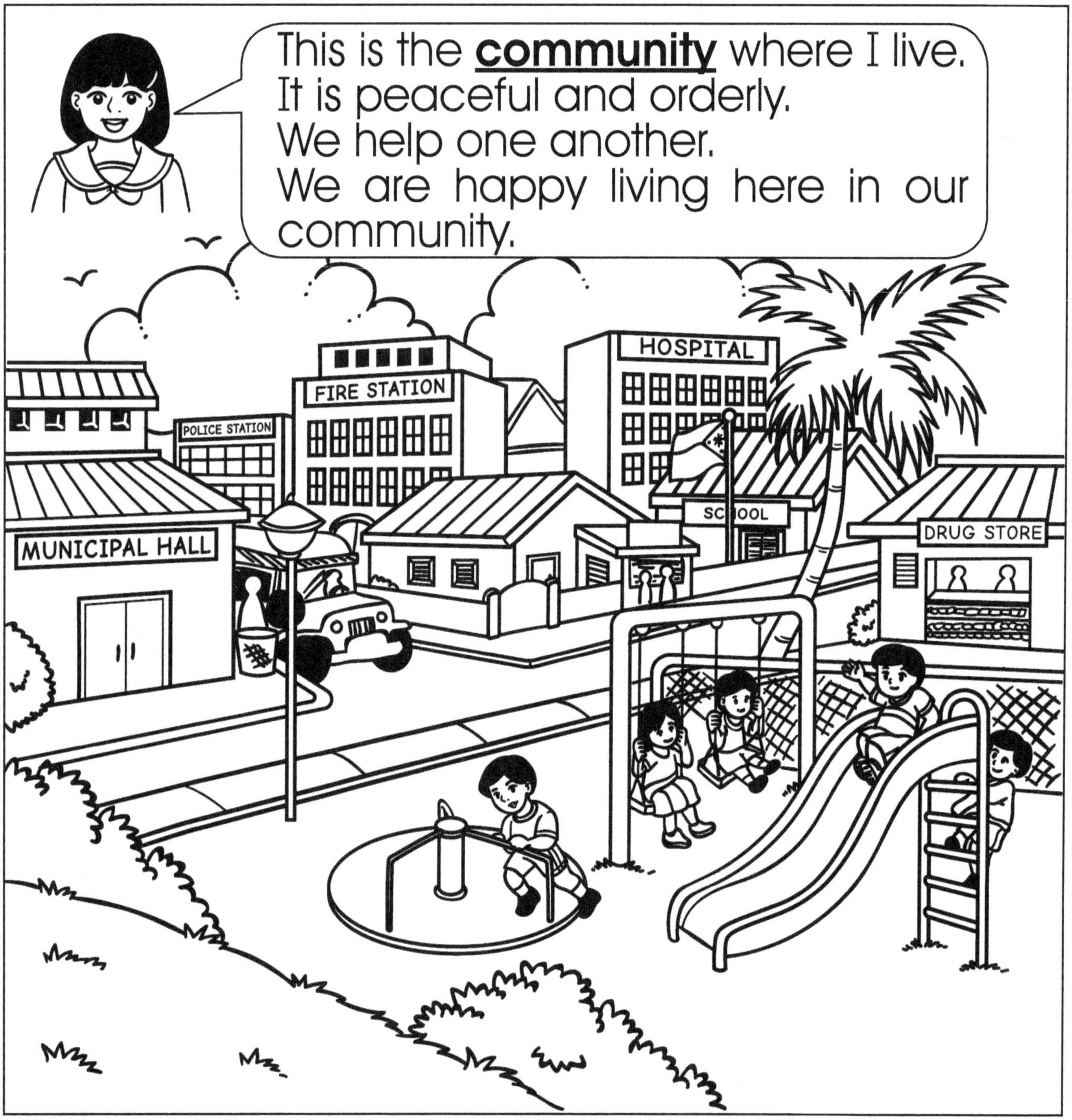

These are the different places in our community.
(Color the places where you have already been.)

home

This is where our family lives.

school

This is where we learn how to read, write, and count.

market

This is where we buy food and other needs.

bakery/bakehouse

This is where we buy bread and cookies.

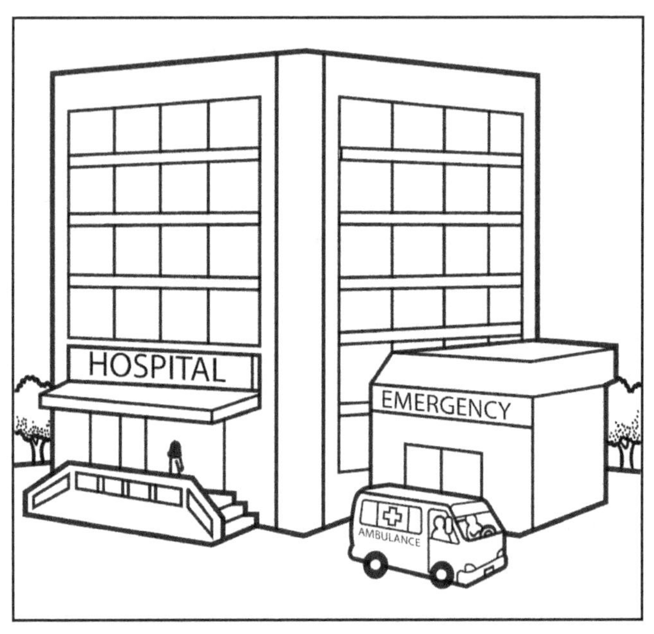

hospital

This is where we go when we are sick or injured.

drugstore/pharmacy

This is where we buy medicine.

barbershop/parlor

This is where we get our haircut.

restaurant/food house

This is where we eat special food.

bank

This is where we keep our money safe.

post office

This is where we get and send letters and packages.

police station

This is where we call for help when bad people harm us.

fire station

This is where we call for help when there is fire.

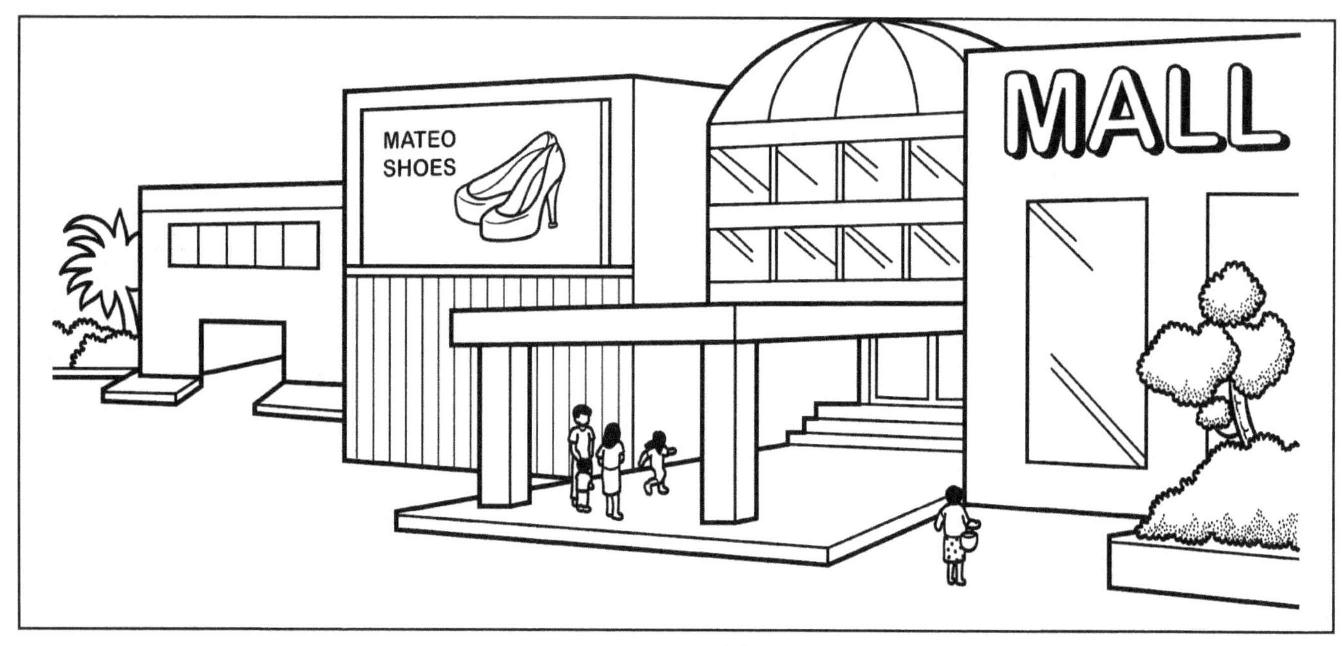

mall

This is where we shop and have fun.

park

This is where we stroll, play, and relax.

These are the special places in a community.
(Color the place where you go.)

church

This is where our Catholic brothers and sisters hear mass.

chapel

This is where our non-Catholic brothers and sisters worship God.

mosque

This is where our Muslim brothers worship.

SUGGESTED ACTIVITIES FOR THE DIFFERENT LANGUAGE SKILLS

SKILLS	ACTIVITIES
Listening and Speaking 	Have a pretend play with the children. Make an improvised "telephone" by inserting a funnel on each end of a plastic hose. One end of the "telephone" serves as the mouthpiece while the other end serves as the earpiece. Pretend that you need to call a police station to report an accident, or a restaurant to order food, or a fire station to report a fire. Start making the call while a child answers on the other line. Have the children take turns calling and answering "phone calls." 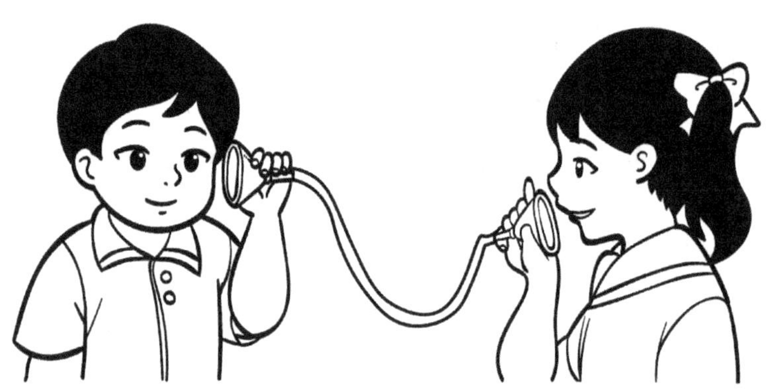
Reading and Writing 	• Encourage the children to think about the houses and buildings in a community and build them together with blocks or LEGO sets. Add some labels (mall, market, restaurant, hospital, fire station, etc.) and some tape. Let the children place the labels on the different buildings. Add street signs (and street names for older children), toy people, and cars. • Have a Restaurant Pretend Play! Make several copies of menus of items that will be served at a restaurant. To make the menu, cut out pictures of food from magazines and write the names and prices on each menu item. 

<u>Direction</u>: How many of the different places in the community have you visited? Paste pictures of yourself taken in these places. *(10 points)*

# ACTIVITY 1

SCORE: _______

Connect the things to the places where they are found.

1. 

2. 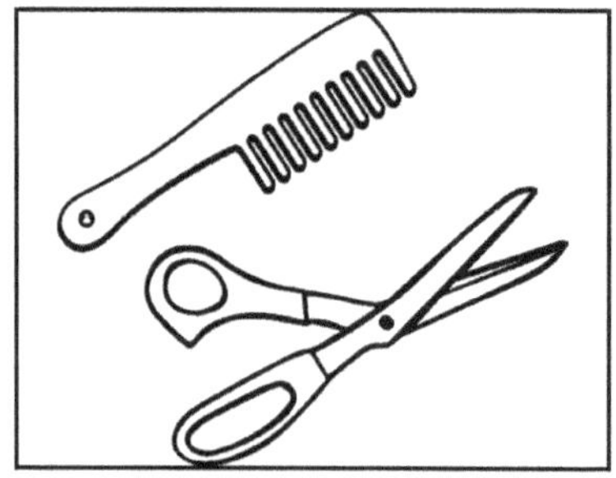

3. 

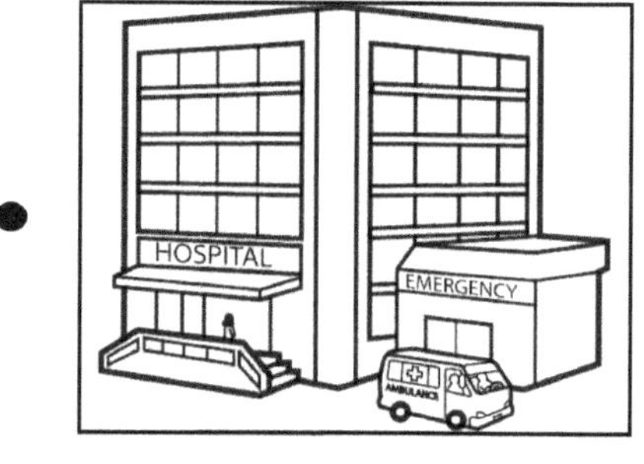

4. 

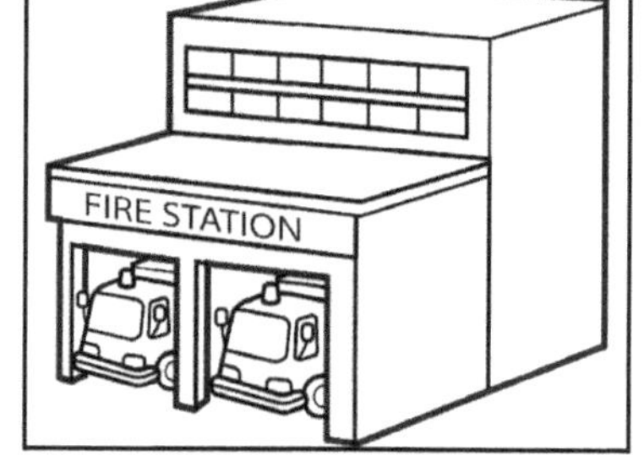

5. 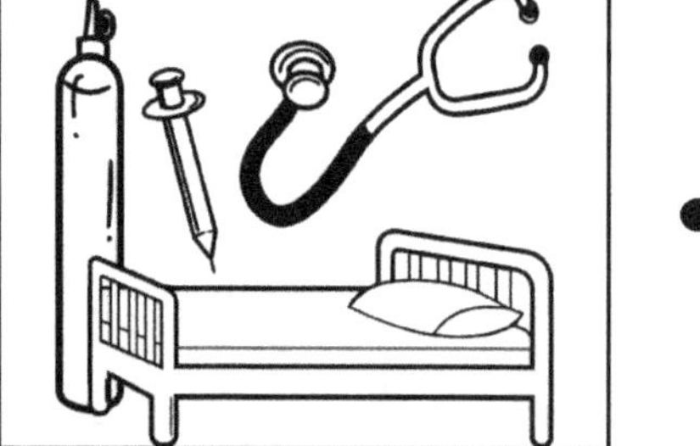

6. 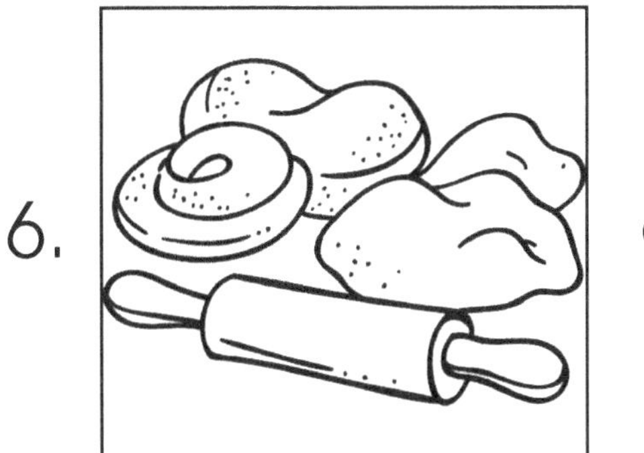   •   • 

7.    •   • 

POST OFFICE

FRAGILE

PHILIPPINE BANK
ATM
ATM

ST.MATTHEW'S LEARNING SCHOOL

MATH
CRAYON

QUEEN'S BAKERY

8. 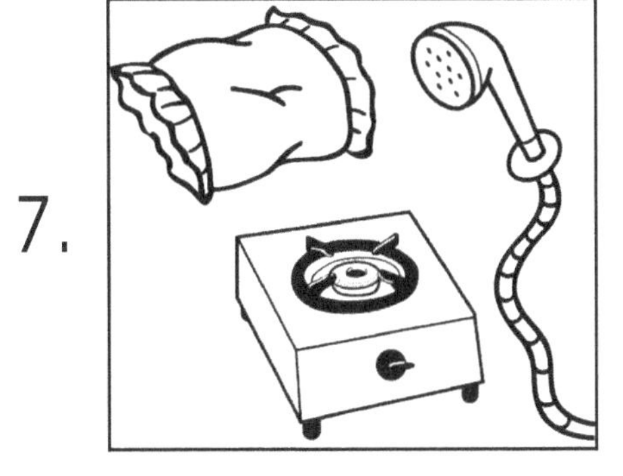   •   • 

9. 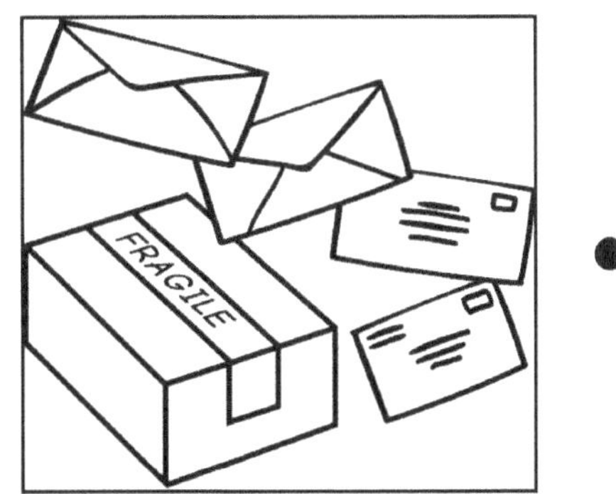   •   • 

10.    •   • 

QUIZ NO. 1

SCORE: _______

Direction: In what place can you find the following? Check the correct answer.

1.	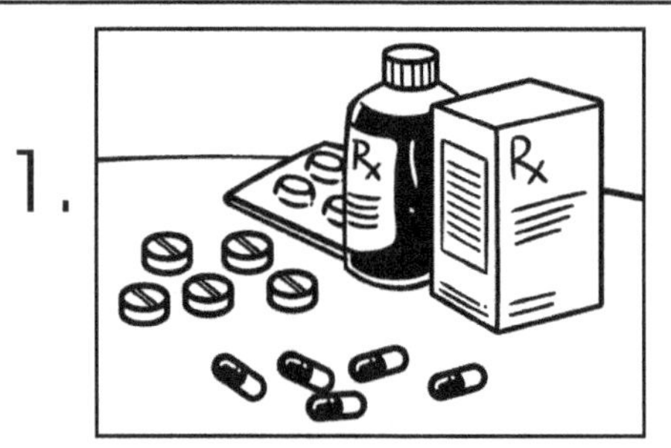		
2.			
3.			
4.			
5.			

QUIZ NO. 2

SCORE: _______

Direction: Connect each activity to the place where it is done.

1.  •

  • 

2.  •

  • 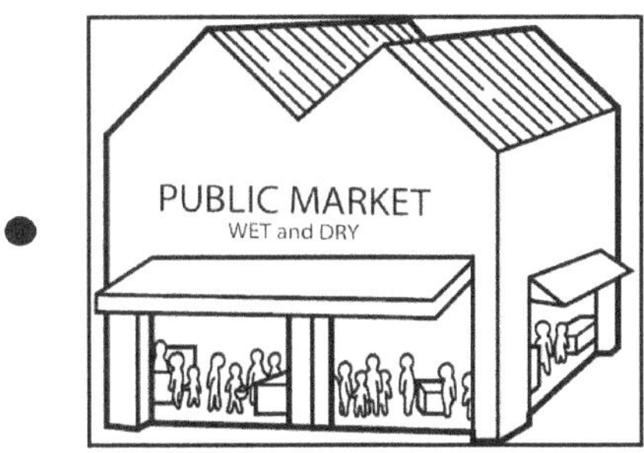

3.  •

  • 

4.  •

  •

5. •

  • 

6.  •   • 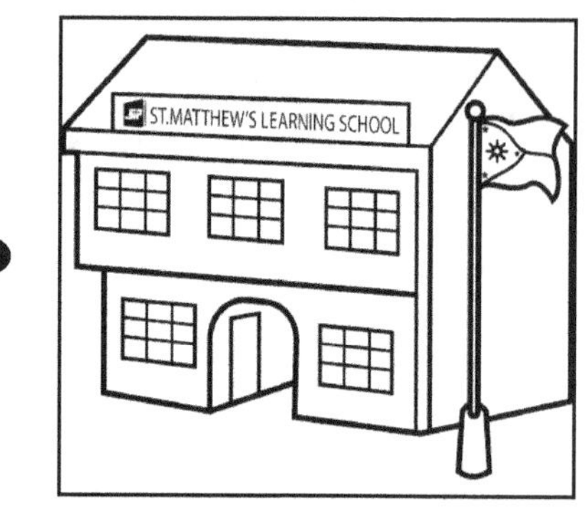

ST.MATTHEW'S LEARNING SCHOOL

HOSPITAL
EMERGENCY
AMBULANCE

BEAUTY PARLOR & BARBER SHOP

RVC
FASTFOOD
VALUE

QUEEN'S BAKERY

7.  •   • 

8.  •   • 

9.  •   • 

10.  •   • 

CLASS ACTIVITY 1

Guide: Gather the class in a circle and play a guessing game with them. Think of a place in a community. Dramatize what they do in this particular place. Let the children guess what place it is. Have them take turns dramatizing, while the rest of the class guess each place. You may also divide the class into two groups: the first group dramatizes while the other guesses; or you may schedule small trips to the different places in the community.

CLASS ACTIVITY 2

Guide: Gather the class in a circle and play a guessing game with them. Think of a community helper and act out what he or she does. Let the children guess whom you are imitating. Have them play out the rest of the game, with each pupil taking turns to dramatize.

cinema

This is where we watch movies.

hotel

This is where we stay when we are traveling.

airport

This is where airplanes land and take off.

gasoline station

This is where we have our cars fueled.

swimming pool

This is where we swim and have fun.

auto shop

This is where we have our cars fixed.

pet shop

This is where we buy pets and pet food.

veterinary clinic

This is where we go when our pet is sick.

beach

This is where we go when we want to swim and relax in the sea.

amusement park

This is where we have rides, games, and different forms of entertainment.

In what place can you find the things on the left? Color the box of the correct answer.

1.

2.

3.

4.

5.

QUIZ NO. 3

SCORE: _______

Direction: Connect each activity to the place where it is done.

1.  •   • 

2.  •   • 

3.  •   • 

4.  •   • 

5.  •   •

6.

7.

8.

9.

10.

Check (✓) the pictures of those you have already met. (Color the picture of the person you want to be when you grow up.)

father and mother

Father and Mother take care of us. They help us grow into good persons.

teacher

The teacher teaches us to read, write, and count.

vendor

The vendor sells things we need.

baker

The baker bakes bread and cookies.

postman

The postman delivers letters and packages.

traffic aide

The traffic aide directs traffic and helps us cross the street.

fireman

The fireman puts out fires.

policeman/policewoman

The policeman or policewoman protects us from harm.

doctor

The doctor treats the
sick and the injured.

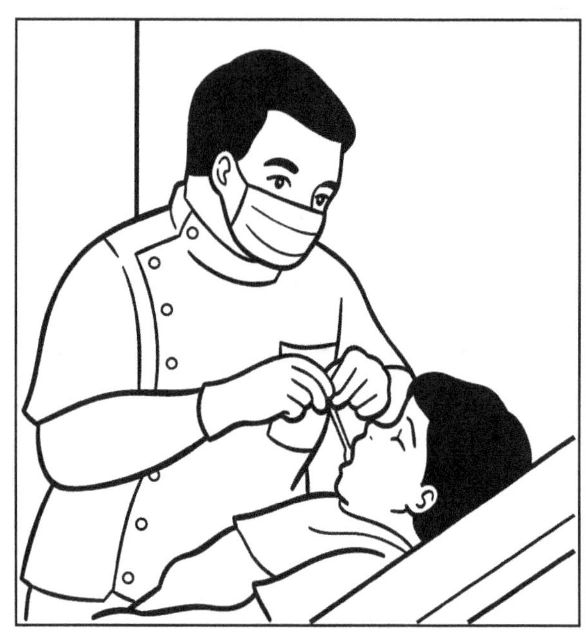

dentist

The dentist helps us
take care of our teeth.

nurse

The nurse takes care
of the sick.

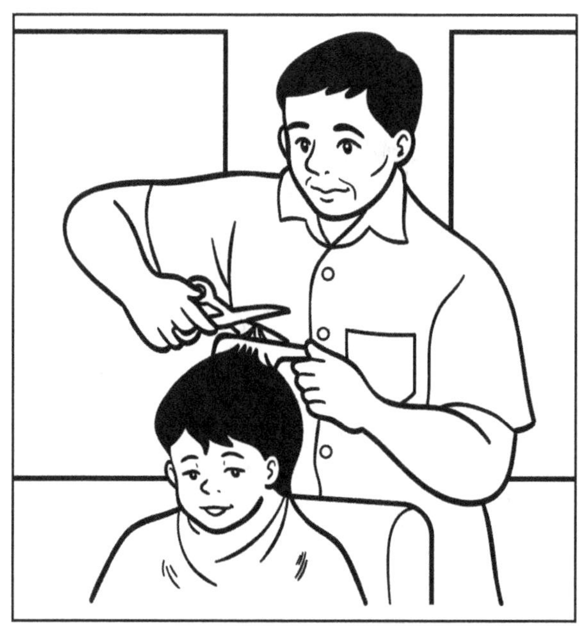

barber

The barber trims and
grooms men's and
boy's hair.

flight attendant

The flight attendant helps us with our needs while the plane is in flight.

garbage collector

The garbage collector gets the garbage from our houses.

mechanic

The mechanic fixes our cars.

pilot

The pilot flies airplanes.

fisherman

The fisherman catches fish and other sea creatures.

driver

The driver drives cabs, buses, and jeepneys.

seamstress/tailor

The seamstress or tailor cuts out and makes garments for men and women.

carpenter

The carpenter builds and repairs houses.

farmer

The farmer plants rice and other crops.

Check (✓) the person who teaches you about God.

priest

The priest says mass and helps us become good Catholics.

pastor

The pastor helps us learn more about God and His teachings.

imam

The imam helps us know more about Allah and His teachings.

SUGGESTED ACTIVITIES FOR THE DIFFERENT LANGUAGE SKILLS

SKILLS	ACTIVITIES
Listening	Try to invite community helpers to visit your classroom to talk about their jobs to the children. They can bring items from their trade and hand out flyers or cards about their business for children to take home. Also, ask the visitors to tell stories about their experiences in their work.
Speaking	Talk to the children about what they want to be when they grow up. Encourage them to tell why they want to be such. Let them tell about what they would do in their job and how they would help other people.
Reading	Print pictures of different community helpers (fireman, teacher, policeman, etc.) and some objects that relate to each community helper (firetruck, mail bag, books, police cap, etc.). Let the children match the object with the community helper.
Writing	"My Community Helper Book" In advance, using copy paper for the pages and construction paper for the cover, assemble booklets for each child. Encourage the children to print their own name and decorate the covers which you have pre-printed with "My Community Helper Book" as the title. Have the children draw different helpers to make the book. If they find it hard to draw, have them cut out pictures from old magazines instead.

ACTIVITY 3

SCORE: _______

Encircle (O) the person who uses and carries the things on the left.

1.			
2.			
3.	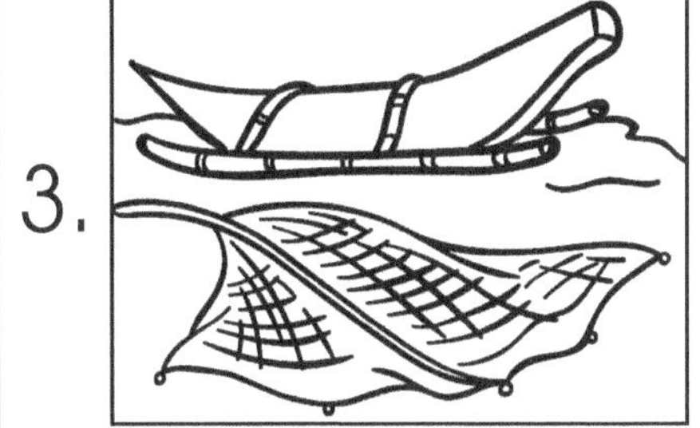		
4.	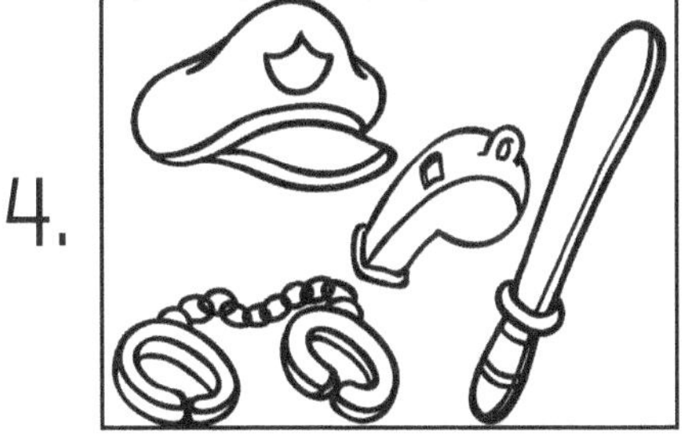		
5.			

6. 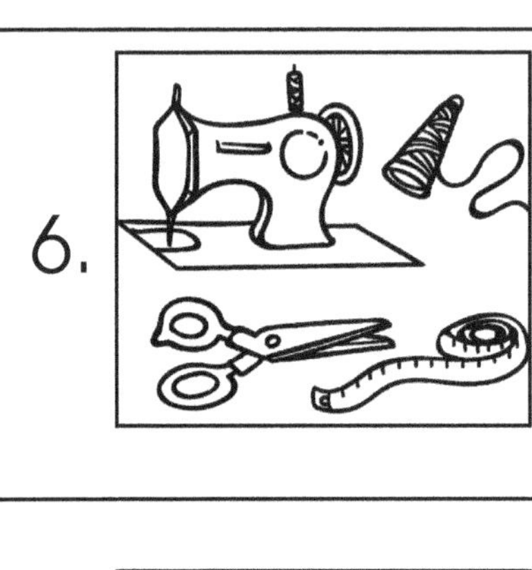  

7.  

8.  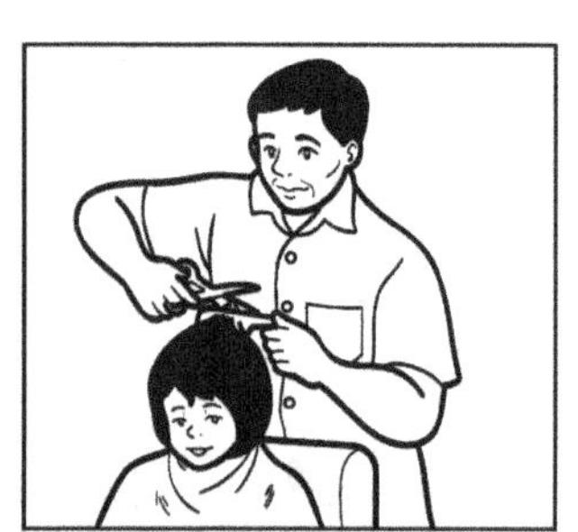

9.  

10.  

11.   

12. 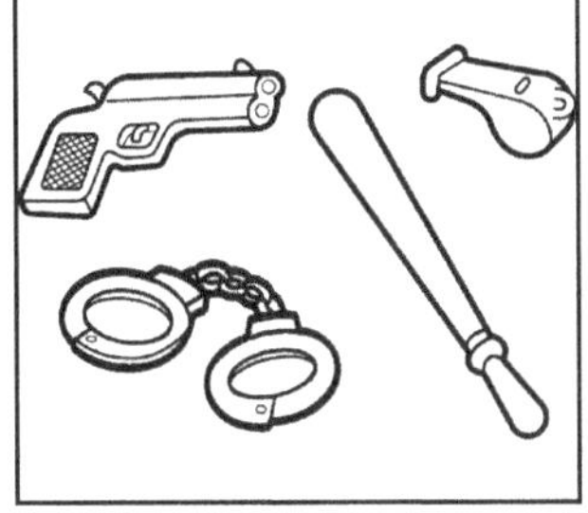  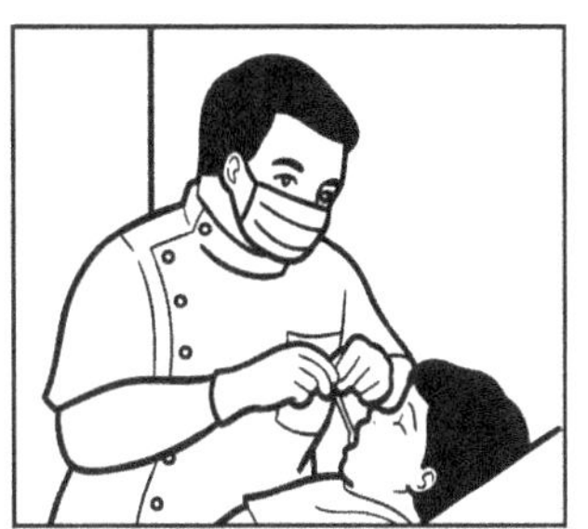

13.   

14. 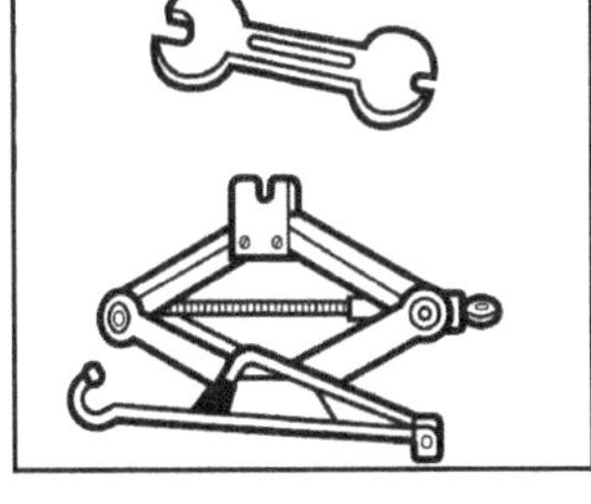  

15.   

QUIZ NO. 4

SCORE: _______

Direction: Connect the things to the person who uses or wears them.

1.

2.
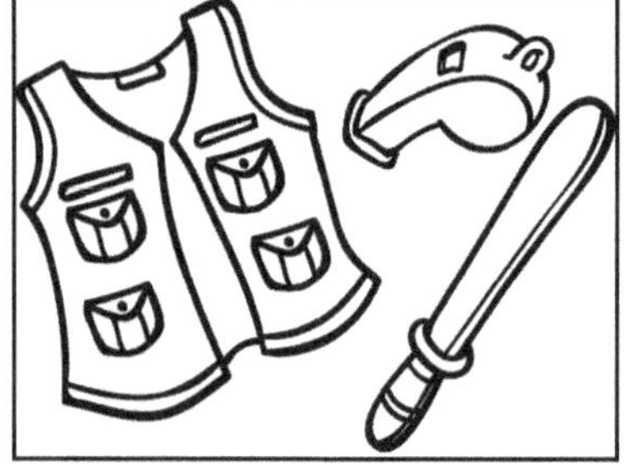

3.
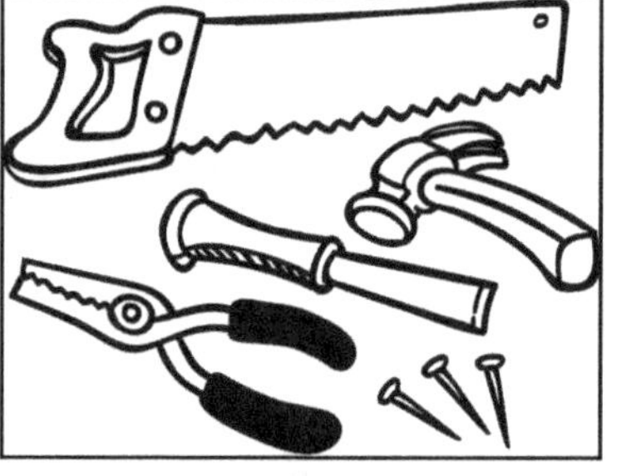

4.
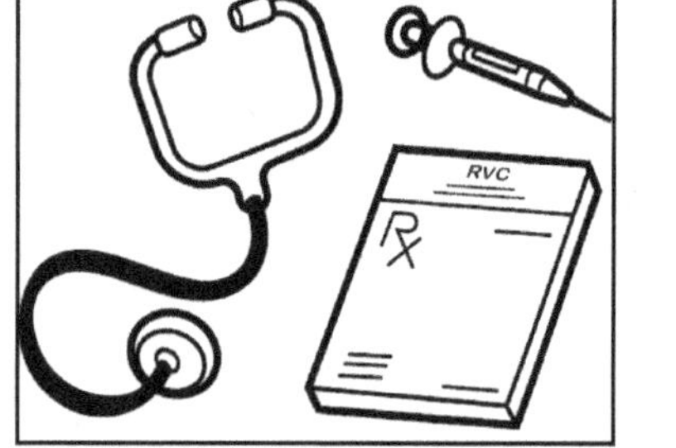

5.

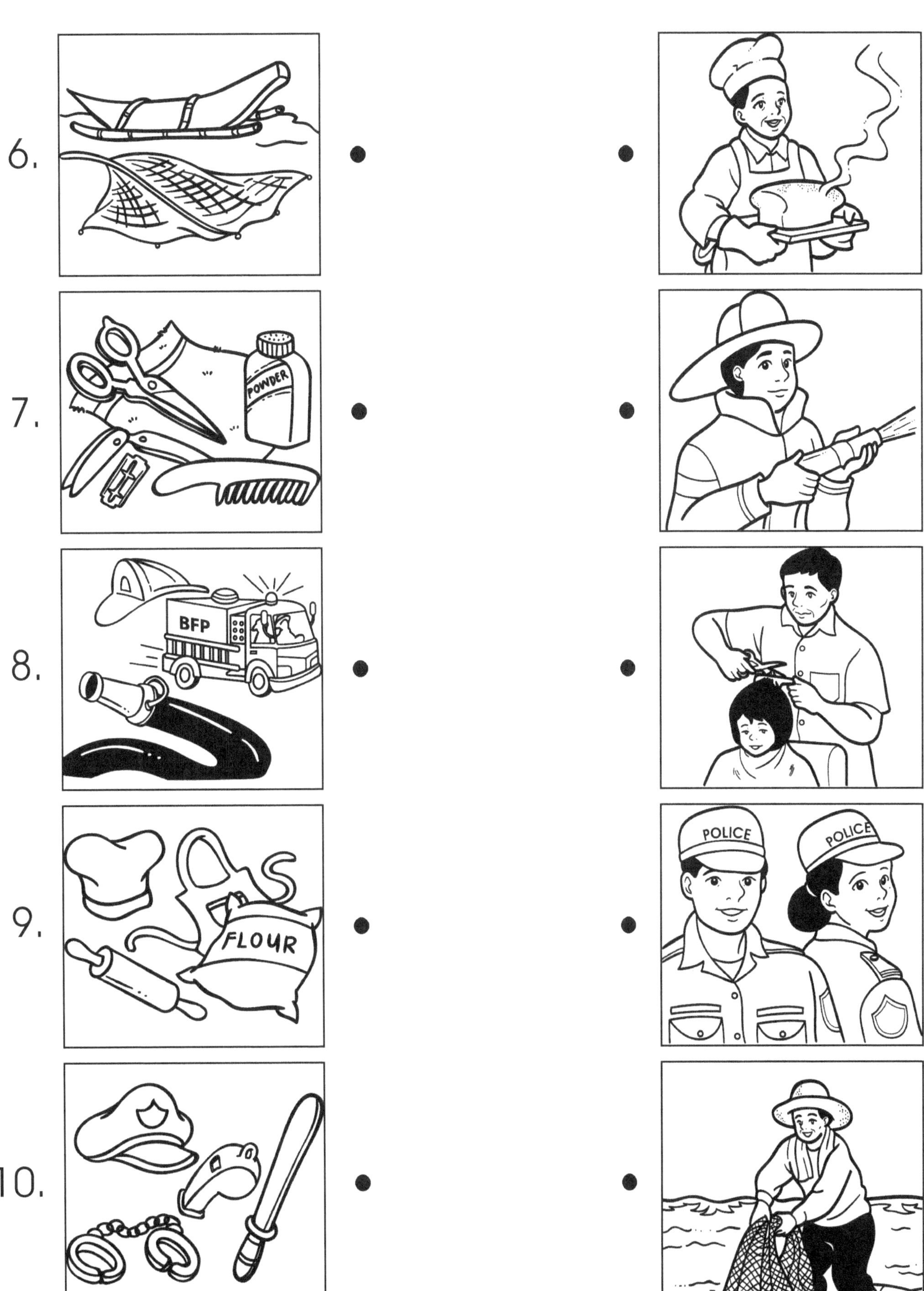

6.

7.

8.

9.

10.

Baker or Chef Tissue Paper Roll Craft

Materials:
- toilet paper tube
- glue
- scissors
- crayons
- colored marking pens

Procedure:
1. Color the template pieces as appropriate and cut them out.
2. Glue the large rectangular piece around the toilet paper tube.
3. Glue on the arms and the head.
4. Glue the chef's hat onto the head.
5. Glue the feet onto the bottom of the toilet paper tube, bending the tabs to make a 3D effect.
6. Glue the cake onto the hands.

QUIZ NO. 5   SCORE: _______

<u>Direction:</u> Check (✓) the correct picture for each name. (Your teacher will read the names for you.)

1. barber

2. nurse

3. farmer

4. postman

5. pilot

6. carpenter

7. dentist

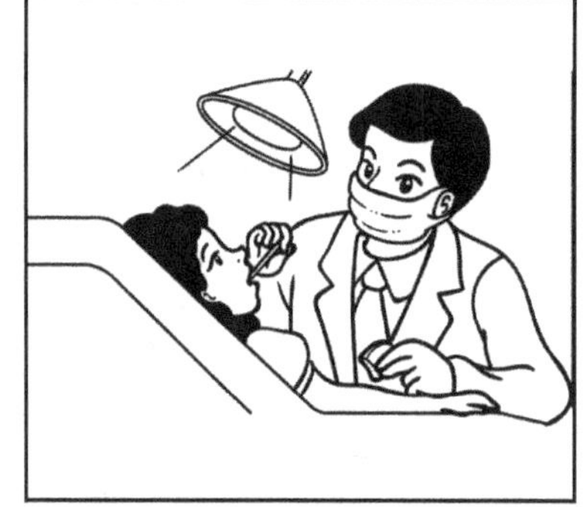 

8. fireman

9. driver

 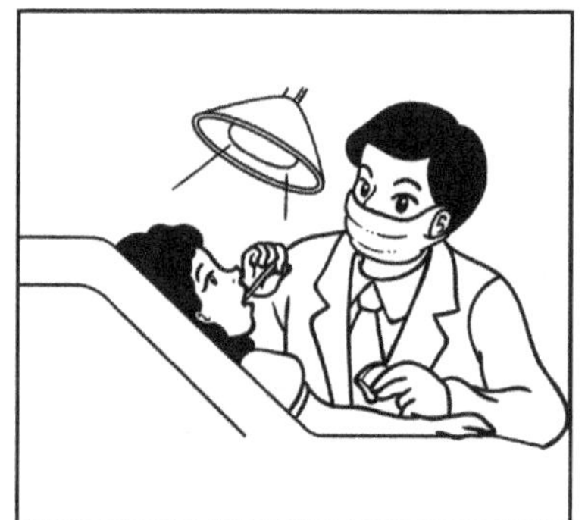

10. seamstress

 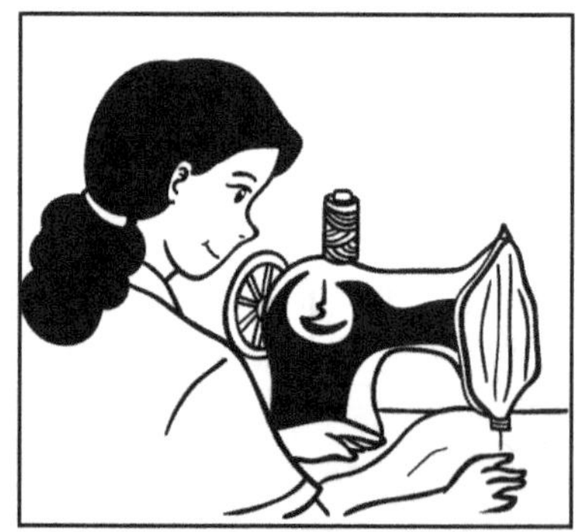

Direction: Connect each community helper to the place where he or she works.

1. 

2. 

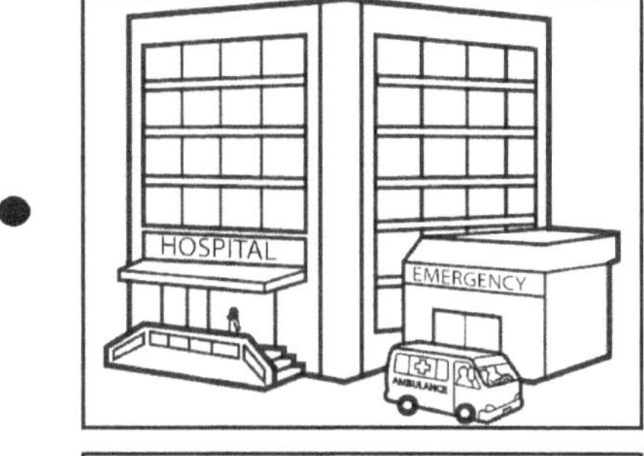

3. 

4. 

5. 

6. 

7.

8.

9. 

10.

WORDS THAT TELL WHERE
In, On, and Under

Guide: Show a doll to the class and introduce it as "Aya." Place the doll <u>in</u>, <u>on</u>, and <u>under</u> different places in the classroom. Play a "question-and-answer" game with the children while singing the song on the next page. You may substitute the doll with the things found in the classroom and use <u>over</u>, <u>below</u>, <u>left</u>, <u>right</u>, <u>up</u>, <u>down</u>, <u>inside</u>, and <u>outside</u> in the succeeding lessons.

The rat is **in** the box.

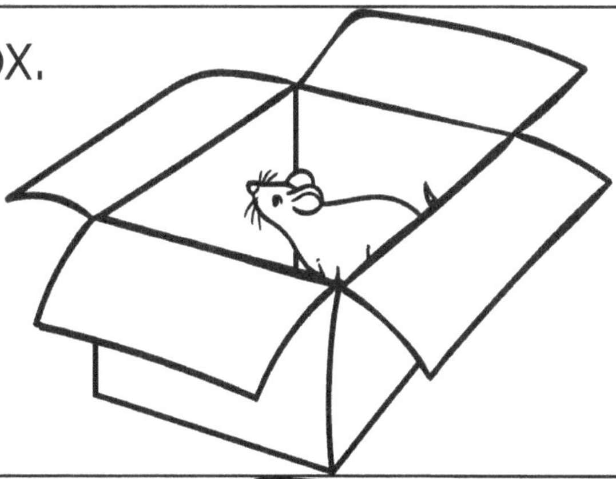

The rat is **on** the chair.

The rat is **under** the chair.

Tune: "Where is Thumbman?"

Teacher: Where is Aya? Where is Aya?

Pupils: On the chair,
On the chair.

Everybody: Aya is a doll,
Aya is a doll,
On the chair,
On the chair.

Variation: In the box
In the bag
On the mat
On the rug
Under the chair
Under the bed

SUGGESTED ACTIVITIES FOR THE DIFFERENT LANGUAGE SKILLS

SKILLS	ACTIVITIES
Listening	Play "Simon Says" using the prepositions <u>in</u>, <u>on</u>, and <u>under</u>. Not only will children get to work on these words, but they'll get extra practice following directions, too. Example: *Simon Says put the ball in the box, on the table, and under the chair.*
Speaking	Play a treasure hunt with the children. Hide a toy or snack somewhere in the classroom, then tell the children where they can find it using <u>in</u>, <u>on</u>, or <u>under</u>. Example: *The toy is in the bag, on the tray, and under the table.* For a twist, have the children hide something from you and direct you to it using <u>in</u>, <u>on</u>, and <u>under</u>.
Reading	Prepare several flashcards with the words <u>in</u>, <u>on</u>, and <u>under</u>. Make another set of flashcards with pictures that show the meaning of <u>in</u>, <u>on</u>, and <u>under</u>. Have the children match the two sets of flashcards.
Writing	Display the flashcards with the words <u>in</u>, <u>on</u>, and <u>under</u> on the classroom wall. Make it a part of your word wall where children can practice reading and writing the words.

ACTIVITY 4

SCORE: _______

Cross out (✗) the pictures that show the meaning of <u>in</u>.

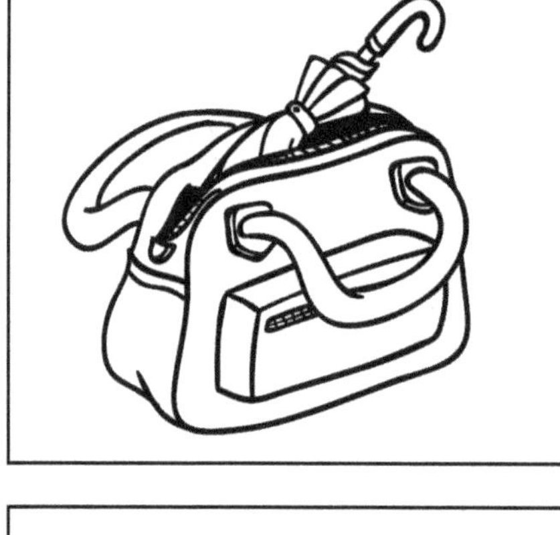

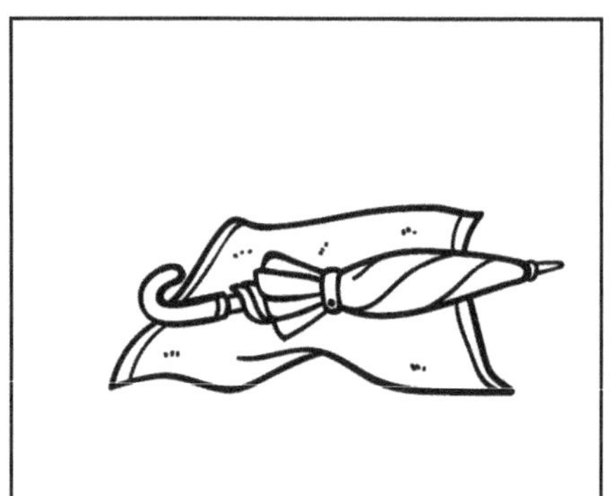

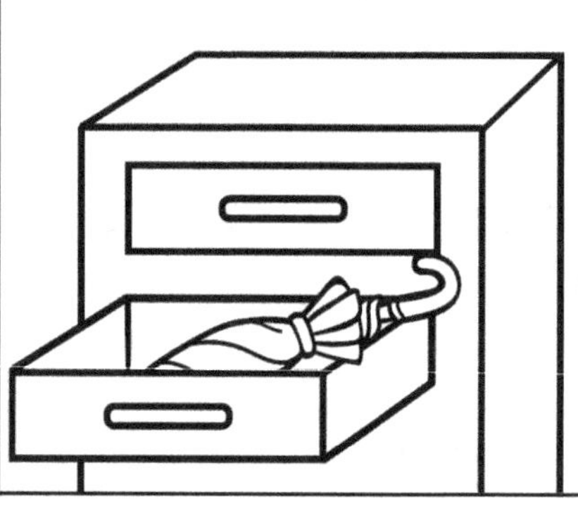

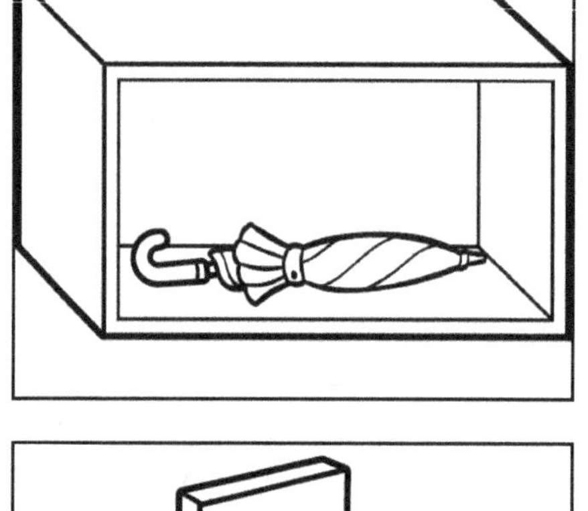

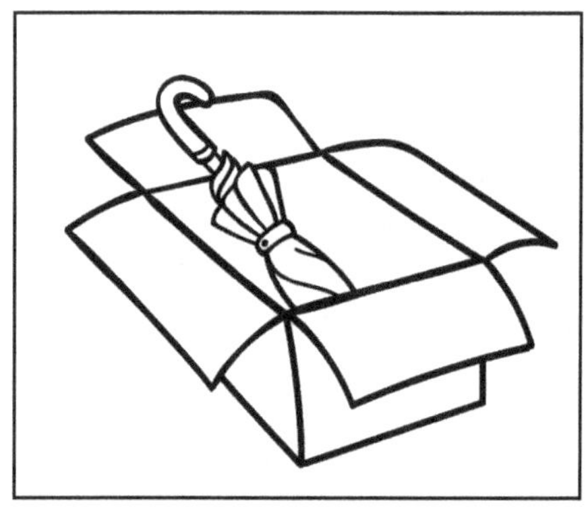

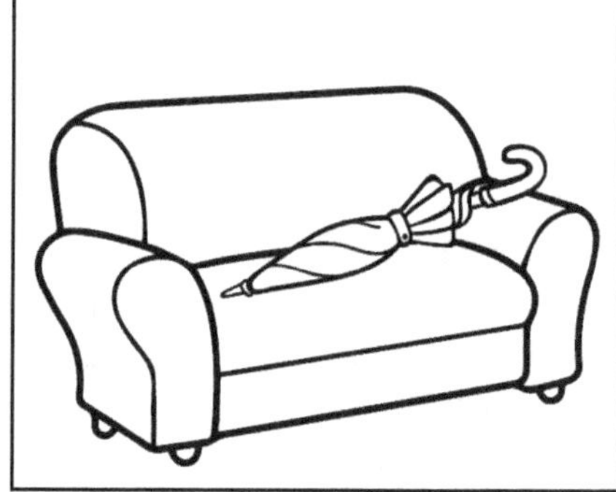

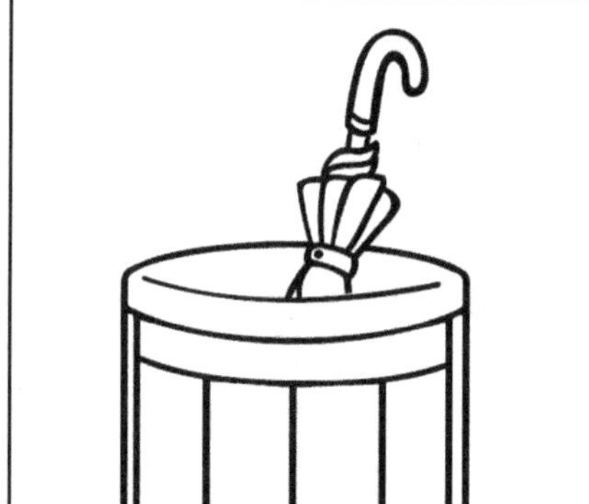

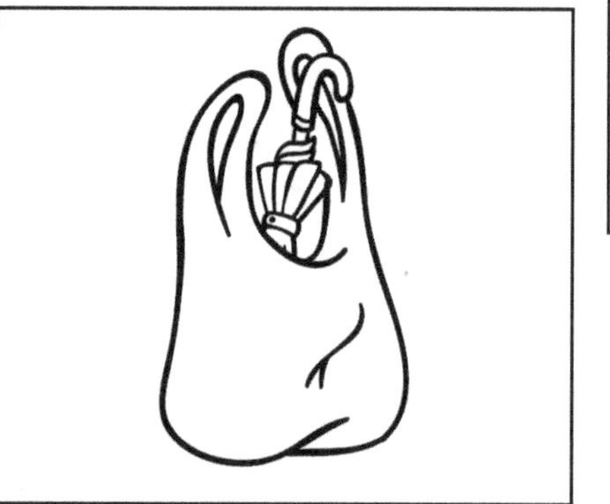

ACTIVITY 5

SCORE: _______

Where is the cap? Connect the pictures to the correct word.

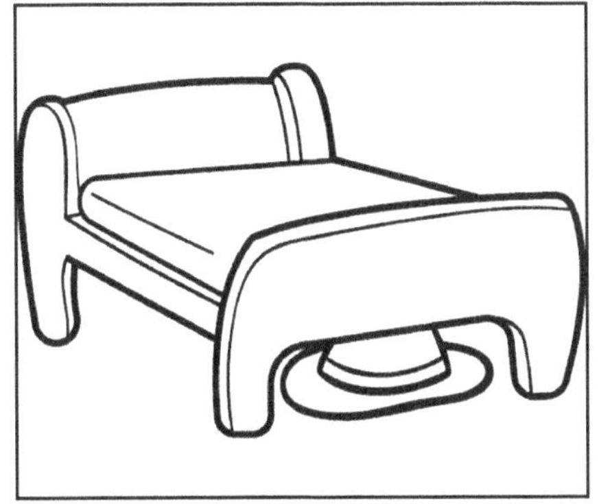

on

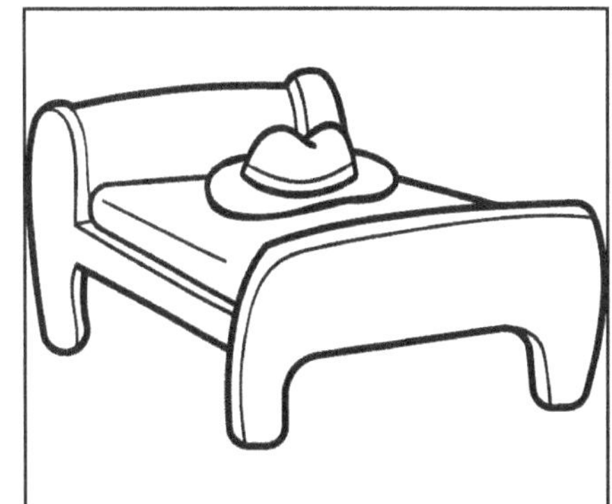

under

HOME ACTIVITY 2   SCORE:_______

Direction: Draw a ball (⊕) as directed.

1. in the drawer

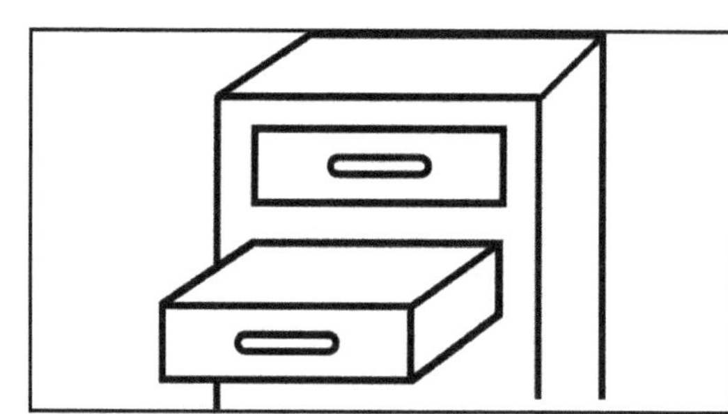

2. on the table

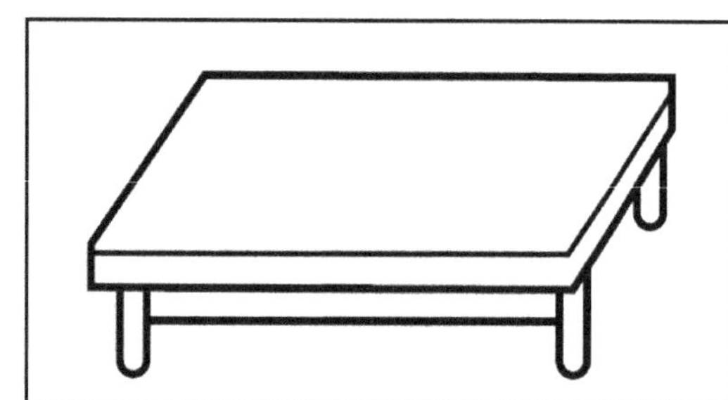

3. under the chair

4. under the stool

5. on the box

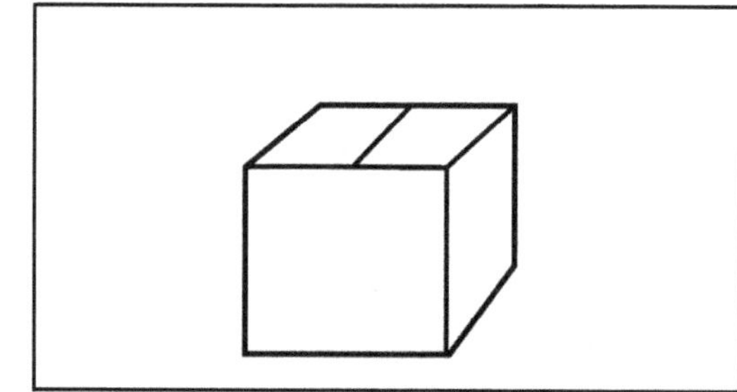

QUIZ NO. 7   SCORE: _______

Direction: Where is the cat? Connect each picture to the correct word.

	in	
	under	

	on	
	in	

	under	
	in	

	under	
	on	

	in	
	on	

Up and Down

ACTIVITY 6

SCORE: _______

Check (✓) the pictures of things or animals that are <u>up</u>. Cross out (✗) those that are <u>down</u>.

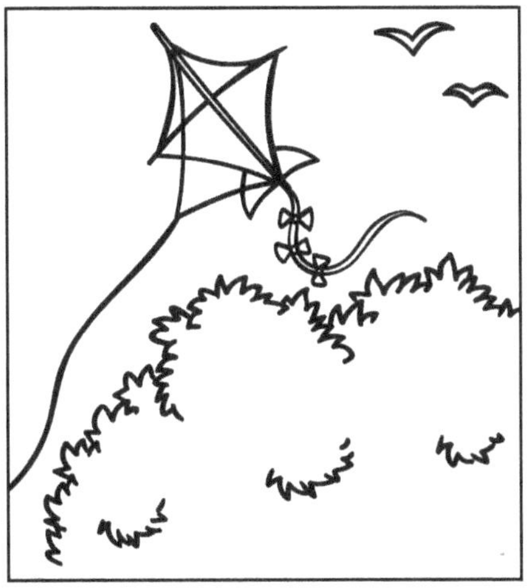

QUIZ NO. 8

SCORE: _______

Direction: Where is the mouse? Color the box with the correct answer.

1. 

| up | down |

2. 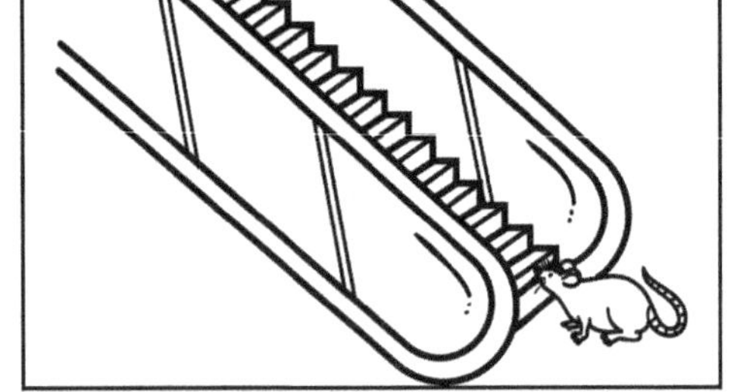

| up | down |

3. 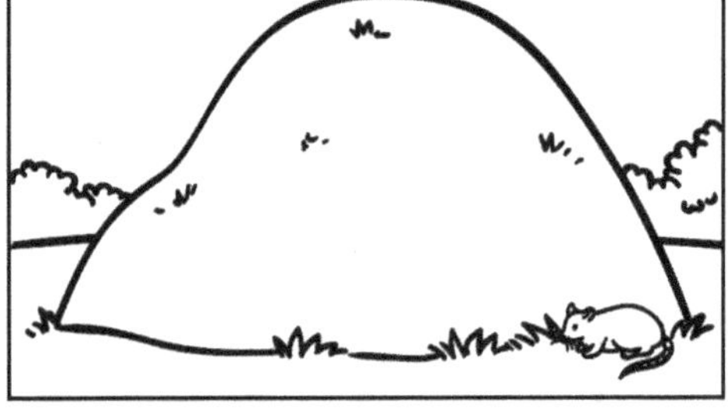

| up | down |

4. 

| up | down |

5. 

| up | down |

Over and Below

The airplane is **over** the clouds.

The airplane is **below** the clouds.

SCORE: _______

Where is the bee? Write <u>O</u> for over and <u>B</u> for below.

______ 1. 

______ 4. 

______ 2. 

______ 5. 

______ 3. 

______ 6. 

QUIZ NO. 9

SCORE: _______

Direction: Where is the bee? Connect each picture to the correct word.

over

below

over

below

over

below

over

below

over

below

Left and Right

The girl is on the **left**.
The boy is on the **right**.

The boy is facing **left**.
The girl is facing **right**.

SONG

Guide: Sing the songs with the children, putting appropriate actions to them.

Up and down and clap, clap, clap;
Up and down and clap, clap, clap;
Clap to the left and clap to the right;
Turn around, and clap, clap, clap.

** Change the word "clap" to "sway," "shake," etc.*

Tune: "Twinkle, Twinkle, Little Star"

Up to the ceiling,
Down to the floor,
Left to the window,
Right to the door.
Kiss me, Mama,
Kiss me, Papa,
For I know where
I should be.

ACTIVITY 8

SCORE: _______

Where is the spoon? Write <u>L</u> for left and <u>R</u> for right.

_____ 1. 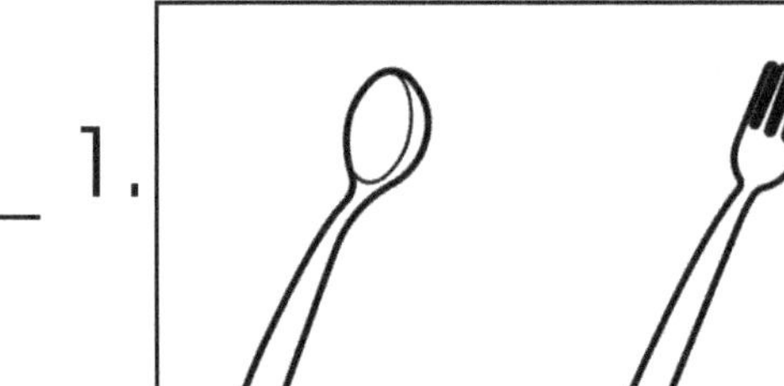

_____ 2. 

_____ 3. 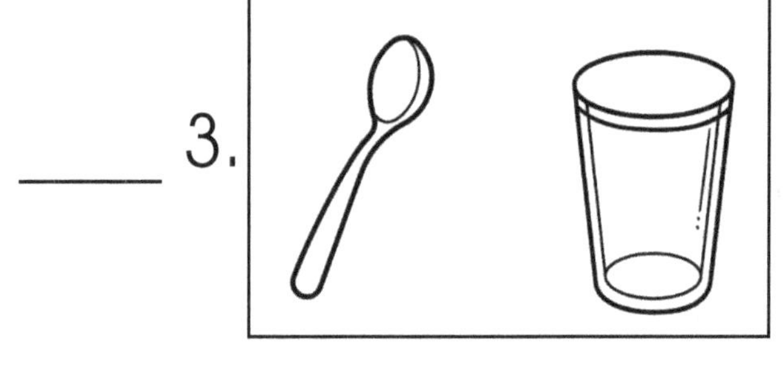

_____ 4. 

_____ 5. 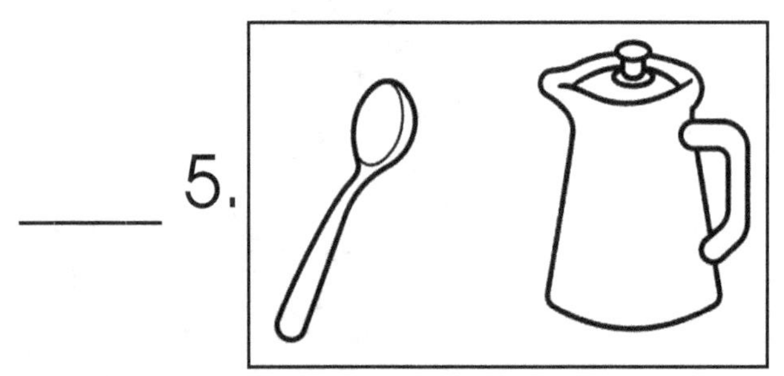

_____ 6. 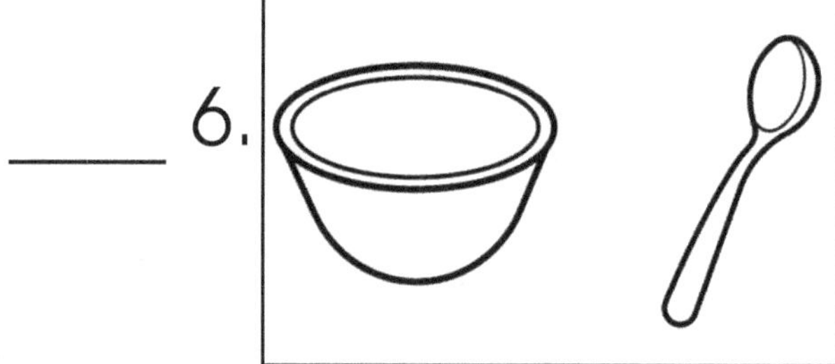

_____ 7. 

_____ 8. 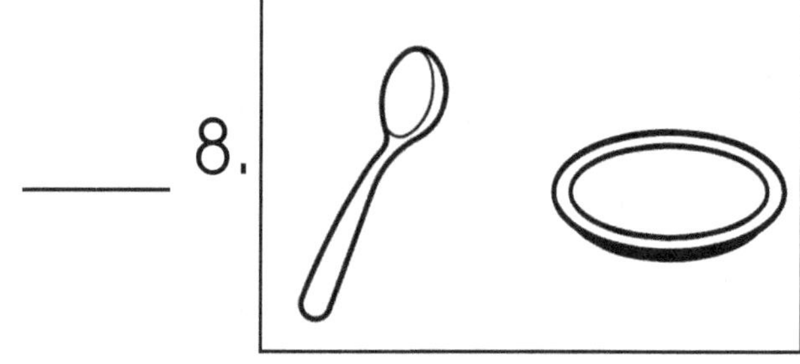

_____ 9. 

_____ 10.

QUIZ NO. 10   SCORE: _______

Direction: What direction is each animal facing? Write <u>L</u> for left and <u>R</u> for right.

_____ 1. 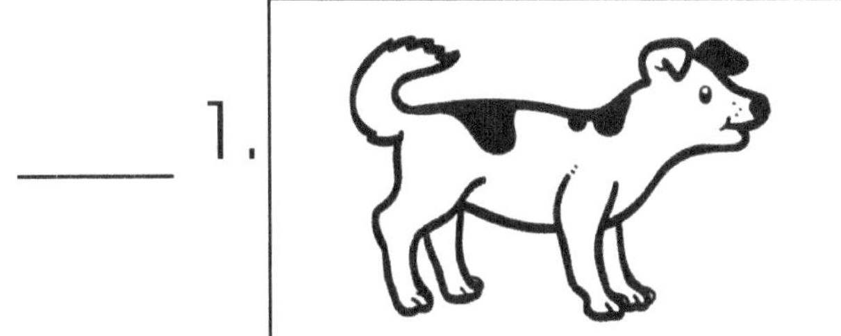

_____ 2. 

_____ 3. 

_____ 4. 

_____ 5. 

_____ 6. 

_____ 7. 

_____ 8. 

_____ 9. 

_____ 10. 

Inside and Outside

The chickens are **inside** the coop.
The ducks are **outside** the coop.

ACTIVITY 9

SCORE: _______

Encircle the animals that are inside the yard. Check the animals that are outside.

Direction: Where are the animals? Connect each picture to the correct word.

inside

outside

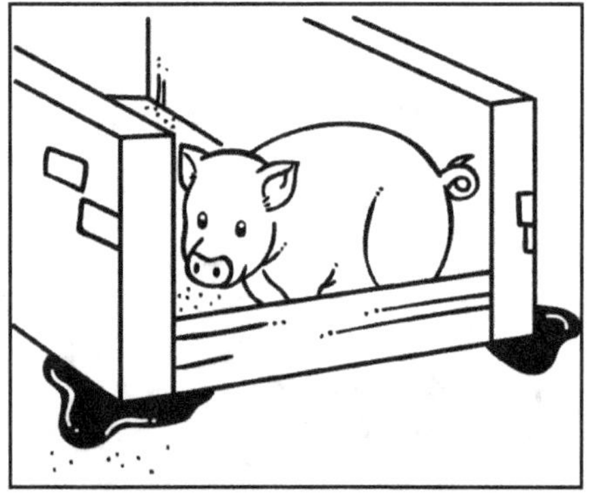

THIRD QUARTERLY TEST

Name: _________________________________   Score: ____________

Level: ________________   Date: ______________

I. Help each person find his or her way by connecting each picture to the correct place to go.

1.    •   •   

2.    •   •   

3.    •   •   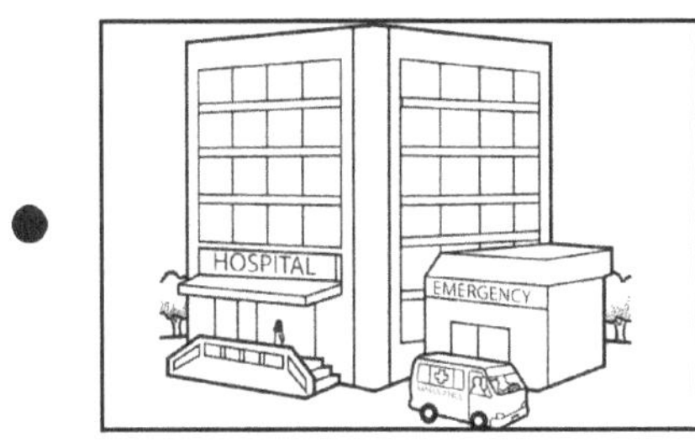

4.    •   •   

5.    •   •   

1. carpenter

2. vendor

3. traffic aide

4. dentist

5. farmer

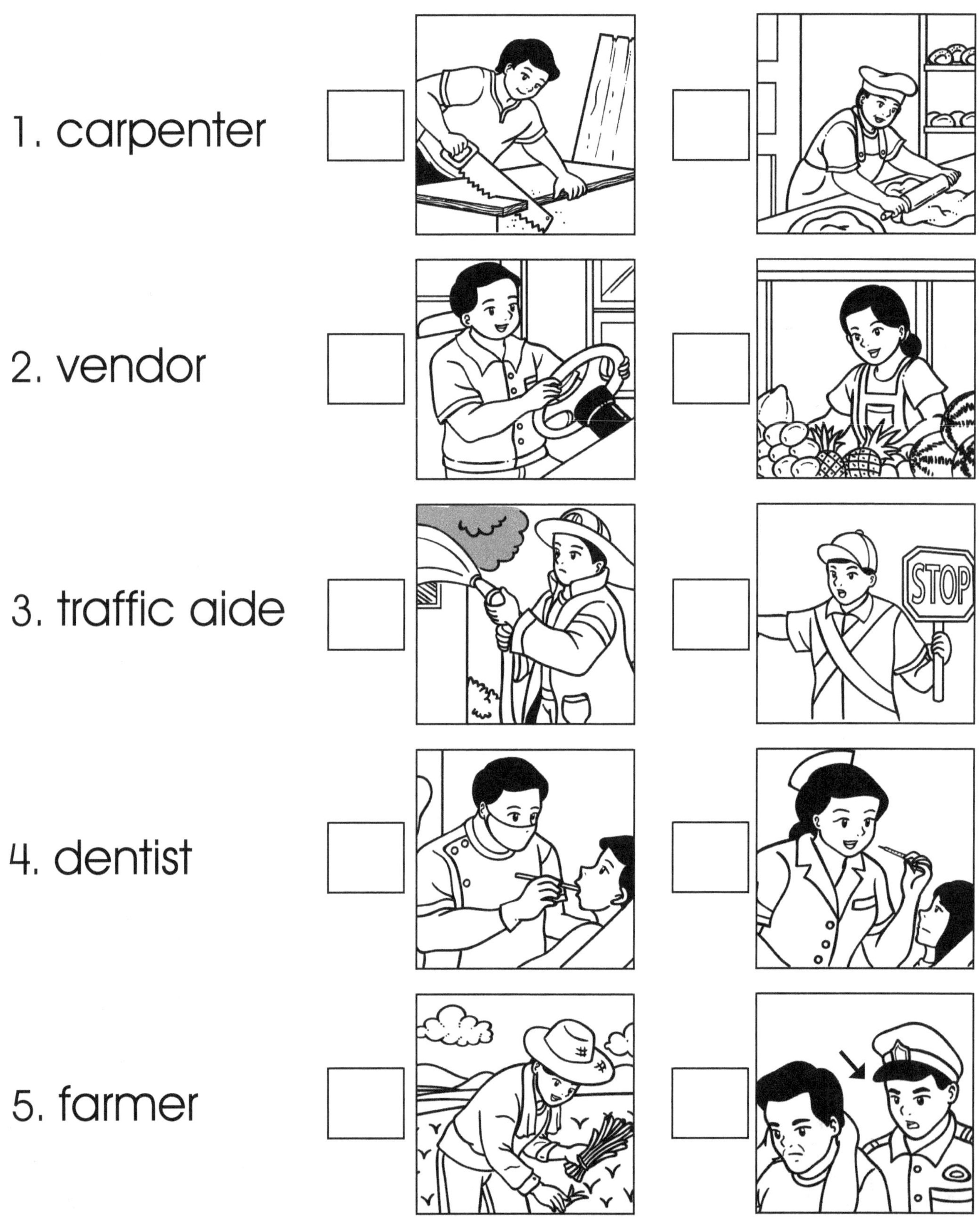

III. Where is the cat? Underline the correct answer.

PROGRESS CHART
THIRD QUARTER

Name: _________________________________ Level: _______________

ACTIVITY	No. of Items	My Score	HOME ACTIVITY	No. of Items	My Score	Quiz	No. of Items	My Score
1	10		1	10		1	5	
2	5		2	5		2	10	
3	15					3	10	
4	10					4	10	
5	10					5	10	
6	9					6	10	
7	6					7	10	
8	10					8	5	
9	10					9	10	
						10	10	
						11	10	
TOTAL	85		TOTAL	15		TOTAL	100	

___________________________   ___________________________
Parent's/Guardian's Signature   Teacher's Signature

FOURTH QUARTER
SPECIAL WORDS

Teacher's Objectives and Student Evaluation

Lesson	*At the end of the activities, the child should be able to:*	NI	S	E
1	1. differentiate <u>behind</u> from <u>in front</u>			
	2. know when to use <u>beside</u> and <u>between</u>			
	3. use the words learned properly in sentences			
2	4. understand the meaning of describing words			
	5. identify describing words			
	6. tell the opposite of some describing words			
	7. increase vocabulary			
3	8. understand the meaning of action words			
	9. identify action words			
	10. tell the correct word for each action			
	11. act out action words			
4	12. enumerate and recite the seven days of the week in their correct order			
	13. identify the correct spelling of the days of the week			
	14. be observant of the daily weather conditions			
	15. develop keenness of observations			
	16. develop good judgement and analytical thinking skills			
5	17. recite the months of the year			
	18. know the different celebrations and events each month			

Legend:
NI — Needs Improvement   S — Satisfactory   E — Excellent

LESSON 1

OTHER WORDS THAT TELL WHERE

In front and Behind

Guide: Play a different version of "Hide and Seek," with the children being the "it." Let them close their eyes as you hide behind the door. Tell them to count from 1 to 5. When they finish counting, let them look for you. When they find you, tell them you were behind the door but now, you are in front of the door. Do the activity again, hiding behind a table, chair, bookshelf, etc.

The boy is **in front** of the car.

The boy is **behind** the car.

SUGGESTED ACTIVITIES FOR THE DIFFERENT LANGUAGE SKILLS

SKILLS	ACTIVITIES
Listening	Build a model of a community with the children. Use Lego sets, toy cars, and small dolls for the activity. Tell directions such as: "Place the car beside the street light," "Place the car in front of the market," etc.
Speaking	Encourage the children to talk! Hide behind the door, go in front of the table, stand beside a boy, or sit between two girls, and ask the children to tell where you are.
Reading	Prepare several flashcards with the words behind, in front, beside, and between. Make another set of flashcards with pictures that show the meaning of behind, in front, beside, and between. Have the children match the two sets of flashcards.
Writing	Display the flashcards with words behind, in front, beside, and between on the classroom wall. Make it a part of your word wall where children can practice reading and writing words.

ACTIVITY 1

SCORE: _________

Color the pictures that show the meaning of <u>in front</u>.

Cross out (✖) the pictures that show the meaning of <u>behind</u>.

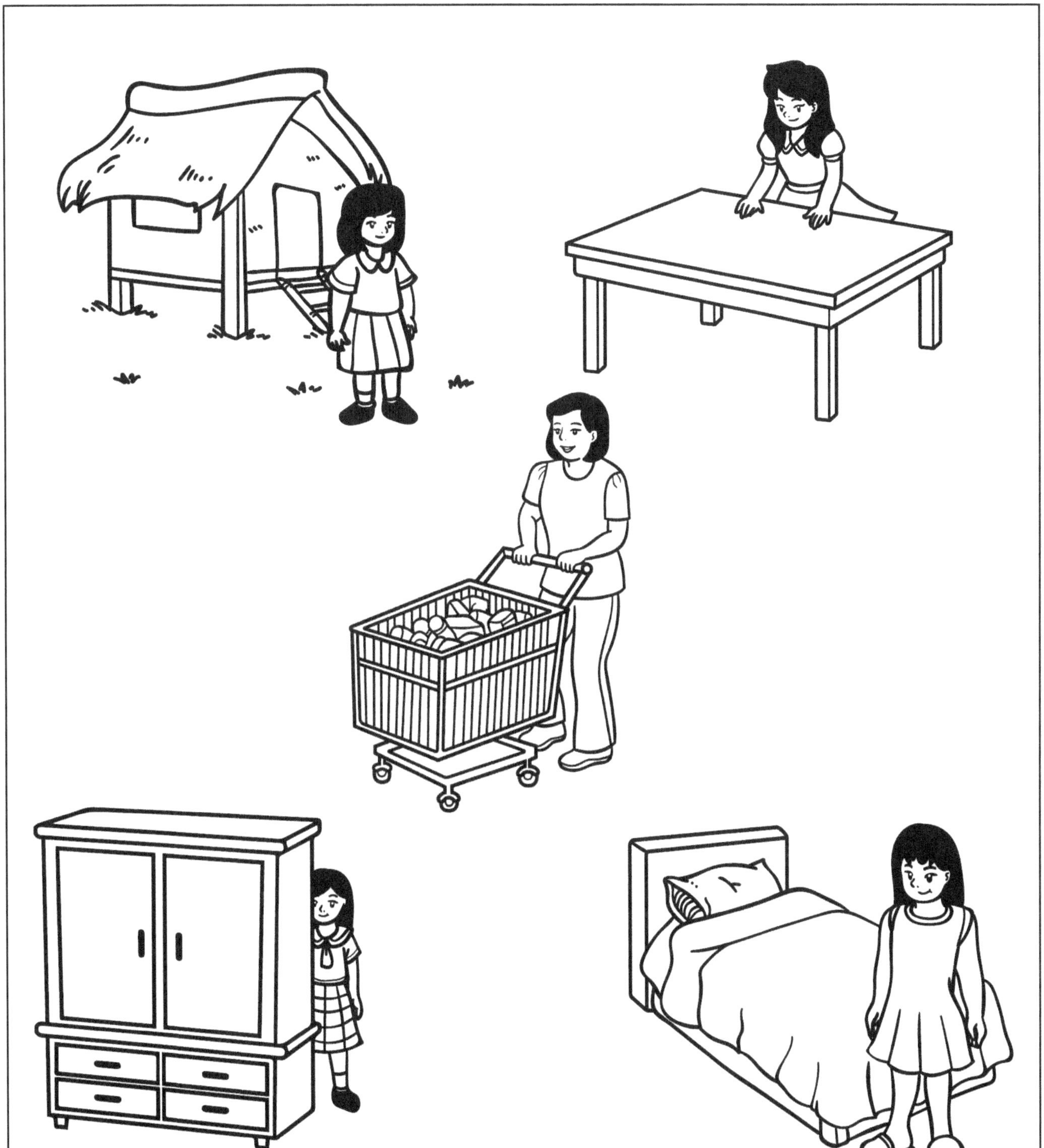

HOME ACTIVITY 1   SCORE:______

Direction: From old magazines, cut out pictures of 5 animals with 4 legs and 5 animals with 2 legs. Paste all the two-legged animals in front of the gate. Paste all the four-legged animals behind the gate. *(10 points)*

Direction: Where is the dog? Underline the correct word.

1.   behind   in front

2.   behind   in front

3.   behind   in front

4.   behind   in front

5.   behind   in front

6.    behind   in front

7.    behind   in front

8.    behind   in front

9.    behind   in front

10.    behind   in front

Beside and Between

The glass is **<u>beside</u>** the plate.

The glass is **<u>between</u>** the two plates.

ACTIVITY 3

SCORE: _______

Where is the glass? Check the correct picture for each word.

beside		
between		
beside		
between		
between		

Direction: Where is the lizard? Color the circle beside the correct answer.

1.    ○ beside   ○ between

2. 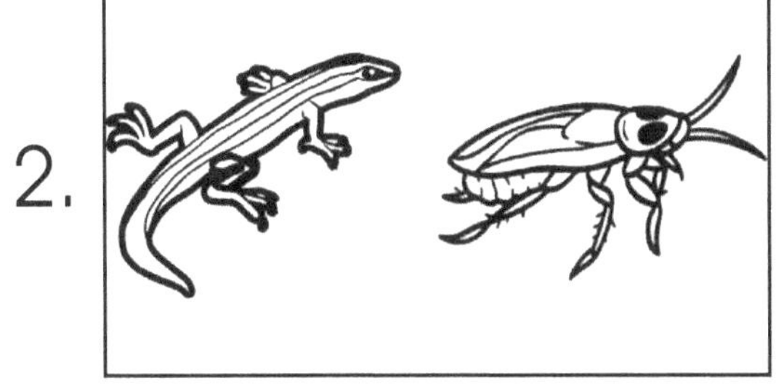   ○ beside   ○ between

3.    ○ beside   ○ between

4.    ○ beside   ○ between

5.    ○ beside   ○ between

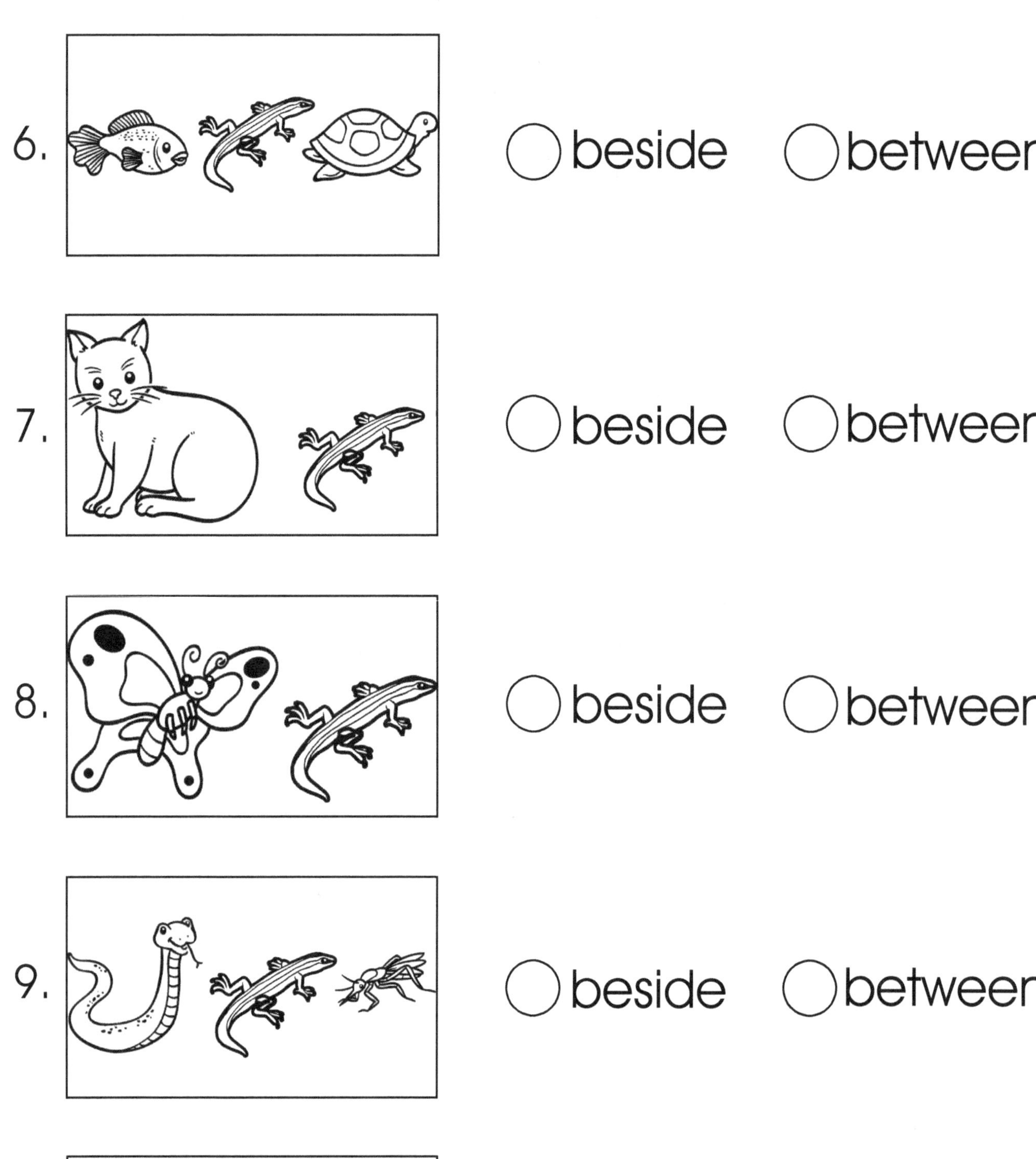

6.
beside   between

7.
beside   between

8.
beside   between

9.
beside   between

10.
beside   between

QUIZ NO. 3

SCORE: _______

<u>Direction</u>: Where is the cat? Connect each picture to the correct word.

behind

between

in front

behind

between

in front

beside

between

beside

in front

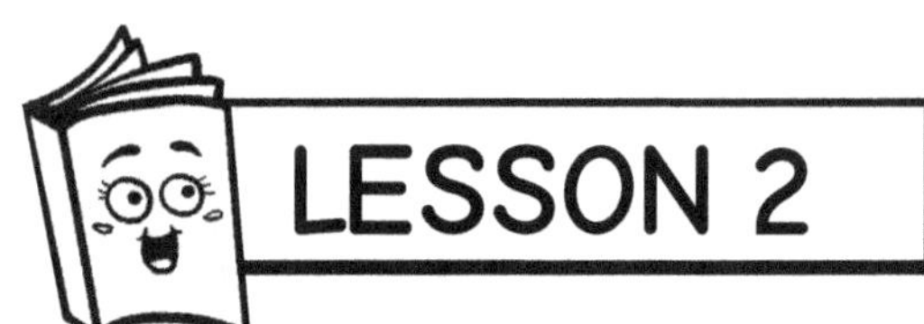

LESSON 2 DESCRIBING WORDS

Guide: Show your different emotions to the class: happy, sad, mad, etc. Invite the children to show different emotions, too. As you show an emotion, say the word. Tell the children that these words describe how you feel. Encourage the children to talk about their favorite person, pet, or toy, then have them say something about it.

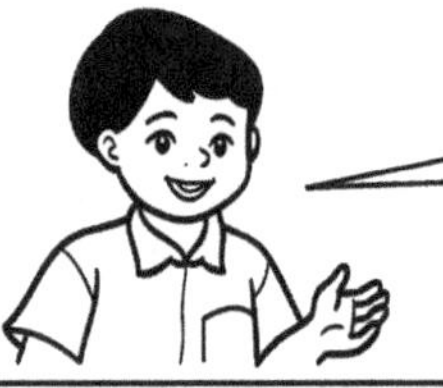

happy	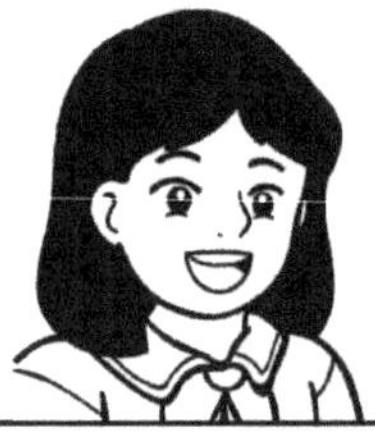	hot	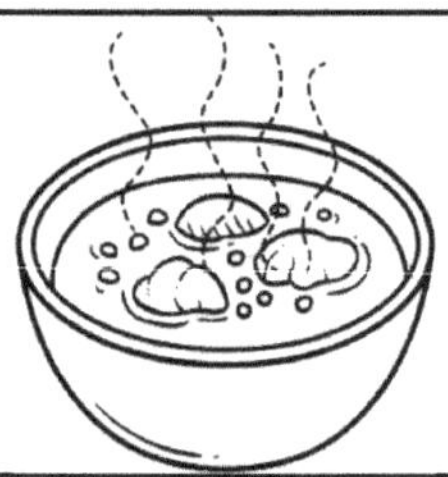
pretty	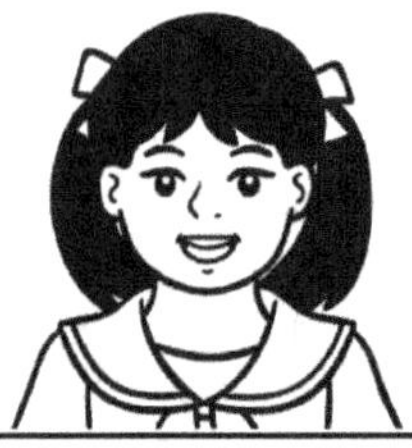	fat	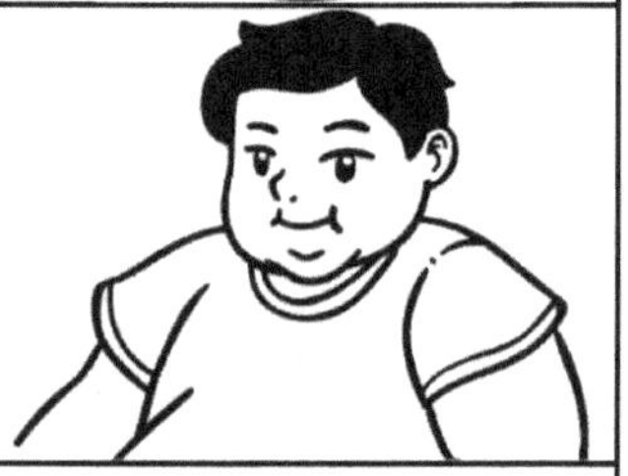
small	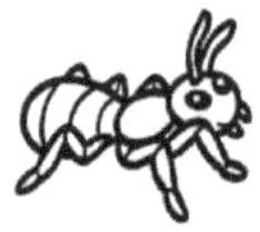	clean	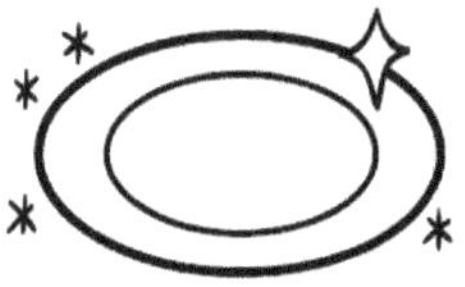
long	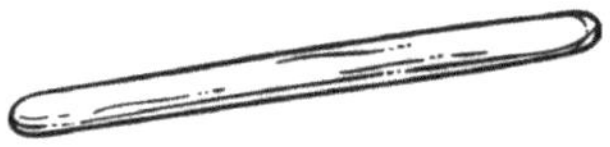	sad	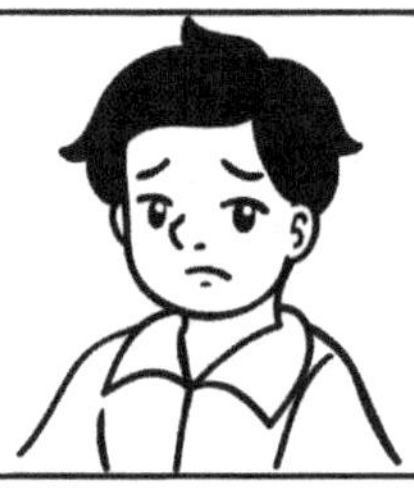

Remember:

Describing words are words that tell about a person, animal, place, or thing.

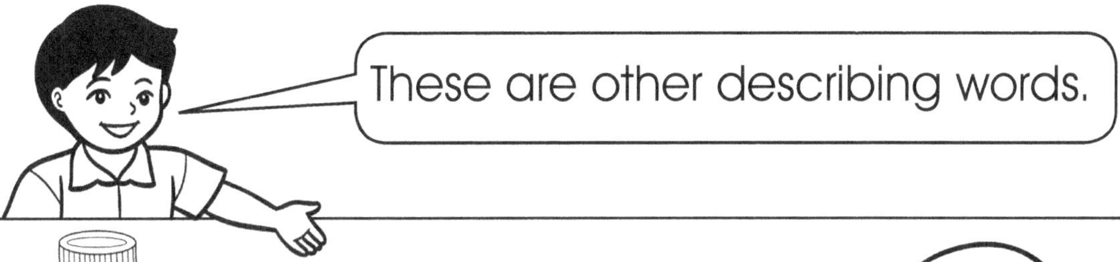

sweet

old

tall

soft

wet

thin

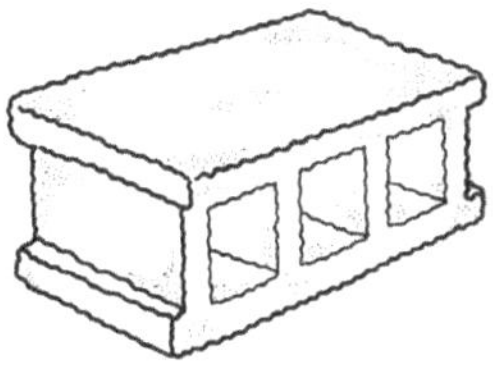

heavy

mad

smooth

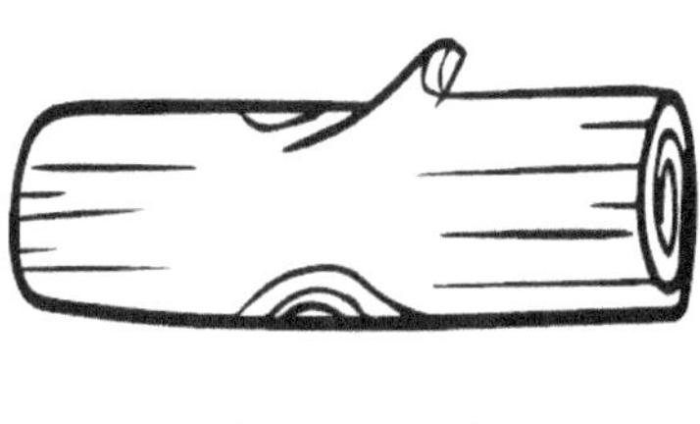

hard

SUGGESTED ACTIVITIES FOR THE DIFFERENT LANGUAGE SKILLS

SKILLS	ACTIVITIES
Listening and Speaking  	Make an Adjective Bingo! Create a table with three (3) rows and four (4) columns. Glue pictures of different people, animals, and things, e.g. a baby, an old man, a new dress, an old hat, vinegar, candy, hollow blocks, etc. on the cells. Scan the bingo cards and laminate them. Make a set of "calling cards" (with adjectives) that the caller (you or the children) can use to call out words during the game. Use inch cubes or small blocks as bingo markers.
Reading and Writing  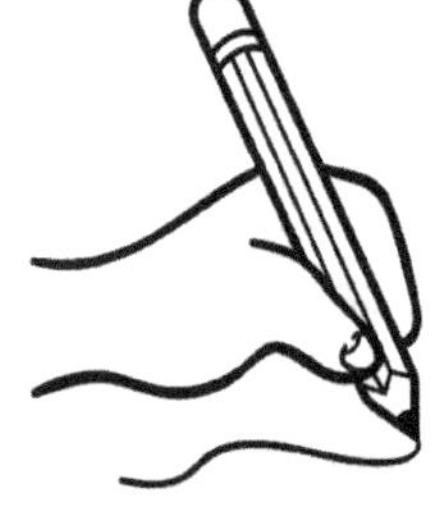	Hang the Adjective Bingo cards in a visible place where children can see them everyday. Occasionally, ask the children to tell something about the pictures in the bingo cards. Have them read the "calling cards" and match them with the pictures. Adjective Bingo Card Calling Cards 

ACTIVITY 4

SCORE: _______

Connect each describing word to the correct picture.

1. long •

2. pretty •

3. clean •

4. happy •

5. fat •

6. small •

7. hot •

8. tall •

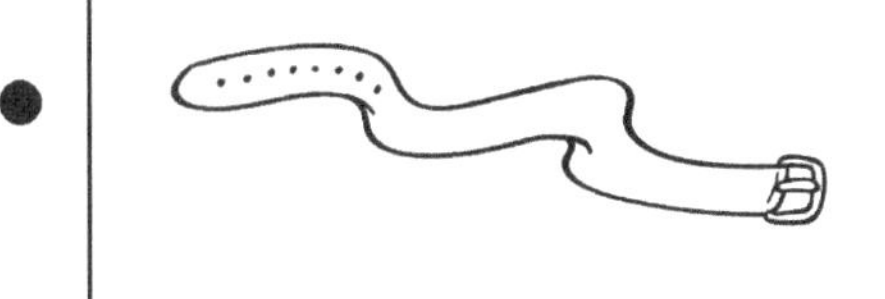

QUIZ NO. 4

SCORE: _______

Direction: Color the box beside the picture that matches each describing word.

1. sad

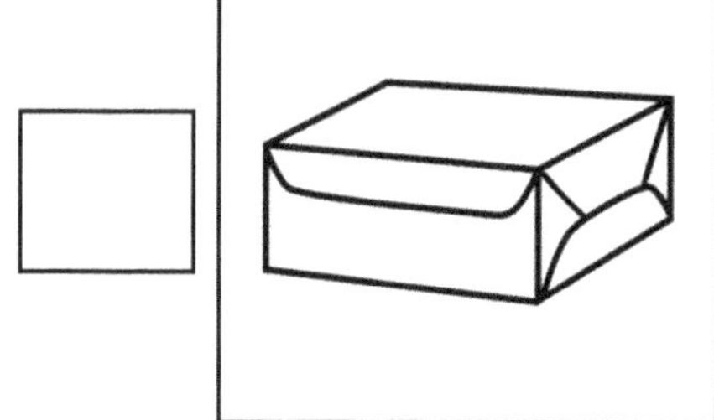 

2. old

3. big

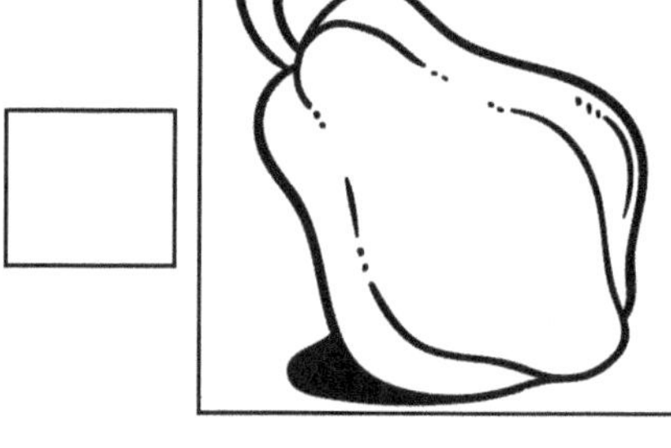 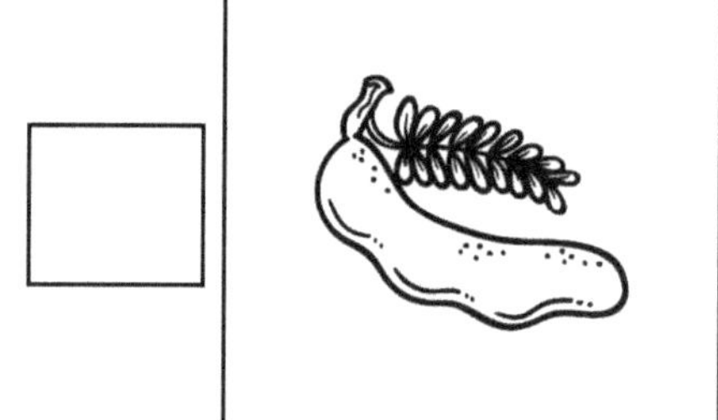

4. soft

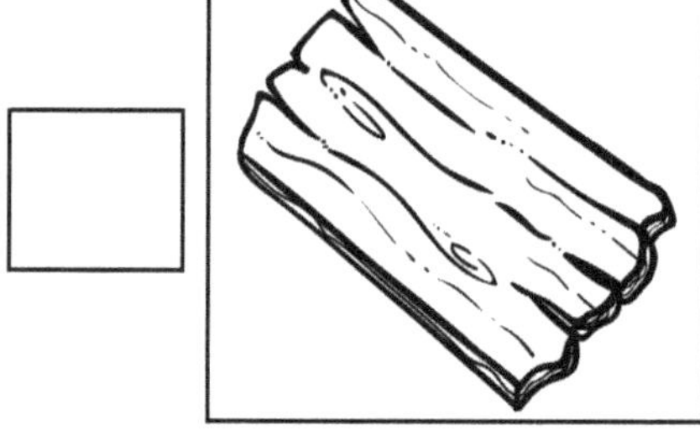 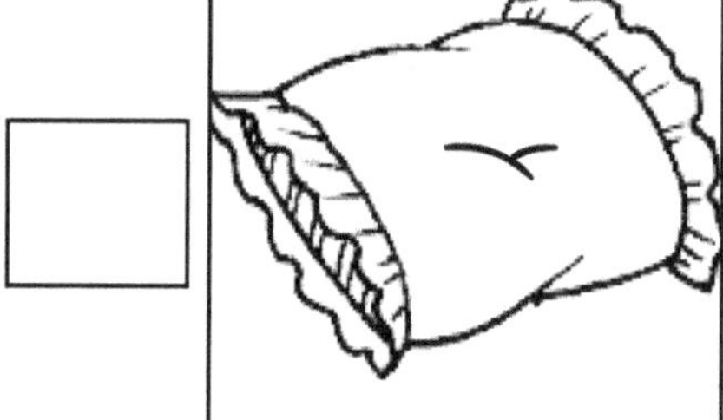

5. dirty

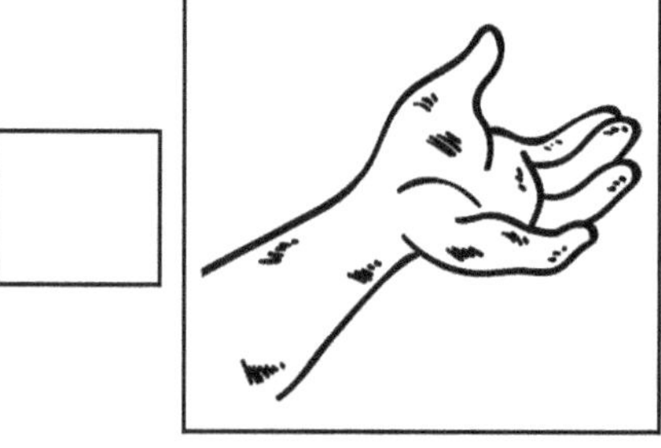 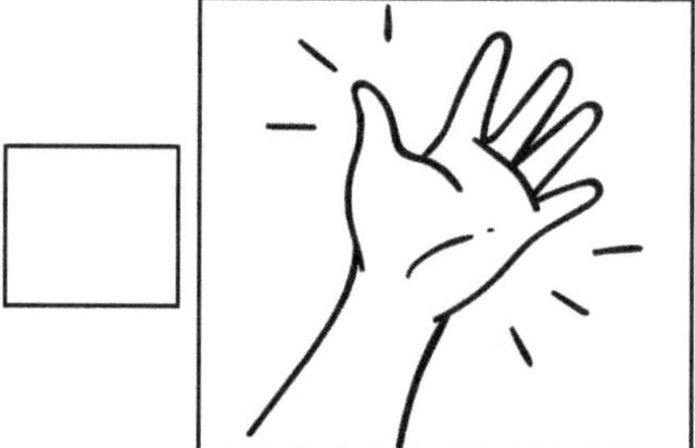

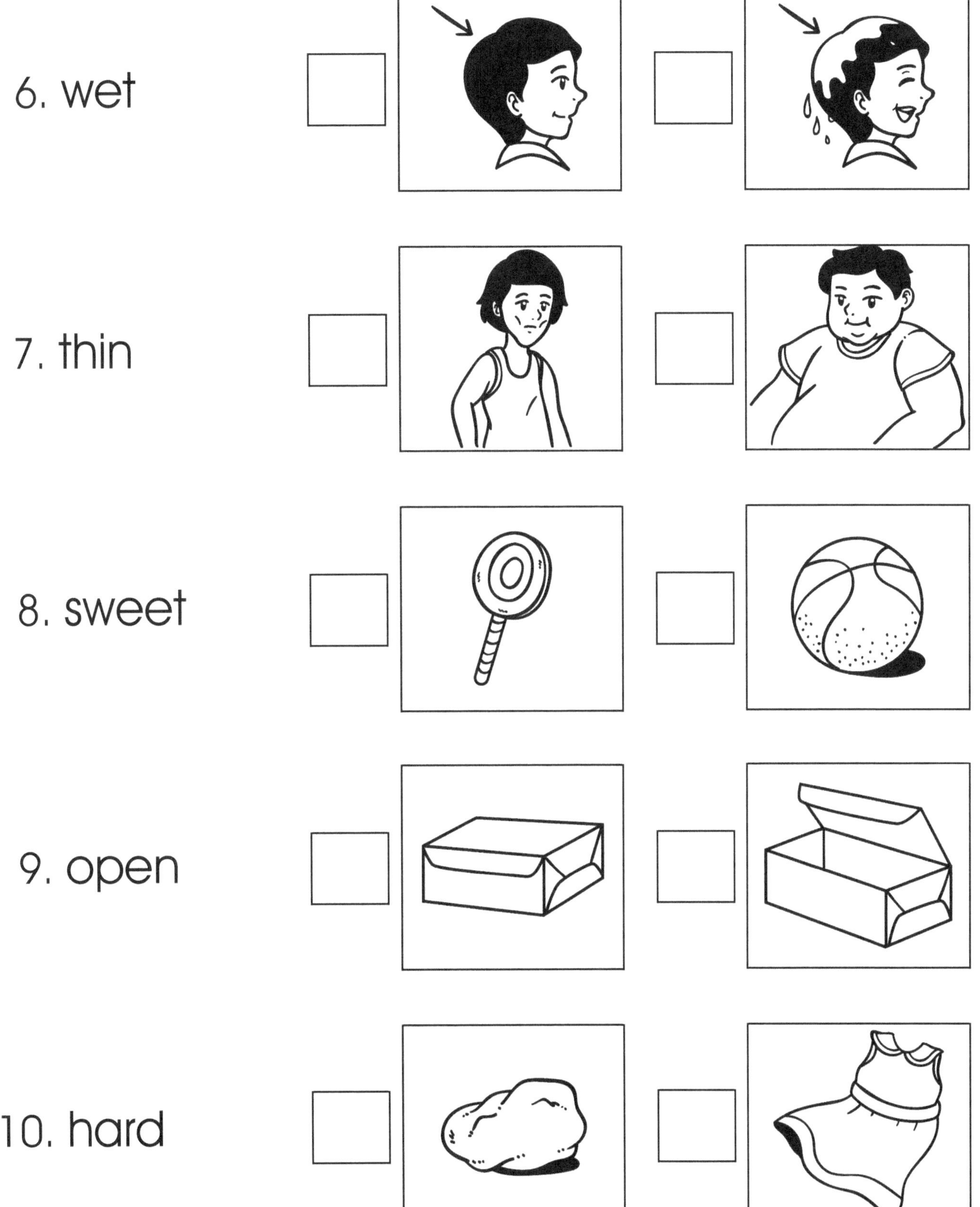

6. wet
7. thin
8. sweet
9. open
10. hard

11. mad

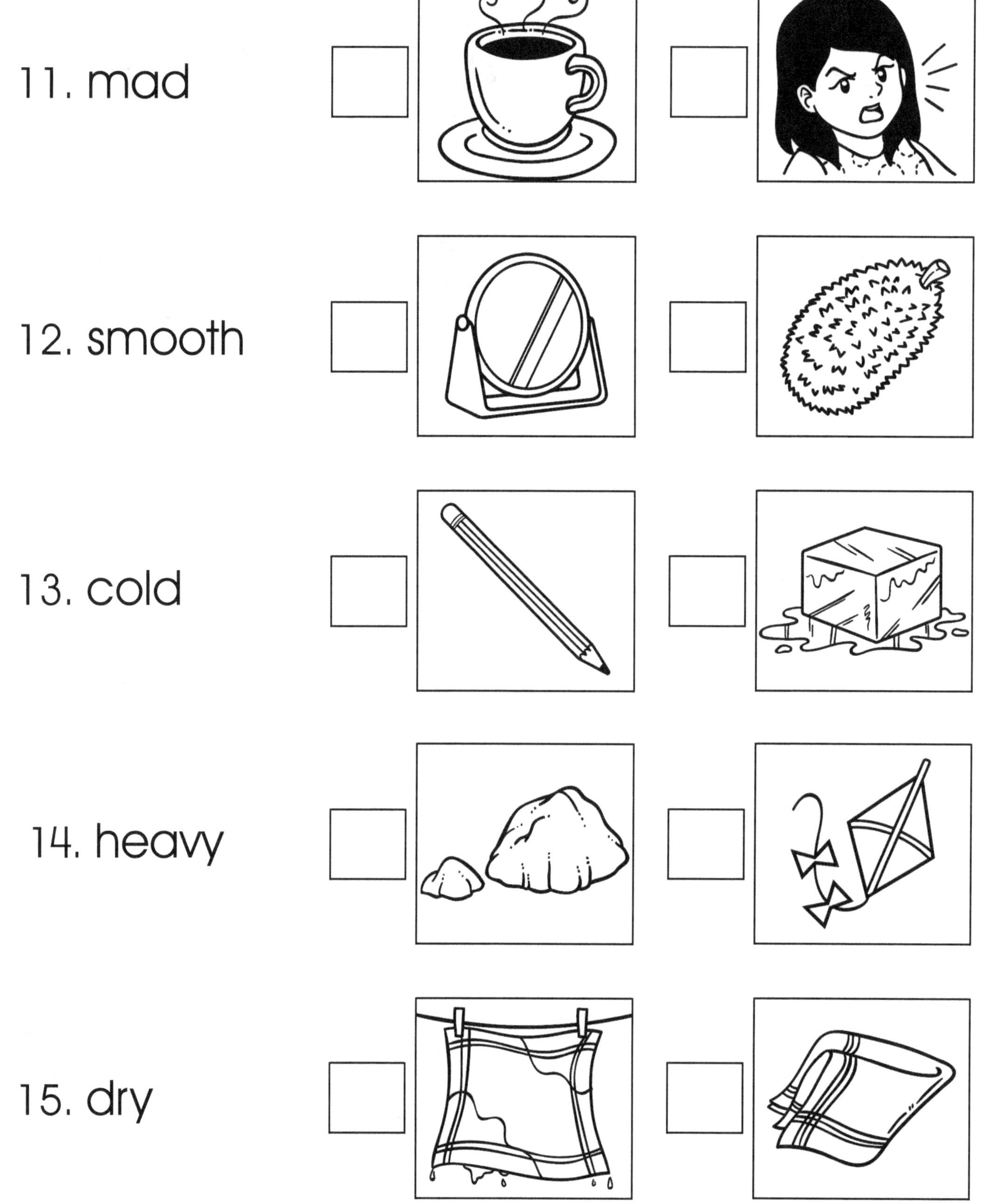

12. smooth

13. cold

14. heavy

15. dry

Opposite Words

The words in each pair below have **opposite** meanings. Let's study them!

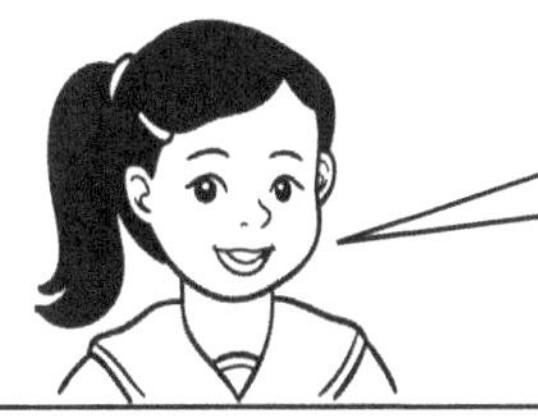

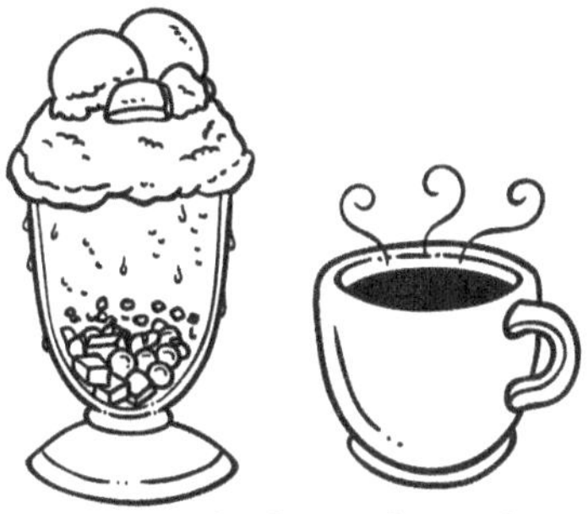

cold – hot

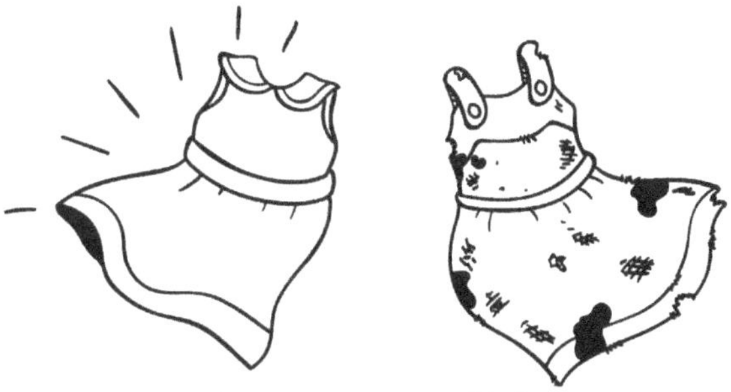

clean – dirty

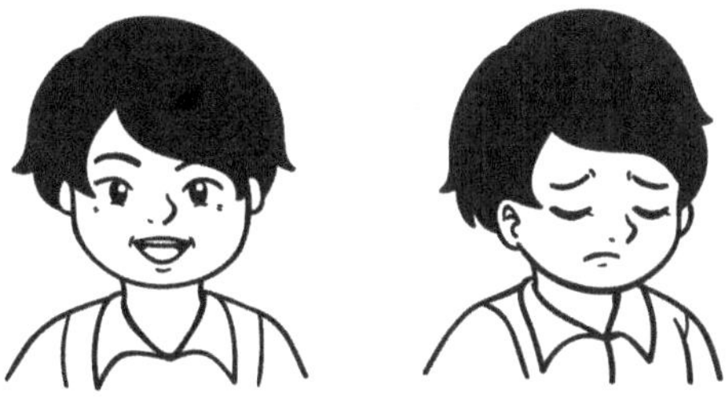

happy – sad

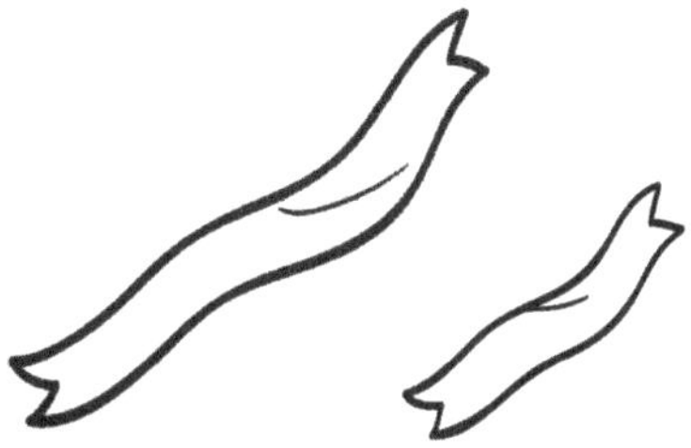

long – short

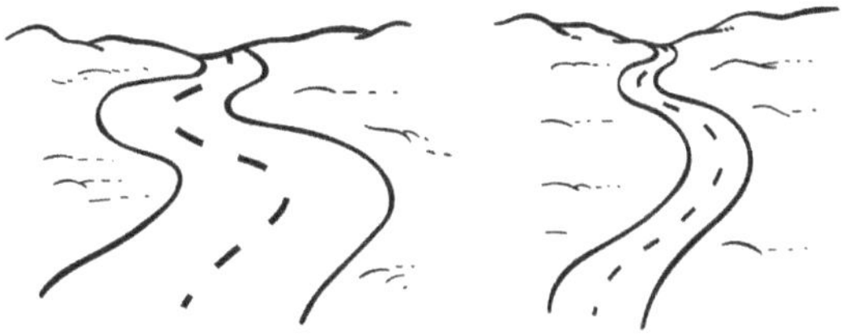

wide – narrow

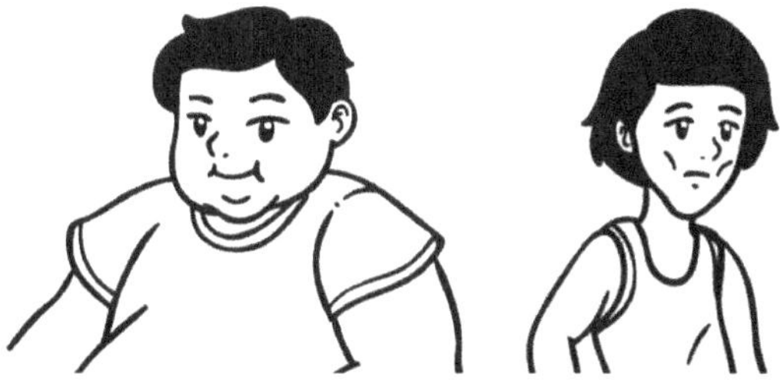

fat – thin

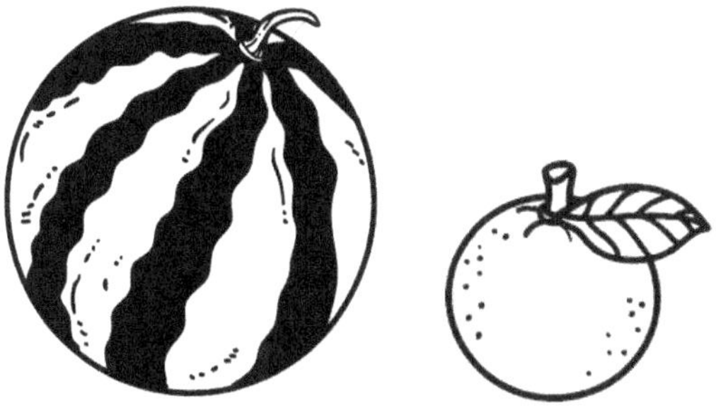

big – small

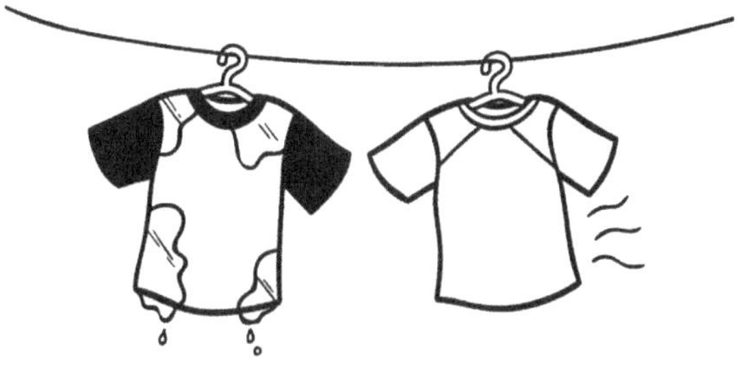

wet – dry

closed – open

old – young

tall – short

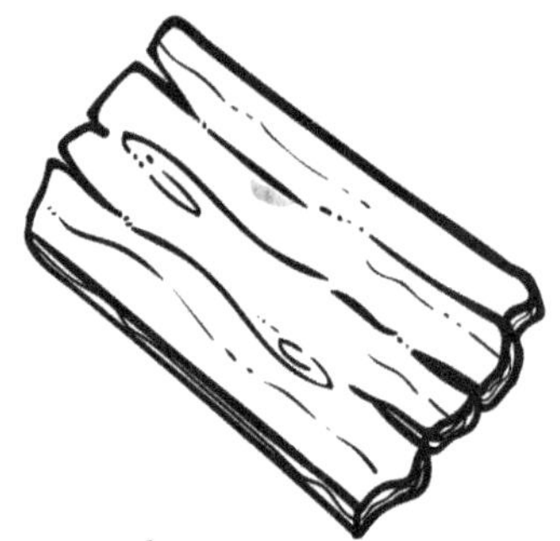

soft – hard

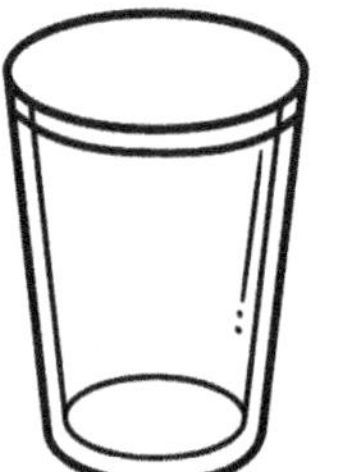

loud – soft

smooth – rough

old – new

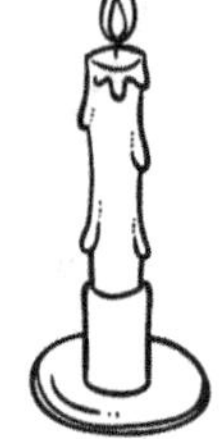

bright – dim

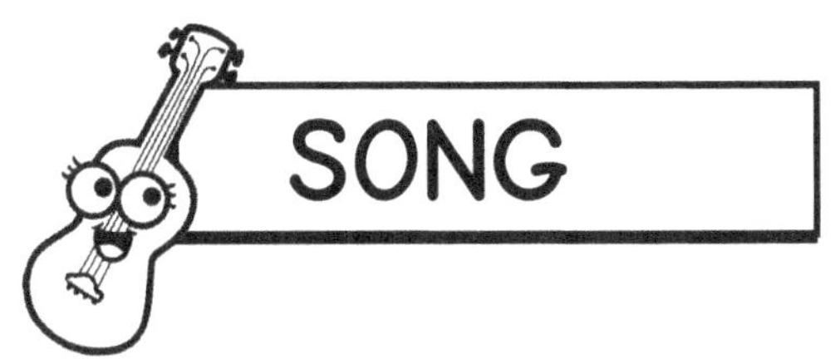

Deep and Wide

Deep and wide, deep and wide—

There's a fountain flowing deep and wide.

Deep and wide, deep and wide—

There's a fountain flowing deep and wide.

Variations:

- Big and small, big and small—
  There are two balls bouncing big and small.

- Fat and thin, fat and thin—
  There are ladies walking fat and thin.

- Long and short, long and short—
  There are pencils writing long and short.

- High and low, high and low—
  There are buildings standing high and low.

- Far and near, far and near—
  There are two birds flying far and near.

- Loud and soft, loud and soft—
  There are two men talking loud and soft.

ACTIVITY 5

SCORE: _______

Color the opposite of each picture on the left.

1. 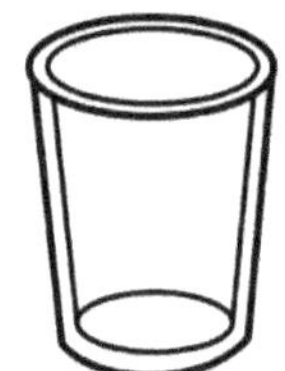  

2.   

3.   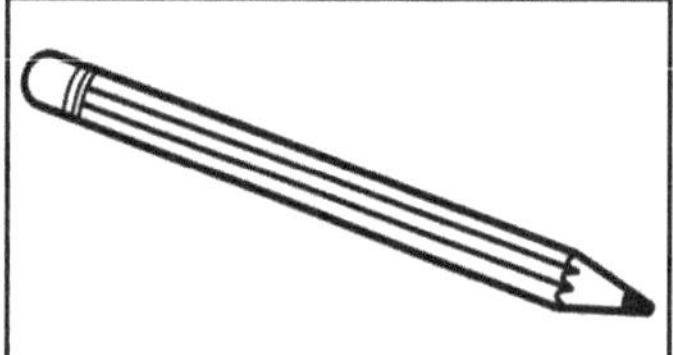

4.   

5.   

6.  

7. 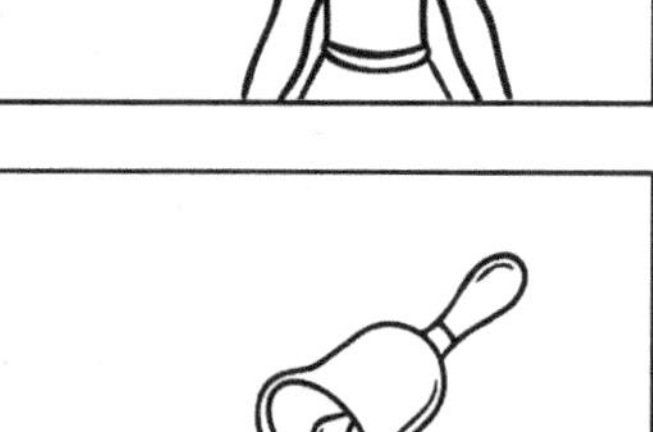

QUIZ NO. 5

SCORE: _______

Direction: Connect each picture on the left to its opposite on the right.

1.    •   •   

2.    •   •   

3.    •   •   

4. 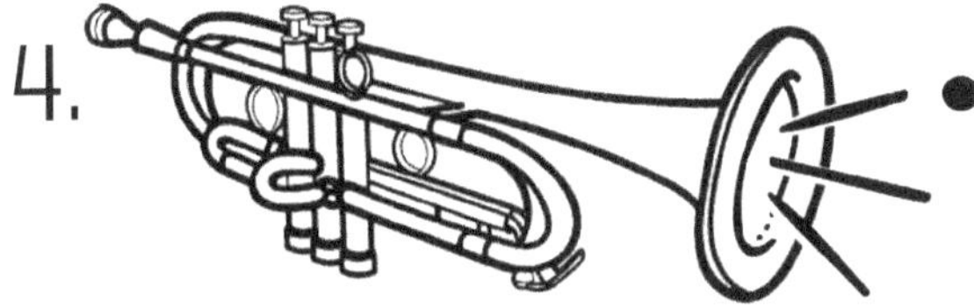   •   •   

5.    •   •   

6.

7.

8.

9.

10.

QUIZ NO. 6

SCORE: _______

Direction: Connect each word to the correct picture.

long

short

thick

thin

closed

open

rough

smooth

old

new

ACTION WORDS

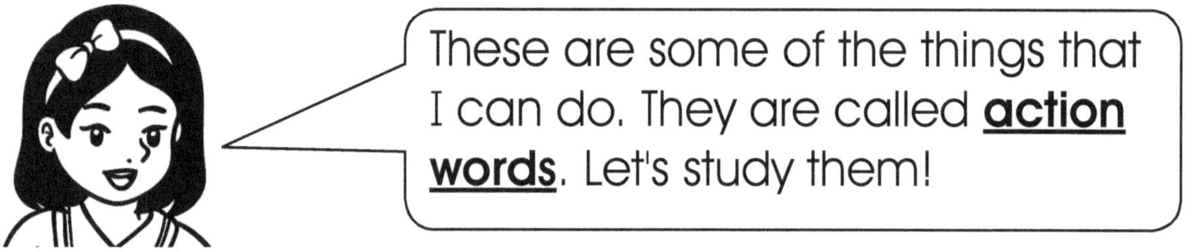

Remember:

Action words are words that tell what we can do.

run

read

eat

pray

sit

stand

play

sleep

walk

swim

SONGS

Guide: Teach the children the song "Ten Little Indians" first. Then change the lyrics substituting different action words for **clap** while acting out the words.

Tune: "Ten Little Indians"

Clap, clap, clap,
Little Indians.
Clap, clap, clap,
Little Indians.
Clap, clap, clap,
Little Indians.
Clap, little Indian children.

Guide: Form a circle with the children. Move in a clockwise direction while acting out each word. You may use other action words for variation e.g., swimming, dancing, jumping, jogging, playing, etc.

Tune: "Where is Thumbman?"

Walking, walking,
Walking, walking;
Hop, hop, hop,
Hop, hop, hop;
Running, running, running,
Running, running, running;
Now, let's stop.
Now, let's stop.

SUGGESTED ACTIVITIES FOR THE DIFFERENT LANGUAGE SKILLS

SKILLS	ACTIVITIES
Listening	**Attention Commands** Call out commands such as: Attention, salute, march in place... stop; sit down, stand up, walk in a circle, wave your hands... stop; jog in place... stop; crawl around... stop; jumping jacks... stop; etc. At first, the children will copy you but later, they should be able to do commands without you. Have the children give the commands themselves.
Speaking	**Action Word Charades** Have one student come to the front of the class and whisper an action word to him or to her. The child acts out the word and the first one to guess can be the next player. This works very well with action words (e.g., hop, spin around, wave, swim, etc.). Later, you can give more complex patterns such as open a door, fly an airplane, slice some cake, eat ice cream, etc.
Reading	**Verb Races** Make several flashcards with action words. Line the students up and have them read the action word that you show. When you shout "Go!" that's the time that the children go for the race. Actions include: jump, hop, gallop, skip, and jog. Later, make it more difficult like big hops, little steps, crawl like a snake, fly like a bird, gallop like a horse, hop like a rabbit, walk quickly/slowly, and so on.
Writing	Distribute the verb flashcards to the children. Let them copy the words on a sheet of paper. Have them draw themselves doing the action word.

ACTIVITY 6

SCORE: _______

Check the pictures that show what you can do.
Cross out those that show what you cannot do.

ACTIVITY 7

SCORE: _______

Color the correct picture for each action word.

1. dance

2. write

3. sing

4. jump

5. eat

<u>Direction:</u> Paste pictures of each family member (including you) doing something. Let an adult label each action. *(10 points)*

 **QUIZ NO. 7**   SCORE: _______

Direction: On the blank, write the letter of the correct picture for each action word.

_____ 1. pray

_____ 2. read

_____ 3. jump

_____ 4. cry

_____ 5. swim

a. 

b. 

c. 

d. 

e. 

_____ 6. eat

f.

_____ 7. wash

g.

_____ 8. play

c.

_____ 9. sleep

i.

_____ 10. draw

j.

QUIZ NO. 8

SCORE: _______

Direction: Connect each action word to the correct picture.

sit

stand

walk

run

sing

dance

play

pray

read

write

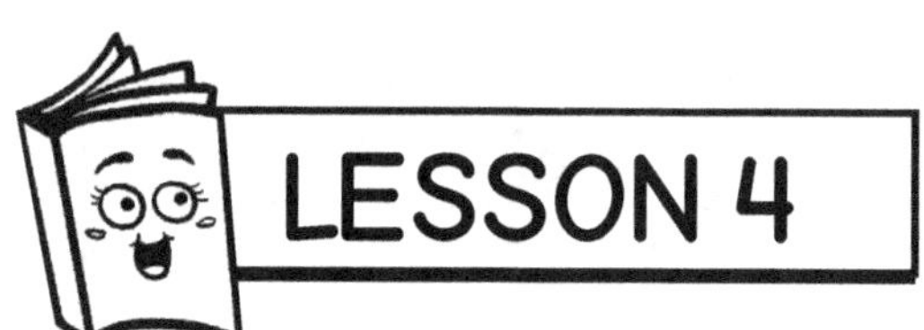

LESSON 4

DAYS OF THE WEEK

DAYS OF THE WEEK

Sunday, la la la

Monday, la la la

Tuesday, la la la

Wednesday…

Thursday, la la la

Friday, la la la

Saturday,

Seven days a week.

SUGGESTED ACTIVITIES FOR THE DIFFERENT LANGUAGE SKILLS

SKILLS	ACTIVITIES
Listening 	Use fun familiar songs to teach the children the days of the week. Singing songs works well for memorization because the familiar pattern is easy for the brain to absorb. In addition, each song can be sung virtually anywhere giving the children even more time to practice and to learn the concept that is being taught.
Speaking 	Use P.E. periods or movement time to teach the days of the week. While children are exercising, they can recite the days of the week instead of counting. They can also do this when forming a line. The first child is Sunday, the second is Monday, and so on.
Reading 	• Find picture books that deal with the topic of the days of the week and read them to your class. If the children are able, have them read the book to you, or even try to explain the pictures and events. • Show the children the days of the week on a calendar. Show them that one row makes one week. Print out each of the days and color code them to make them easier to distinguish, e.g. red for Monday, yellow for Tuesday, etc.
Writing 	Let the children make their own calendar. First show them a calendar and have them say the days' names with you. Then, with a blank calendar page, have the children create a new calendar. Have them tell what happens on each day of the week. Let them use pictures cut from magazines or appropriate stickers to "tag" each day of the week so that it is easier for them to remember. Have them copy the names of the days of the week on a sheet of paper.

ACTIVITY 8   SCORE: _______

Underline the name of the day of the week in each set of words.

1.	wet	want	Wednesday	wig
2.	fin	fish	fry	Friday
3.	sun	Sunday	sack	sell
4.	sand	soy	Tuesday	sell
5.	Monday	men	month	milk
6.	Sunday	swim	sick	suck
7.	tin	tan	ten	Thursday
8.	Friday	for	first	flower
9.	moon	Monday	many	March
10.	soon	say	Saturday	sit

HOME ACTIVITY 3   SCORE:______

Direction: Observe the weather from Sunday to Saturday. Color the picture that shows the weather for each day. On the last column, draw what you do in school and at home. *(10 points)*

Day	Sunny	Cloudy	Rainy	What I Do
Sunday				
Monday				
Tuesday				

Day	Sunny	Cloudy	Rainy	What I Do
Wednesday				
Thursday				
Friday				
Saturday				

QUIZ NO. 9   SCORE: _______

Direction: From each pair of words, choose the name of the day with the correct spelling. Color the triangle (△) beside it.

1. △ Tuesday   △ Toosday

2. △ Staurday   △ Saturday

3. △ Firday   △ Friday

4. △ Sunday   △ Sanday

5. △ Wednesday   △ Wenesday

6. △ Monda   △ Monday

7. △ Thursday   △ Tursday

MONTHS OF THE YEAR

January – New Year's Day

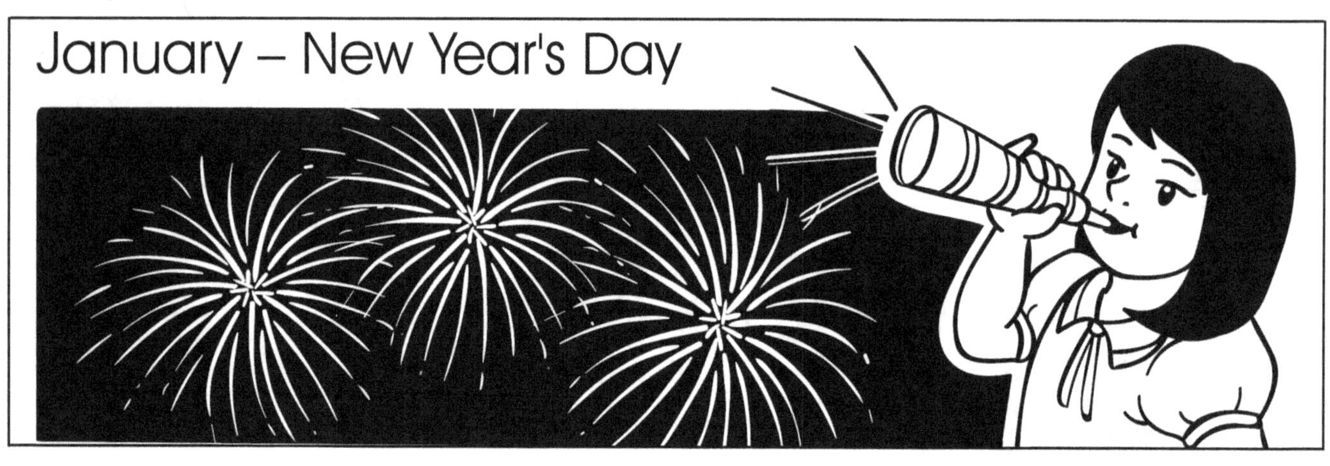

February – Valentine's Day

– Chinese New Year

March – Graduation Month

April – Holy Week (Catholics)

May – Mother's Day

– Labor Day

– Flores De Mayo (Catholics)

June – Opening of Classes
SCHOOL

July – Nutrition Month

August – Filipino Month
WIKANG PAMBANSA

October – United Nations' Day

November – All Saints' Day (Christians)

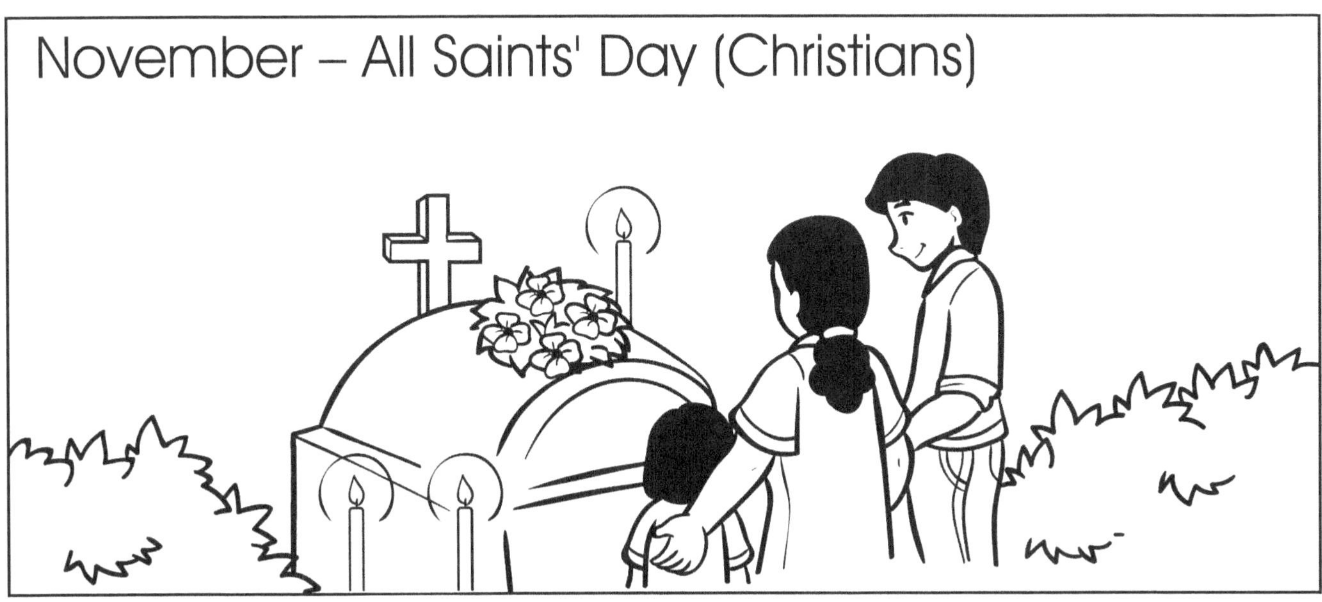

December – Christmas (Christians)

Note: Some celebrations, events and holidays may vary in months and dates.

SKILLS	ACTIVITIES
Listening and Speaking 	Show the children a calendar. Flip through the pages, pointing out the names of the different months. Talk about how there are twelve months in an entire year and how a year starts in January and ends in December, then starts over again. Print out favorite days and holidays in each month and pay special attention to each child's birthday so that the children have events to relate to each month. When talking about the months, mention about two seasons (dry or sunny and wet or rainy) and how they happen during the same months every year. Encourage the children to talk about their experiences during these months.
Reading and Writing 	Type and print a flashcard for each month. Include a picture that represents something that happens during that month, for example a holiday or a celebration. If possible, laminate them so that they will last longer. Spread the flashcards on the floor and have the children help you put them in the correct order. Next, have the children stand in a line next to January and jump to February, March, etc. Next, mix up the cards so that the children have to jump back and forth to the next month. Have the children practice writing the names of the months of the year.

ACTIVITY 9

SCORE: _______

Shade the box beside the picture that shows the event or the celebration on each month.

1. April

2. December

3. January

4. August

5. May

6. March 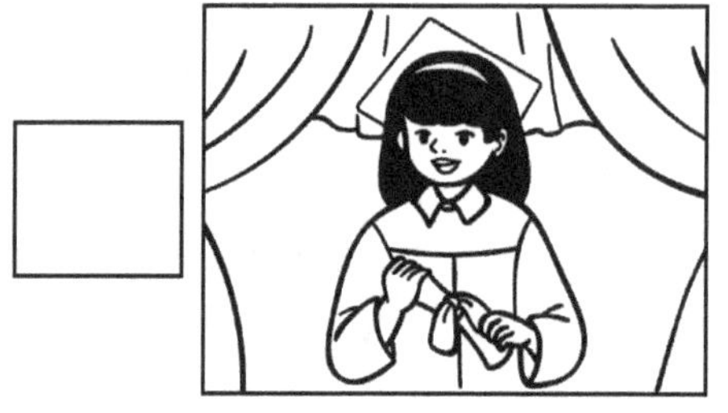 

7. July  

8. February  

9. June  

10. November  

<u>Curved-Flap Envelope Craft</u>

Make unique folded envelopes/cards with curved flaps. This project is made out of construction paper, gift wrapping paper, or pretty wallpaper scraps. This can be used for all occasions to go with the different celebrations in a year.

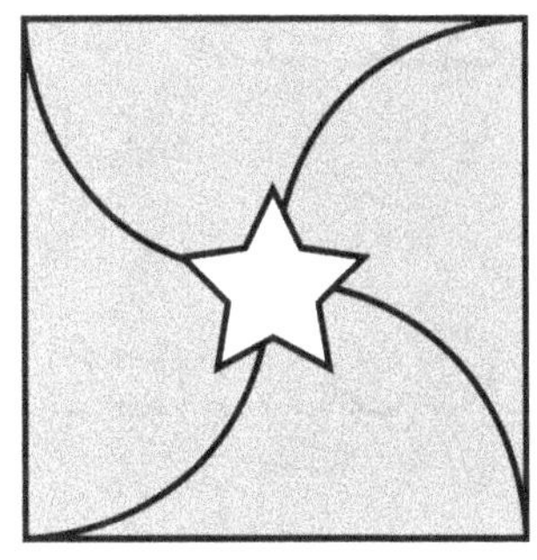

<u>Materials:</u>

- construction paper
- pencil
- scissors
- crayons
- colored marking pens

<u>Procedure:</u>

1. Draw a crisscross of two oblongs on a sheet of construction paper.
2. Carefully cut out the envelope (you could use pinking shears instead of a regular scissors to give your envelope an unusual jagged finish).
3. Write your message on the inside of the envelope.
4. Fold over the flaps, one at a time, on top of the central square. When you get to the last flap, gently push one edge of the flap under the first flap.
5. Address your envelope on the other side.
6. You now have a unique envelope/letter with curved flaps. If you want to seal it, you can either tape the flaps down securely or put a pretty sticker where the four flaps meet.

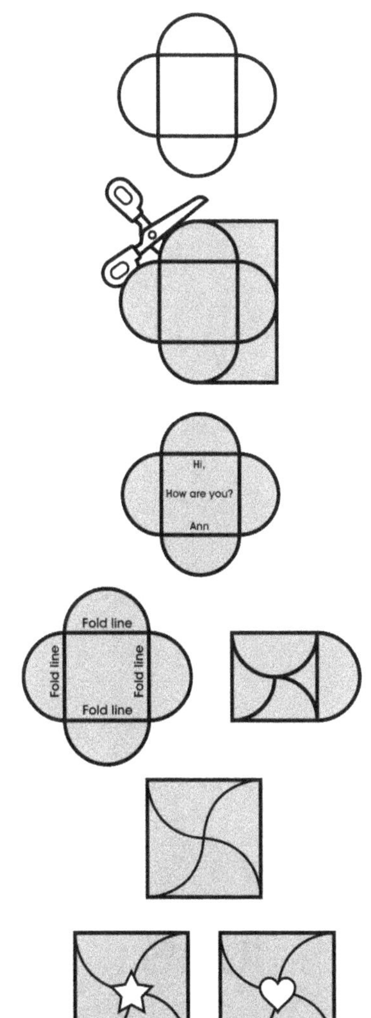

SCORE: _______

Direction: Connect each month to the event or celebration.

1. December •

2. August •

3. March •

4. February •

5. November •

6. January •

7. October •

8. June •

FOURTH QUARTERLY TEST

Name: ______________________________ **Score:** __________

Level: ______________ **Date:** __________

I. Where is the boy? Shade the box of the correct answer. *(10 points)*

1. ☐ behind ☐ in front

2. ☐ behind ☐ in front

3. ☐ behind ☐ in front

4. ☐ behind ☐ in front

5. ☐ behind ☐ in front

II. By underlining the correct answer, tell where
the turtle is. *(10 points)*

1.  beside   between

2.  beside   between

3.  beside   between

4. beside   between

5.   beside   between

1. thick

2. young

3. pretty

4. clean

5. smooth

6. old

7. cold

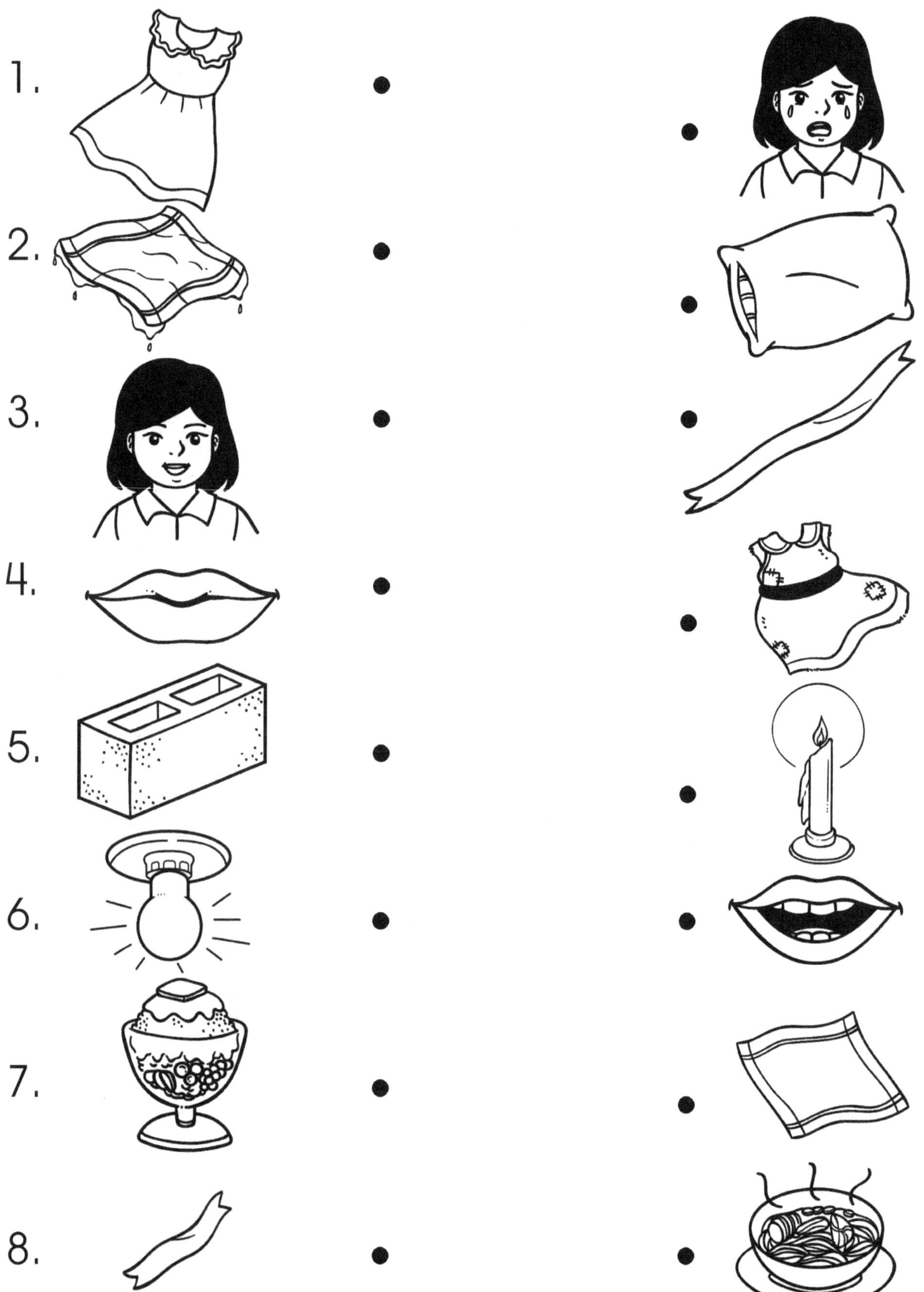

IV. Connect the pictures that are opposites.
1.
2.
3.
4.
5.
6.
7.
8.

V. Encircle the star beside the correct picture
   for each action word.

1. clap

2. draw

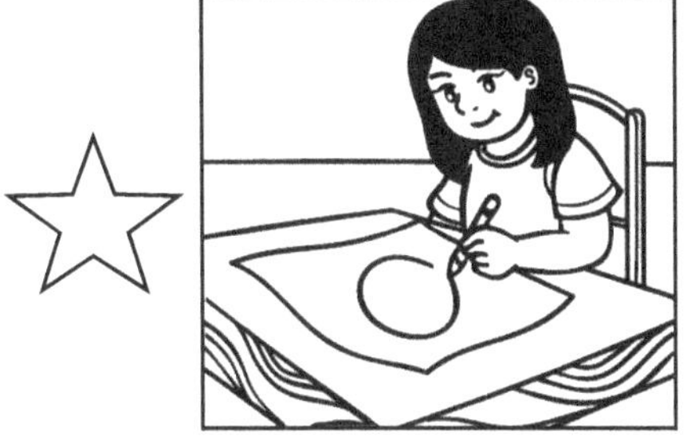

3. swim

4. cry

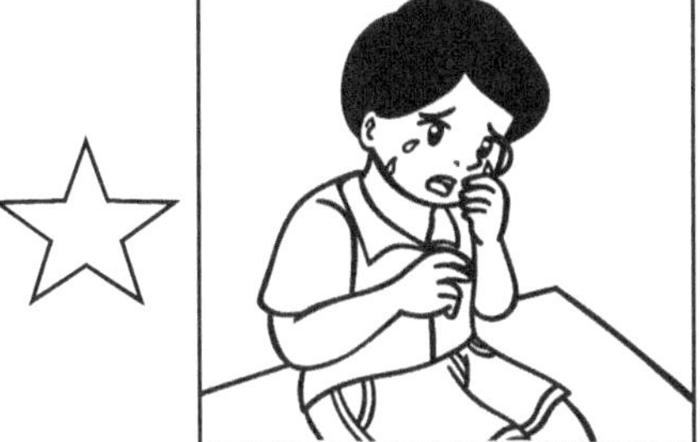

5. read

Name: ________________________   Level: ________

ACTIVITY	No. of Items	My Score	HOME ACTIVITY	No. of Items	My Score	Quiz	No. of Items	My Score
1	5		1	10		1	10	
2	5		2	10		2	10	
3	5		3	10		3	10	
4	8					4	15	
5	7					5	10	
6	10					6	10	
7	5					7	10	
8	10					8	10	
9	10					9	7	
						10	8	
TOTAL	65		TOTAL	30		TOTAL	100	

Parent's/Guardian's Signature   Teacher's Signature

HAZEL DOMINGO BABIANO

Hazel Domingo Babiano is the directress of the Steppingstone Progressivist School, which has campuses in Fairview, Quezon City and Caloocan City.

She leads a dynamic life in the education field as an Instructional Manager for the Department of Education in the National Capital Region, an Educational Consultant for the Child Development Center of Sirkulo ng Kababaihan sa Pasig (SIKAPIN), Vice-Chairperson on Education, Urban Poor Institute for Community Building (UPICOB), and official trainor/facilitator of BKP (Bagong Kulturang Pinoy) Philippines.

She finished both her degrees in Bachelor of Arts in Psychology and her Masters in Education, major in Special Education from the University of the Philippines.

ACKNOWLEDGMENT

This book wouldn't have been possible without the precious assistance and support of the following people:

- my awesome kids, the sources of my inspiration — Donovan, Alathea, Bohari, and Adzel — for the overwhelming support, understanding, concern, love, and yes, for everything;
- Dada and Aeden — for adding color to my life;
- the teachers and staff of STEPPINGSTONE — Layra L. del Rosario, Mitchel T. Pula, Eva Mascariola, Lizette Don, and Ofelieta O. Saladaga — for taking charge of the school while I am busy writing books and conducting seminars;
- Dhoris L. Dela Cruz — for helping me with the other details of this book;
- Jean L. Pascual and Susan S. Nuñez — for being with me through rain and shine;
- my sisters, Josie, Loida, and Lorna — for the weekend get togethers;
- my publishers — the fabulous Raymund and the alluring Isabel Catabijan — for the special bonding spiced with some "jokes";
- the magnificent sisters, Regine and Wowie — for guiding me through the digital aspects of book-writing;
- the staff of St. Matthew's Publishing — Sarah, Maricar, Janet, Josie, Gina, Darren, Orly, Gio, Eunice, Sol, and, of course, Rollie — for all the fun and for their patience with my "kakulitan";
- the gorgeous agents, sub-agents, and artists of Saint Matthew's Publishing — for their hard work and perseverance;
- all teachers — not only for helping me touch the lives of children, but also for making a difference in all the lives that we touch;
- all children — for inspiring me and helping me learn the greatest lessons in life;
- my great love — for believing in me and bringing back my self-esteem, for the laughter, the words of encouragement, the many sacrifices, the respect, the love, and the simple gestures of kindness… for being my best friend… and for trudging with me through life's endless journey;
- above all, our Almighty God — for the good health and for the gifts of humor, wisdom, perseverance, resiliency, and extraordinary strength; and for the outpouring blessings despite the tough journey… thanks, Lord!

Hazel Domingo Babiano